INVITATION
TO A MURDER

GAIL ABBOTT
ZIMMERMAN

Pocket Books

New York   London   Toronto   Sydney

Pocket Books
A Division of Simon & Schuster, Inc.
1230 Avenue of the Americas
New York, NY 10020

First Pocket Books paperback edition November 2008

POCKET and colophon are registered trademarks of
Simon & Schuster, Inc.

For information about special discounts for bulk purchases,
please contact Simon & Schuster Special Sales at
1-800-456-6798 or business@simonandschuster.com.

Cover design by Anna Dorfman
Cover photo by Ben Stockley/Getty Images

Manufactured in the United States of America

10 9 8 7 6 5 4 3 2 1

ISBN-13:978-1-4165-4659-7
ISBN-10:   1-4165-4659-6

FOR ONE DETECTIVE,
THE CASE WAS FAR FROM CLOSED.

What troubled Detective Doug Williamson most was that crumpled piece of paper he had seen on the front seat of Roger Harrington's car. It turned out to have Mark Winger's name and address written on it, and, most perplexing, a time—"4:30."

Winger told the police he did not know the man who attacked his wife. He said he had never met Roger Harrington. He said nothing about having an appointment with him. Yet here was a piece of paper that seemed to indicate that a time and place had been set.

Detective Charlie Cox agreed that the note was disturbing, but he guessed there was probably a logical explanation he simply was not seeing at the moment. Crazy people do crazy things for crazy reasons. Roger Harrington had not been in his right mind.

The evening after the homicides, the police met to discuss the case. Cox and Williamson were there, as were the other two detectives on the major case squad who had also been to the scene. They all stated their positions to their superiors, who would ultimately decide how the case would be handled.

Cox made it clear that he was confident the case was resolved. Williamson urged them to keep it open.

"I was argumentative," he says. "I pointed out red flags, pieces that don't seem to fit, all over the place."

He was turned down flat.

For my husband of thirty-five years, Albert,
who is my inspiration; and for my parents,
Ben and Lola Abbott, who have always encouraged me.

ACKNOWLEDGMENTS

This is a sad story, but ultimately one of survival. People who lost a loved one to murder found a way to carry on their with own lives. Authorities who bungled an investigation ultimately fought hard for justice. Many of them helped me tell this tale.

I cannot overstate the input from Sara Jane and Ira Drescher. Sara Jane let me read her insightful, heartfelt writings that chronicled the events through her eyes. This was invaluable, as she is a highly skilled writer and her words painted a vivid, beautiful portrait of her daughter. Thanks to her rich anecdotes and observations—interspersed throughout these pages—this is a story about Donnah's life as well as her tragic death.

Ira Drescher, a wellspring of information, was extremely generous with his time. I have never known anyone to document events as thoroughly as he. I read through hundreds of neatly typed, organized pages as well as notes hastily scribbled on scraps of paper. Never one to hide his feelings and opinions, Ira made sure his

passion for detail kept me on my toes. Ira and Sara Jane
are true heroes. They continue to make their own lives
meaningful while keeping Donnah's memory alive by
raising charitable funds in her name (they were recently
honored by the organization Women in Distress).

Roger Harrington's parents—Ralph and Helen—
and his sister, Barbara Howell, also suffered a great
loss. They are good, caring people who spoke from
the heart, with honesty and candor. The Harringtons
probably do not realize how much the people who
rushed to judgment have learned from them. They
handled their ordeal with grace and dignity. I thank
them for their time and their sincerity.

Considering the history of the case, the *48 Hours*
team did not, at first, expect a lot of cooperation from
the authorities. We were pleasantly surprised. Virtually everyone in the police department and State's
Attorney's office talked openly with us, even expressing their personal feelings. I am grateful for that, and
thank, in particular, Doug Williamson (now a deputy
chief of police), Charlie Cox, Jim Graham, and Assistant State's Attorney Steve Weinhoeft.

At the request of Mark Winger's second wife, I
have used a pseudonym for her and the members of
her family, including Donnah's adopted daughter.
"Jessica" is concerned about protecting the privacy of
her children. She, her mother, and her brothers are re-
silient, loving people who were tested by extraordinary
circumstances and thrived. I am grateful to them for
giving me their perspective.

Television production is a collaborative effort and a lot of the information in this book was gathered for the television program. Most of the quotations I used come from interviews conducted by *48 Hours* correspondent Richard Schlesinger. Richard is a master at soliciting thoughtful responses. Producer Doug Longhini was on this case long before I was, and he did the lion's share of the investigation and getting people to speak with us. Producer Ian Paisley worked tirelessly on the project. We always had the support of Senior Producer Hal Gessner. Executive Editor Al Briganti is the force behind the *48 Hours Mystery* books and I thank him for his guidance. Thanks to Clarissa Striker for organizing the photos. And I am always grateful to Executive Producer Susan Zirinsky—a true broadcasting giant— for allowing me this opportunity.

A word about the source material used for this book: it comes from formal interviews, casual conversations, court records, depositions, police reports, evidence reports, personal correspondence, emails, and journals. I reconstructed some incidental dialogue, based on documents or the memories of the participants. Inevitably, peoples' memories differ, and I acknowledge that some incidents are recalled from a particular point of view. Unfortunately, there were a few people I was unable to track down.

I thank two great print reporters, Sarah Antonacci and Linda Rockey, who covered the case in real time and helped us prepare our program. They both allowed me to pick their brains. Thanks also to Rabbi

Mike and Jo Datz (who gave a great deal of thought and time to my questions), Dave Barringer, Ray Duffey, Michael Metnick, and John Nolan.

Finally, thanks to the colleagues, friends, and family members who listened to me blather on and on and let me bounce ideas off of them. Paul LaRosa and Peter van Sant—two experienced authors on our staff—helped enormously. Thanks to everyone—especially my parents, Ben and Lola Abbott—who excused my absences while I devoted time to this project. And special thanks to my husband, Albert, for his patience and for being my first reader. His advice—as always—was sound.

CONTENTS

xii • Contents

INTRODUCTION
A Cry for Help

The call came from a tranquil residential neighborhood in the heart of Springfield, Illinois. The caller was frantic.

"Emergency! Emergency! There's a man—he beat my wife—and I shot him! My God, my wife's bleeding!"

The 911 operator dispatched responders to the scene as she gathered whatever information she could. "Is the man still in your house?"

"Yes! He's lying there on the floor with a bullet in his head!"

"Did you shoot him?"

"Yes, I shot him; he was killing my wife!"

The operator thought she heard a human sound in the background. The caller paused, then blurted, "My baby's crying! I'll call you back!" He hung up.

The operator muttered an obscenity. It was 4:27 in the afternoon. The call came from a part of town where even petty crime was rare, especially in broad daylight. The telephone number was assigned to Mark and Donnah Winger. The operator swiftly tried to reestablish the connection. The panicked man picked up.

"Yes! Yes! Hello!"

"Mr. Winger?"

"Yes!"

The operator spoke firmly. "This is the police department. I've got officers en route. I need to know what is going on there."

"My wife is dying on the floor!" Winger was panting.

"Who is this man who attacked her?"

"I don't—I don't know who he is!"

"Is he still inside the house?"

"Yes, he's lying on the floor! I gotta hold my wife, I gotta get to my wife!"

"Okay, are you Mark Winger?"

"Yes, I am; yes, I am."

"Okay, and your wife is Donnah?"

"Yes, she is."

"When did the man get there?"

"I don't know, a few minutes ago . . ." Winger's voice trailed off, then grew urgent. "Please—let me get to my wife! I won't hang up! My door is open."

"Okay, but—" Before the operator could give further instructions, Winger dropped the phone. The operator gave brief instructions to the crews as she strained to hear what was happening in the house.

There were sirens in the distance but the man's pleading voice came through.

"Don't die!" he shouted. "Oh, my God, Donnah, don't die!"

Beneath the wailing, there was another sound: a low-pitched moan.

1

A Model Couple

Mark and Donnah Winger were newlyweds when they left Hollywood, Florida, for Illinois in 1989. Donnah knew she'd be homesick for her family, but Mark, a nuclear engineer, had a job offer that was too good to pass up. They eventually settled into a modest four-bedroom redbrick ranch house on a tree-lined street a few miles west of the sites famously associated with Abraham Lincoln. Donnah loved hearing the sounds of children playing in nearby yards. Both she and Mark were eager to have a family of their own.

Donnah had an unshakable commitment to family. She was close to her two younger sisters. Her best friend was her mother, Sara Jane Drescher, whom Donnah included in every aspect of her life.

"She would tell me *everything*," Sara Jane told *48 Hours* correspondent Richard Schlesinger.

Back when Donnah was single, the men she dated may have found her a little more old-fashioned than they expected her to be. A striking beauty with thick, dark wavy hair, she dressed in the latest fashions. Her disarming smile and slim, athletic build all but guaranteed an active social life. But her vivacious spirit and willingness to have a good time belied her traditional nature.

"She did not have a history of appropriate young men in her life," Sara Jane said.

Donnah did not consider any of the men she dated to be worthy of becoming part of her family, until, at age twenty-four, she met Mark Winger.

At the time, Donnah was a surgical assistant in a busy hospital. The training had been rigorous, requiring an ability to concentrate throughout lengthy, tedious procedures. Donnah persevered, overcoming a learning disability that made it hard for her to study written material. Her heart was set on having a job that would have a positive impact on peoples' lives. She had developed a strong passion—and stomach—for the medical profession.

"Mom, I had the most incredible morning," Donnah once enthusiastically told Sara Jane during a break. "I did an amputation. It was fabulous!" She hung up, saying it was time for her lunch.

"If she didn't have the learning disability, she would have been a physician, because she just had that instinct to know the right thing to do at the right time," Sara Jane said.

One day at work, Greg Winger, a nurse anesthetist, told Donnah that his brother, Mark, had just returned from a year in Korea. Mark had been an army lieutenant and had a degree in physics from the Virginia Military Institute. He thought Donnah would like Mark and offered to fix them up. Donnah had reservations and, as always, turned to her mother for advice.

"How bad could it be? Just go."

Mark Winger exceeded all of Donnah's expectations. He was soft-spoken and polite. His round glasses and bushy eyebrows gave him a bit of a goofy look, but, like Donnah, he kept himself fit. He was five foot ten, but his broad shoulders and soldier's posture gave him a taller appearance. Donnah was struck by his intelligence and wry sense of humor. Even that first night he easily made her laugh.

Mark did not expect his blind date to be so attractive. He was drawn to Donnah's large brown eyes and the way they made him feel important. He also liked Donnah's lack of guile. The party was a blast, he thought, but the best moment came when he walked her to her car. There was the inevitable awkward silence when she turned to him before leaving. What should he say? Should he kiss her? Wave good-bye? Before he could do anything, Donnah spoke up.

"I had a great time," she said, adding bluntly, "I knew I'd like you from the moment we met."

Mark stumbled his way through a response but let Donnah know that the feeling was mutual.

"We kissed good-bye," Mark said, seemingly savoring the moment. "It seemed to linger long after it was done." There was no turning back.

He told his family she was a breath of fresh air. He had never met anyone like her.

"You could tell they clicked right away," said Mark's brother, Greg. "They were just right for each other."

Sara Jane and her new husband, Donnah's step-father, Ira Drescher, could not have been more pleased. Mark came from a good family. He had graduated college. He was on a solid career path—a nuclear engineer, no less! To top it off, he was, like Donnah, Jewish.

"It could not have been a better scenario," Sara Jane said.

Ira agreed. Sara Jane's high-estrogen family was a new experience for him. He came from an unabashedly macho background.

"My father was a professional boxer," he said proudly.

Ira had three children from his previous marriage, two athletic sons and a daughter who played quarterback on the powder-puff team. Still, he warmed quickly to his stepdaughters, especially Donnah.

"Donnah and I would watch boxing together," he said. "She liked boxing."

Mark was the perfect balance for Donnah. He was a little on the quiet side and pragmatic: the Dreschers affectionately called him "the geek." Donnah, bursting with energy, was not necessarily always focused. Their attraction for each other was striking. They could not stand to be apart, and when they were together, they could not keep from touching each other. They held hands, put their arms around each other, or simply cuddled. They had become soul mates.

"They were really cute," Sara Jane said. "I can remember times when Donnah might get upset about something and Mark would say something funny and she would laugh. Then they would be giddy and silly with each other."

"They loved each other very much and that love rubbed off on everybody around them," said Mark's mother, Sallie.

To the delight of both families, Mark proposed to Donnah six months after they met. They celebrated with a dinner at a Springfield restaurant. Knowing it would be a big night, Mark arranged for his parents to be there, along with Ira and Sara Jane Drescher.

"Amazingly, she said yes," Mark announced proudly. The older couples slipped into easy conversation. Mark and Donnah held clasped hands on the table. They were lost in their own little world.

"They were adorable, a model couple," Sara Jane said.

Sara Jane, who divorced her first husband when Donnah was seventeen, knew how hard a failed marriage could be on a family. She had told her daughters that she would pay for their first weddings, but if they remarried they were on their own. She was confident that her oldest daughter was getting it right the first time. She and Donnah would spend the next nine months working out every detail of the wedding.

"It was the most wonderful time of our lives," Sara Jane said. "We were working together, mother and daughter. I wish every mother could have the experience I had with Donnah."

There was never any tension, only joy.

Sara Jane remembered the night Donnah called her to say she finally found *the* wedding dress.

"She started the conversation with this shriek that almost knocked the phone away from my ear," Sara Jane recalled.

Donnah, an expert shopper, knew which clothes best suited her shapely figure. Still, she wanted her mother to take a look. They went to the bridal shop the next day.

Donnah directed Sara Jane to a chair and disappeared into a back room. A few minutes later, she emerged.

"You can turn around," she told her mother softly.

Sara Jane slowly pivoted in her seat. Donnah stood above her, on a platform, in front of a three-way mirror.

"I focused on the vision I saw in front of me. It was my oldest daughter in a wedding gown," Sara Jane said later. "Tears welled in my eyes and I saw her smile, so proud and so happy."

"What do you think?" Donnah asked.

Sara Jane finally found her voice.

"Oh, Donnah, it is just beautiful. You are just beautiful. It's perfect."

Donnah had chosen a graceful princess gown with long tapered sleeves. She stood tall and sashayed around the small space, looking very much like a professional model to her mother. Sara Jane walked to her daughter and embraced her. They held each other tightly, savoring the moment.

The rest of the planning went just as smoothly.

"There was never a time when either one of us felt stressed," Sara Jane said. "We were always on the same page."

The big event took place on March 4, 1989. One hundred thirty guests gathered at the temple for the ceremony. It was sunny with the temperature in the mid-seventies—the type of day that inspires people to move to the Sunshine State.

"Donnah looked more beautiful than I had ever seen her," Sara Jane said. "She glowed." Even better, she was marrying a man who loved her unconditionally and would take care of her.

Mark, looking unusually sophisticated in his tuxedo, was flanked by his parents when he walked down the aisle. Ira, trim and tan, smiled from ear to ear as he escorted the mother of the bride. Sara Jane, petite and blond, was dressed in an elegant pale pink gown. Donnah's sisters—bridesmaids who bore a striking resemblance to the bride—could barely hold back their tears as they made their entrance.

Donnah was radiant. She held the attention of everyone in the room. Walking down the aisle alone, she stopped halfway. Mark met her and took her hand, and they walked the rest of the way together. They stood under the chuppah, the canopy used in Jewish weddings. They recited their vows, exchanged rings, and, following tradition, Mark smashed a glass with his foot. The crowd shouted "Mazel tov!" wishing them good luck. The music resumed and they strolled back up the aisle together, never letting go of each other's hand.

The newlyweds made their debut dancing to "I Only Have Eyes for You." It was the perfect choice. Although Donnah loved being surrounded by family and friends celebrating her joy, for the moment Mark was the only one who mattered. She loved being showered with his affection. She felt protected. She had grown to idolize him.

"The smile that Donnah walked down the aisle with never left her face," Sara Jane said. It lasted through the reception, the dinner, the dancing, the toasts.

Sara Jane was the first to pay tribute on the wedding video.

"It's the happiest day of my life for two of the most beautiful young people I know," she said. "I love you both."

Ira focused on the future. "We wish you a lot of beautiful, healthy babies."

The party ended and the two families hugged. Everyone was elated that Mark and Donnah had found each other. Donnah loved her new in-laws and they returned the affection. Sara Jane felt that Donnah had found a real-life prince.

"I was blessed and I knew it," she said.

The following day, before leaving for her honeymoon, Donnah made a quick call to her mother.

"I just had to tell you when Mark and I were getting ready to go to bed, he took off his tuxedo pants and he was wearing Cleveland Browns boxers," she reported.

They laughed. That was Mark, a die-hard Browns fan with a great sense of humor. That was Donnah, candid as always, filling Sara Jane in on every intimate detail of her life.

2

A New Arrival

Springfield, Illinois, may not be the most exciting place to live, but its hundred ten thousand citizens have access to the best of both worlds: reasonable urban amenities and a small-town lifestyle. Downtown, residents are outnumbered by tourists in search of Abraham Lincoln, Springfield's revered son. It's an association Springfield will not let you forget—not for a second. Lincoln's name is shamelessly omnipresent: on streets, businesses, and seemingly countless historic sites. These include the Lincoln family home (the only one he ever owned), the Lincoln law office, thirty Lincoln storyboards mapping out a walking tour, and the Abraham Lincoln Presidential Library. In 2005, the Abraham Lincoln Presidential Museum opened, with elaborately staged—and highly entertaining—vignettes in which actors interact with holographic historical figures.

Despite Springfield's commitment to preserving its heritage, the city's character is more defined by its role as state capital. An abundant supply of government jobs makes it a safe haven, even in hard economic times. It's a white-collar town with good housing, ten-minute commutes, and a clean, safe, downtown with—people there tend to point out—plentiful free parking.

Springfield suited the Wingers well. Mark was an engineer for the state's Department of Nuclear Safety. His job involved developing equipment to monitor effluent discarded by the nuclear power plants across the state. He was well trained and intelligent, and he rightfully expected to be promoted in the not-too-distant future.

Donnah landed a job in the day surgery unit at Memorial Hospital. She quickly became a favorite with doctors and patients alike. She befriended an attractive but shy surgical nurse named DeAnn Schultz. They went to the gym together and began hanging out on their days off. DeAnn came to value Donnah as a trusted confidante. They were relieved that their husbands got along well.

The Wingers joined a synagogue, forging friendships within Springfield's small but tight-knit Jewish community. Donnah made fast friends with the young rabbi's wife, Jo Datz. Jo, a native of South Africa, met and fell in love with her husband, Rabbi Mike Datz, when he traveled to her homeland. Like Donnah, Jo was outgoing, attractive, and energetic. As married women planning to have children soon, they formed a tight bond. Rabbi Mike also enjoyed the Wingers' company, and the two couples socialized often.

Despite Donnah's gregarious nature and widening circle of friends, her closest ties remained with her family. She spoke with her mother, Sara Jane, up to four times a day—at a time when long-distance calls could be costly. On weekends they had a ritual.

"Sunday mornings we'd have coffee together," Sara Jane told Richard Schlesinger. "She'd have coffee in Springfield, I'd have coffee in Florida, but we did it together."

Donnah would imagine her mother dressed in fashionable shorts, sitting in the sun-drenched kitchen so familiar to her. She soaked up the family news and reported everything happening in her own life, including the efforts she and Mark were making to have a baby.

"She really would tell us everything," Sara Jane said. "Sometimes she told me more than I wanted to know! She just let it all come out. We knew every detail of her life. She shared it with me, she shared it with her sisters."

Donnah also kept her friend, Jo Datz, up-to-date.

"She told me when and how often and where they had sex," Jo said later. "She was very open about that. We talked about it a lot, as I was also trying to conceive."

Sara Jane Drescher may have been a little taken aback by her daughter's candor, but her heart ached for her. Donnah had been very excited about trying to get pregnant, and Sara Jane had always been supportive. Her own three daughters were the joy of her life.

As months of trying stretched into years, it was apparent it would not be so easy for Donnah.

Donnah and Mark had fallen into a routine, sitting together at the dining room table, staring at a pregnancy test strip.

"We'd be elbows on the table, looking at each other," Mark remembered. "And then looking down at the test, to see if it developed."

Each time they were optimistic they would see a positive result, they would wait the agonizing minutes, but there would be no change.

"And then we'd think: maybe we're jinxing ourselves. And so we'd have a contest to see who could not look at the little test the longest. And we'd have the time set on the stove for the five minutes or whatever."

The timer would go off, Mark said, and they would stare at each other. The result was always the same: negative. After dozens of tests, Mark no longer tried to lighten the mood with humor. Something was clearly wrong.

The problem was traced to a defect in Donnah's fallopian tubes that made it impossible for her to conceive. The remedy would not be new fertility technology but an age-old practice. It began with a conversation Donnah had with a colleague.

In December, 1994, an ob-gyn at the hospital told Donnah about a fifteen-year-old patient who was four months pregnant. The girl wanted to put her baby up for adoption. This was more than coincidence, Donnah believed: it was the answer to her prayers. Mark agreed they should seize the opportunity.

For the next five months, the Wingers were on pins and needles. They worked through an attorney, abiding with every rule and regulation. There was a nail-biting delay while the biological father, who showed up at the eleventh hour, grappled with signing away his parental rights. In the end, he realized that the Wingers would provide his baby a safe and secure home.

On May 27, 1995, a baby girl was born. The Wingers named her Ruby in honor of Donnah's grandmother. Their dream to become parents was finally fulfilled.

Five days later, early in the morning, Mark and Donnah stood outside their house, waiting for Ruby's arrival. Sara Jane recorded the occasion on video.

"A very special baby is coming," she announced, panning to Donnah, "and there's the Mommy! She's so excited, she hasn't slept for days."

Feeling a bit light-headed, Donnah smiled and gave a little wave. It was, appropriately, the height of spring. The blossoms were unusually fragrant. The young leaves were a vibrant, shimmering green. Springfield had fully emerged from the drab gray midwestern winter.

Donnah was more grateful than ever to have Mark beside her to keep her grounded. He kissed her forehead as she buried herself in his arms.

Mercifully, Sara Jane stopped recording until, after

what seemed like an eternity, a red Lincoln turned up the street. Within minutes, the Wingers' lawyer handed tiny Ruby to her new parents. They held her together, between them, squeezing close to each other. Both sobbed while Ruby slept, blissfully oblivious to the commotion.

"She's so perfect. So delicate. So perfect." Donnah said softly, tears welling in her eyes. "Oh! Sweet!" She was too choked up to utter another word.

Ruby Winger had chubby cheeks, a full head of hair, and deep-set eyes.

"I loved her from the moment she was placed in my arms," Mark said later.

For the next few days, virtually every event in Ruby's life was documented on video. Donnah recorded as Mark rocked her in his arms. Mark recorded as Donnah fed her on the couch with DeAnn watching.

"Here's Aunt DeAnn," Donnah said.

DeAnn smiled. "This is just my sweetest little niece I've ever seen."

Rabbi Mike Datz performed a touching and joyful naming ceremony in the Winger living room. He lifted Ruby so that the friends and family witnessing the ritual could see her, then he handed her to her father. As the rabbi recited prayers welcoming Ruby to the family, she grew restless in Mark's arms. Donnah gently stroked her brow.

Afterward, while Ruby napped in her crib, Mark tiptoed into the darkened room to capture the moment.

"I just wanted to have a little time alone with you and let you know how much Daddy loves you," he whispered. "And I want to get it on video because I know you are going to grow up so fast, I'll wonder where the years went."

Three months later, Mark Winger was calling 911, begging for help. Donnah's blood was everywhere. He held her tightly, he said, as he "helplessly watched her life pour out of her."

3

Photo Op

Patrolman Dave Barringer was the kind of cop who joined the force for all the right reasons. The affable officer with the boyish face had a genuine sense of commitment to his community. He could be counted on to help run charitable events and document them with photos. His ability to defuse volatile situations and comfort people in distress had earned him accolades from his superiors and letters of praise from Springfield's citizens. Despite having five years on the force, he was neither jaded nor ambitious for promotion. He was happy being out in the streets with the people he served.

On August 29, 1995, Barringer was leaving a hospital, heading back to the station. It was a hot, humid day, and an uneventful one—until a call came on the radio at 4:29 p.m. A homeowner on the west side had shot an intruder. Gunfire in that part of town was highly unusual at any time, let alone midday.

Barringer was far away. Figuring that eight to ten officers could get to the scene before him, he hesitated—but only for a moment. What if they needed his help? "I made good time getting there," he said later, smiling.

When Barringer pulled up to 2305 Westview Drive, he was relieved to see that no crowd had gathered, at least not yet. There was, however, a vehicle that seemed out of place on this street of well-kept homes: a beat-up maroon Oldsmobile parked the wrong way, right in front of the house.

Nodding to the grim-faced officer at the door, Barringer stepped inside. He was struck by the sight and stench of recent violence. There was blood everywhere: on the floor, the walls, even on the ceiling. The victims were in plain sight: a female in the dining area, and a male about five feet away, near the kitchen. The female had gaping head wounds that exposed her brain. Two fire department medics were working on her, but she did not seem responsive. The tall, thin male laying on his back also had severe head wounds. He was clinging to life, taking deep, labored breaths, but his time was probably limited as well. A bloodied claw hammer lay between them on the floor.

Barringer's observations were cut short by the piercing cry of a baby in distress. He followed the sound to a back bedroom, where a distraught man in running shorts—presumably the homeowner who shot the intruder—sat on the edge of a bed, moaning and holding his head in his hands. The baby lay behind him, in the middle of the bed, her arms and legs flailing as she shrieked. An officer trying to talk with the man shot Barringer an exasperated look.

Barringer scooped the baby from the bed, rocking her gently and whispering soothing words. Cradled in the comfort of his arms, the baby ceased crying. Barringer continued cooing to her as he walked back to the hallway. He was drowned out by an arriving ambulance. This was a big incident, he knew, one that might very well end up with two dead victims. He surveyed the scene, absorbing every detail he could when he suddenly remembered he had a way to contribute to the inevitable investigation. He ran outside, hurriedly handing the baby to the startled officer at the door.

Barringer opened his trunk and grabbed his Polaroid camera. Teams of paramedics were entering the home. Their priority would be saving lives. That meant that, within minutes, the scene would be altered. Furniture would be moved and the victims would be taken away. Later, he was sure, the crime scene technicians would document the blood spatter and other evidence. Now was the one and only chance to have a record that showed where the bodies lay.

Barringer mentally reviewed the procedures he had learned in a crime scene photography class: take at least four photos, one from each direction. That would be great, he thought, except he had only three shots left. He stepped back into the hallway as far as he could and snapped the first one, showing the woman and the furniture around her. He laid the picture down and the image slowly materialized. Barringer walked to the opposite side of the room, by the kitchen. From this angle he could see both victims and their relation to each other. As the second picture developed, Barringer carefully set up his last shot, squeezing all the way to his left, backing into a hallway that led to the garage. He framed it so that the male could be seen in proximity to the refrigerator, which was near his feet.

Dave Barringer waited for the images to fully form, then tucked the three photos into his shirt pocket. He would check them into the evidence room later. His immediate concern was helping control the increasing chaos at the scene.

Major case squad detectives Charlie Cox and Doug Williamson arrived at the scene at 5 p.m., half an hour after the call came to 911. Out of 270 police officers in Springfield, four were assigned to this unit. Cox and Williamson had been partners only for a few months, but worked well together. Cox, a soft-spoken nineteen-year veteran with thick graying hair, would lead the case. He had developed good instincts and learned to trust them.

Williamson, at six foot four, towered over his partner but was ten years younger. This was his second homicide. He was methodical and reserved, and had a good head for detail. Like his partner, he sported a mustache.

Cox and Williamson walked past a heart-shaped lawn ornament with the words "Friends Welcome" and up the three steps that led to the door. The officer at the door was, incongruously, holding an infant. He briefed the detectives. There were two victims inside; both were alive but both suffered massive head injuries. The paramedics were preparing them to be moved to the hospital. The woman, Donnah Winger, lived there. The male was an intruder, identity unknown. There were two weapons, a .45 semiautomatic pistol, secured, on the table, and a bloody hammer left where the officers found it: on the floor.

The officer said that Mark Winger, the man who had called 911, was in the dining room when they got there, holding his wife and yelling at her to breathe. They coaxed him away and brought him to a back bedroom. He was an emotional wreck but very cooperative.

Winger told the officers that he had been in his basement, jogging on his treadmill, when he heard a strange noise. He went upstairs to investigate and found his three-month-old daughter on his bed, alone. Then he heard commotion in the living room and became alarmed. He grabbed his gun and ran to the hall. He saw a man beating his wife on the head with a hammer. As the man was about to strike again, Winger shot him. He had no idea who the man is.

The moment the detectives walked through the door, they were thrust into the horror. Cox had served most of his years as a crime scene tech and had seen his share of bloodbaths. This was one of the worst. There was blood and human tissue on nearly every surface he could see. He felt the adrenaline pumping through his veins. This was going to be a high-profile case. He saw his partner wince with revulsion.

Williamson went to the back bedroom to meet Mark Winger while Cox took a quick look around. Something terrible had happened here and it was his job to get to the bottom of it. A dozen or so people were crowded in the small living room/dining room area, most frantically working on the victims.

The male was groaning, his low-pitched moans making the scene more intense for Cox. It was harder to work near someone in pain than it was to work near a corpse. Cox was a religious man, and, as he always did in these situations, he stood beside each victim and said a silent prayer. From the looks of the gaping wounds, he doubted either would survive.

Cox no longer got queasy in these circumstances. To be an effective investigator, he had learned to block out the gore. Cold as it seemed, he had to think of the victims as pieces of evidence. He had to observe every detail about them—and everything else in the room. The early moments of an investigation were critical.

"You have to focus on what's going on," he explained later. "Otherwise, you lose your edge."

The patrol officers had the house well secured. The gun was unloaded and in plain sight. A quick check of the doors and windows revealed no signs of forced entry. Cox's next priority was ID'ing the male victim.

The wounded man was in no condition to talk and

would soon be hauled off to the hospital. Cox gave him a good look: he was thin but muscular and dressed in a rumpled T-shirt and cutoff denim shorts. His face was partially obliterated by the wound and the blood, but Cox thought he looked familiar: he had seen the man before but could not remember where. He patted the man's back pocket and pulled out a wallet.

The name on the driver's license was Roger L. Harrington, age twenty-seven. It did not ring a bell. Cox would run a check on him later, when he was finished talking with Mark Winger.

4

Intruder

Mark Winger was perched on the edge of his bed, clutching his stomach, when Doug Williamson entered the room. He was wearing his running clothes: a red shirt, blue shorts, and sneakers. His arms and hands were streaked with blood.

"Oh, my God! Donnah! Donnah!" he cried out, rocking back and forth.

Williamson introduced himself.

"I was trying to comfort him, ask him if he needed anything," Williamson later told *48 Hours*. "I was letting him know what we were going to do, how the police were going to help him."

Winger asked who the man lying on the floor was. Why was the man in his house?

Williamson promised they would find out. His goal was to calm the distraught man so that Detective Cox could conduct a productive interview. He told Winger he wanted to hear everything he had to say, but they had to wait for his partner. Winger pulled off his T-shirt and wrapped it around his hands. He cried out his wife's name. He asked again about the stranger in his house. Williamson redirected the conversation.

"Your baby is safe," the detective said. "They're taking her to a neighbor's house."

Winger nodded, still fidgeting with his shirt. Williamson made a mental note of that.

When Charlie Cox joined his partner in the bedroom, Winger was considerably less agitated. As the lead detective, Cox would try to connect with Winger and get as much information as he could. Williamson would stay in the background.

"I kept bouncing in and out of the room," he said later.

Winger willingly answered Cox's questions. He said that he lived at the house. That was his wife and an unknown intruder in the other room. He saw the man attack his wife and shot him. He had his gun out because of some weird situations that had been happening.

Cox asked Winger to tell him everything that happened that day.

"Start at the beginning. Tell me what you did when you got up this morning."

Winger said he went to work as he always did. Nothing out of the ordinary happened there, except for an odd phone call he had with a man who had been giving him some problems. Winger said he wanted to reason with the guy and get him to stop bothering his family, but the man started babbling nonsense, as if he were speaking with a third person when there was no one else on the line. Winger said he simply ended the call, telling the man he would be tied up in meetings all day.

Winger was interrupted in mid-sentence by the ear-shattering blare of a siren. Startled, he stared out the window. An ambulance was rushing one of the victims to the hospital.

"Can you check on my wife? Is she all right?" he asked.

Cox assured Winger that Donnah was in good hands. He dared not tell Winger that her chances did not look good.

Winger let out an agonized moan and began rocking again. Cox gave him time before asking the next question.

"How was the man bothering your family? Who was he?"

Winger replied that the trouble began on Wednesday, while he was in Chattanooga at a training center for work. That day, he said, his wife and baby daughter flew back home from a visit with her parents in Florida. They arrived at St. Louis airport where they boarded a shuttle van for the ride to Springfield. The driver was the man Winger had mentioned before. Donnah and her baby were his only passengers. During the ride, the driver did things that bothered Donnah.

"What did he do?" Cox asked.

"He was driving erratically and wildly. Speeding," Winger said. "And he said weird stuff that scared her."

Winger's voice grew tense. His wife was too afraid to say anything to the man, he said, because they were out on I-55, in the middle of nowhere, and she did not want to get him angry.

Cox asked if Winger knew, specifically, what the driver had said. Winger said the man talked about a demonlike creature who had power over him and told him to do violent deeds. Kill people. Plant car bombs. He had some crazy name for this creature.

Winger again twisted his shirt in his hands. He asked the detectives if it was okay to ask his rabbi to come to the house.

"He's a close friend," Winger said.

Cox nodded. He liked the idea of having a spiritual advisor there. He had Officer Barringer make the call.

"Do you remember anything else the driver said?" he asked Winger.

Winger did not hide his disgust. He said the driver told his wife that he liked older women and he invited her to a party at his house. He said they had lots of parties with . . . naked people and wild sex. That made her very uncomfortable but she was afraid to upset him. The whole ride was like that. The man finally dropped her at their house and drove off.

Winger took a long, deep breath. He had another request. His throat felt dry and he wanted something to drink. He asked if someone could get him a drink. There was Diet Coke in the refrigerator. Doug Williamson volunteered. The young detective made his way to the kitchen through the grisly crime scene, where evidence techs were taking photographs and measurements.

Williamson found the soda and closed the refrigerator. He stared at the door. There, hanging smack in front of him, on 8 1/2 x 10" yellow paper, was a handwritten note. The two-page narrative was written, apparently, by Donnah Winger. It was her account of the ride in the shuttle van, the same story her husband had just told. It was an eerie sight—as if Donnah, now so severely brain damaged, was communicating directly with them.

The note described the driver's speeding and the unsettling things he said. "He started telling me about his spirit 'Dahm,'" it read. "He said sometimes Dahm takes him out of his body when he's driving and makes him fly above the treetops." It ended with a summation. "The experience made me feel very nervous and extremely uncomfortable. I felt as if my life and the life of my daughter were in the hands of a nut."

Williamson showed the note to the crime scene photographer. No one had seen it yet. Everyone was busy documenting the bloody mess in the other room.

When Williamson returned to the bedroom, Winger stopped talking and gazed at him. Williamson wondered if he expected an account of what was going on outside the bedroom. His instincts told him not to talk about anything he saw— including Donnah's note. This was Cox's interview.

"Here you go," Williamson said, handing Winger

the soda. Winger put it on the bed beside him and dropped his head into his hands.

Winger continued his story. He said that Donnah didn't tell him about that ride right away because he had a big test Friday morning and she didn't want to burden him. Donnah did tell her friend DeAnn. DeAnn came over and spent two nights with Donnah so she would not be alone.

Cox asked if Winger knew DeAnn's phone number. Winger said not offhand, he would have to look it up. He twisted his shirt in his hands. Cox asked him to continue.

Winger said that after his test on Friday, Donnah called him and told him about her harrowing ride home from the airport. He told her to write it all down, so they would have a record of it. He would register a complaint with the company. Winger shot another glance Williamson's way.

The detectives felt their pagers vibrate. Each glanced discreetly at his belt. The screen displayed a message from headquarters—"1079"—code telling them that the victims were dead. Cox anticipated this, but it still upset him. Winger's life had been shattered in an instant by some lowlife intruder. His baby would never know her mother.

Cox dreaded telling Winger the news and decided not to do it just yet. There was no harm allowing Winger some time to compose himself and have a few more moments of hope. Besides, Cox needed more information, and this—the first hours of the investigation—was the best time to get it. Mark Winger, as the only adult survivor, was bound to be the most important witness.

"Did you talk with the driver again?"

Winger shook his head.

"Did anything else unusual happen at work?"

Winger said that Donnah was there that afternoon, showing off their baby to his colleagues. They left separately; he got home around 3:30 and she got there about ten minutes later.

Winger said when he came in he noticed a hammer lying on the dining room table. He asked his wife about it. She gave him one of her disarming smiles and said it was a subtle reminder for him to hang a hat rack.

"I had been procrastinating," he said. He promised to do it after his workout.

Winger put aside the shirt he had been clutching. He stared at his bloody hands and asked the detectives if he could wash them. Williamson had the crime scene photographer take a shot of them first—just for the record. After Winger washed up, the questions resumed.

Winger stated that he was on the treadmill in his basement for about fifteen minutes when he heard a sound from above—a thump. "I slowed down, then I heard another thump." Concerned that his baby might have taken a fall, Winger said he stopped his workout and started up the stairs. He heard his baby cry.

Cox heard the anguish in Winger's voice.

"I went into the bedroom and saw the baby on the bed—alone." He knew something was wrong. Donnah would never leave her alone like that.

That statement rang true to Cox. He knew from personal experience that you can't leave babies unattended on top of a piece of furniture: they squirm and wriggle and can fall.

Winger said a noise came from the dining room and knew in his gut that something was wrong. His gun was on his nightstand because of the strange things that had been happening that week. He grabbed it and ran to the hallway. There he saw the most awful sight of his life.

His wife was lying helplessly on the floor. A strange man wielding a hammer was kneeling over her. The man swung the tool high, as if he was about to strike again. He turned his head toward the hallway and looked Winger in the eye.

"I shot him!" Winger exclaimed.

Winger was sobbing and shouting, nearly spitting his words. He took a few moments to gather himself.

"I think I hit him," he continued, looking directly at Cox.

Winger said that the man seemed to roll away from his wife. He thought he saw some blood fly in the air. But then the man started to raise his head and shoulders. Winger ran toward the man and fired again.

"I know I hit him that time."

Cox could barely contain his own emotions. Winger's pain permeated the room. He imagined himself in

Winger's position; he would do the same thing to anyone he saw attack his family. If only Winger had come up those stairs just a few moments sooner, he might have saved his wife. Cox feared Winger would forever blame himself for his tragic timing.

"Who is that guy? Do you know who he is?" Winger pleaded. "Is his name Roger?"

Winger could not have been more cooperative, Cox thought. After what he had been through, he deserved the truth.

"Yes. His name is Roger Harrington."

"Oh, my God!" Winger shouted. "That's him!" That man, he said, was the man who had been harassing them all week: the driver who took Donnah home from the airport.

Winger fell on his side, crying.

As senseless as the crime was, the pieces were fitting together. After driving Donnah Winger home, Roger Harrington became fixated with her. He knew where she lived. He stalked her and confronted her, and that confrontation somehow escalated to murder. Detective Cox had most of the information he needed. He would spare Mark Winger further duress and be as delicate as possible with his remaining questions.

"You said Harrington harassed you all week. What do you mean?" he asked.

"We started getting these phone calls," Winger explained. A man spoke in a low, weird monotone voice. He asked for his wife by name.

Donnah's friend DeAnn took one call, Winger said, and DeAnn's teenage daughter took another while babysitting. The Wingers had never gotten calls like that before, and the timing led them to believe that it had to be the crazy driver. That's what prompted Winger to take his gun out of his closet and put it on the nightstand.

Winger wrapped his arms around his body and cried out for his wife.

Williamson left the room again, this time to check out the car parked the wrong way in front of the house. The license plate, "Rog 1001," was indeed registered to a Roger Harrington. Williamson saw a scribbled note on the front seat. He made sure the techs collected it along with everything else in the car.

While Williamson was gone, Winger asked a pointed question.

"Am I going to go to jail because I shot a man?"

"No, not from what you've told us," Cox said. "In most cases, people are victimized and their loved ones have no recourse. In my mind, you are a hero. You shot the creep who was attacking your wife."

Winger did not yet know that Donnah was dead. The detective wanted to console him, but he was cautious.

"It's easy to say the wrong thing; we often do," he later explained, "especially since the mind-set of a cop has to be more in evidence gathering, not in consoling."

To his relief, his words seemed to have an impact. Winger remained composed.

He told Cox that he held Donnah while he waited for help. He watched her life slip away. The man lying on the floor was making noises. Horrible noises. Winger could not stand it. He took the hammer from the man's hand and hit him in the chest a couple of times to shut him up.

As brutal as that seemed, Cox understood. Winger acted in the heat of the moment. The detective made a note to tell the medical examiner about those blows.

The detectives got word that Rabbi Mike Datz was waiting outside. He requested to be the one to tell Winger that his wife was dead. Cox caught his partner's eye; he had no more questions. Doug Williamson spoke up.

"There is one more thing you could do that would help us a lot," he told Winger. "Can you can walk us through what you did and show us exactly where you were when it happened?"

Winger considered that for a moment, then nodded. Cox was impressed that Winger would agree to such a gruesome task. He was one of the most cooperative—and courageous—witnesses Cox had ever dealt with.

"Start here," Williamson said. "Show us where your gun was. What made you get it?"

Winger slowly came to his feet and walked to the nightstand. He had known something was wrong, he said, so he grabbed his weapon and ran out of the room. He led the detectives to the hallway and pointed to the blood-stained carpet, the spot where he said he had seen his wife being beaten. Winger lifted his arm to demonstrate how the man was ready to strike another blow.

"It was like slow motion. Like it wasn't really registering," he said. He said he shot the man and saw him roll off his wife.

Winger said that the gun had been a gift from his father. Both men had been on the pistol team in the military. He was a good shot and was surprised to see Harrington start to get up.

Speaking softly, Winger told the detectives that he was carried by momentum to the area where the wounded man had fallen. He was standing right over him, Winger said, when he fired the second shot. Donnah was in a fetal position. There was a lot of blood.

The physical evidence appeared to perfectly match Winger's story. There was a large pool of blood where Donnah was killed and another where Harrington fell. The paramedics had pointed out a projectile in the carpet that had likely gone through Harrington's head. Cox saw no reason to detain Winger any longer.

By the time they left the house, the hot day was cooling off. Friends and neighbors who had gathered outside ran to Winger and hugged him. They were relieved to see for themselves that he—like baby Ruby—was unharmed. Television news crews waiting at the curb rushed to get shots of Winger and the people surrounding him. Seeking privacy, Rabbi Datz put his arm around his friend and led him to a neighbor's house. Cox followed, keeping a respectable distance.

In the quiet of the neighbor's living room, Cox braced himself for the crushing despair that was about to come crashing down on Mark Winger. He hoped the rabbi would find a way to comfort him. He prayed that Winger's faith would give him strength.

"I shot a man," Winger confessed softly.

Datz nodded. They were seated close together on the couch. The rabbi later recalled that this was new ground for him. He was used to "mopping up" duty, offering comfort to bereaved families. This was a more direct role. He had to tell a good friend what was bound to be the most devastating news he would ever hear.

"I have bad news," he said, his arm clutching Winger's shoulder. "Donnah is dead."

Winger groaned. He fell to his knees and wept.

5

Friends and Family

On Tuesday, August 29, Jo Datz was working later than usual at her office job in the state bureaucracy. Seven months pregnant, her feet were swollen and she felt uncomfortable in the late-summer heat. She heard the screeching sirens of emergency vehicles pass but had no inkling they were headed for the Winger home.

Jo's friends had thrown her a baby shower three days earlier, on Saturday, the same day Mark Winger drove home from Chattanooga. Donnah and DeAnn Schultz arrived at the shower together, leaving Ruby at home in the care of DeAnn's teenage daughter. Jo later recalled that Donnah was her usual effervescent self—even more so because she was thrilled that their children would be so close in age. At DeAnn's urging, Donnah told Jo about the odd ride home from the airport but was far more interested in talking about the babies.

Three days later, in her office, Jo thought about Donnah. The two women spoke every day, as usual, but had not seen each other since the shower. Jo was giving Donnah time to be alone with Mark, who, after all, had just come back from a lengthy business trip. But, Jo felt, it was now time for her to pay a visit. She would go that evening. Her own husband, Mike, the rabbi, had a meeting scheduled.

"I do sometimes wonder what would have happened if I left work on time and dropped in to see Donnah at 4:30, as I often did," she later told *48 Hours*.

While Jo was catching up on work, Mike Datz was in his downtown office. He took a phone call from Officer David Barringer, who told him what had happened and said that Mark Winger requested his presence. Mike's heart raced as he rushed to the scene. He was concerned not only for his close friend but also for his very pregnant wife. He wanted to break the news to her himself, before she found out some other way. He called one of her friends and told her to do whatever she had to in order to distract Jo and keep her away from the television and radio.

"I was very worried that this could send her into early labor or even a miscarriage," Mike said later.

When Jo came home, her friend was waiting in the driveway. She said she wanted to talk about an upcoming event at the synagogue and suggested they sit outside and talk.

"I thought this was a bit odd, as there was really no urgency," Jo said later. But she went along with it to be polite.

A piano tuner working in Jo's home that day came

out to report that the phone was ringing incessantly. Jo went inside to take the call. Her friend followed helplessly, unable to stop her. It was DeAnn Schultz and she sounded hysterical.

"Donnah's been hurt," DeAnn said, panting.

It was impossible to understand another word she said.

Jo assured DeAnn that Donnah would be okay. She was on her way there, she said. Jo's friend had no choice but to drive her to the Winger home. On the way, she said something vague about hearing that there was a problem. It was apparent to Jo that her friend was holding back and something bad had happened. Never for one moment did she imagine how bad it really was.

Jo's heart sank when she saw the yellow police tape cordoning off the house and the strange beat-up car in front of it. She spotted her husband and ran to him. He hugged her and assured her that Mark and Ruby were not hurt.

"I kept on asking about Donnah," she said later. "He finally told me that Donnah was dead. I cannot tell you what a horrifying moment that was."

Jo was hysterical. She could not accept the news. The crazy driver that Donnah had talked about at her shower had actually come back and killed her.

Later, when the police finally released Mark and left, Mike and Jo sat with him in his neighbor's den. They could hear the buzz of other friends and neighbors who had gathered upstairs.

"I killed a man," Mark repeated over and over, shaking his head and looking at the floor.

"At least you killed the man who killed Donnah," Jo said, unknowingly echoing Detective Charlie Cox. It was a small consolation for Jo: not so much as an act of heroism but one of justice.

The Datzes attended to Mark's immediate needs. Mike left a message with Michael Metnick, an attorney who was a member of their temple. Jo called a doctor in an effort to get a prescription for something to help Mark rest. As it turned out, Metnick was on his way over, having heard about the incident on the news. The medication would be unnecessary; before anyone could pick it up, Mark fell asleep on the couch.

Ira and Sara Jane Drescher were born two blocks away from each other, near Yankee Stadium in the Bronx. Sara Jane's family had a spacious apartment in an upscale building. Ira shared a bedroom with his parents in a cramped three-room apartment. He and Sara Jane attended the same elementary school but did not meet until nearly four decades later, in 1984, at a singles party in Hollywood, Florida. By then both of them resided in the oceanfront community, twenty-three miles north of Miami, that dubbed itself "Diamond of the Gold Coast."

Ira was newly divorced after a twenty-eight-year marriage. Tan, with taut muscles, he had an energy and vigor that were the envy of men half his sixty-one years. He had worked his way up in the hotel business and used his smarts to acquire and manage a retirement home. He was the president of the Apartment and Hotel Association of Hollywood. He played hard, too, pitching in regular softball games (fast-pitch on Sundays) and running fiercely competitive sprints (he had won an impressive collection of medals).

Sara Jane, stylish and petite, also kept fit. The daughter of a well-respected longtime circulation director at the *New York Times*, Sara Jane had a childhood home that had been filled with celebrities and high-powered politicians. She had two master's degrees and worked as a teacher when she raised her three daughters. Like Ira, she was proud of her grown children.

Sara Jane enjoyed attending symphonies, ballets, and operas. Ira preferred the Miami Heat, Dolphins, and Marlins. They both loved to travel and entertain, and both were active in community affairs. They had an immediate attraction for each other that, four years later, matured to love. They were married in December 1988, just three months before Donnah and Mark took their vows.

On the evening of Tuesday, August 29, 1995, the Dreschers enjoyed a leisurely dinner with friends at an Italian restaurant and didn't return home to their gated community until sometime after 10:30. They lived in a ranch-style villa situated a mere twenty yards from the eleventh green of a golf course. It was an idyllic setting: immaculately kept grounds that attracted egrets, herons, and occasional flocks of exotic birds they could not identify.

Sara Jane was reading in bed when the phone rang at 11:00. She answered, expecting to hear the familiar voice of the woman who managed Ira's retirement home at night. Ira was a hands-on businessman who insisted on knowing everything in real time. Sara Jane suspected there was a minor crisis; maybe a resident had been taken to the hospital or some drugs were missing. The caller was male—not anyone Sara Jane recognized—and he asked for Ira. Sara Jane handed the phone to her husband .

The man told Ira he was Mike Datz, the Springfield rabbi who was a close friend of Mark and Donnah. He sounded tense.

"Can we talk alone?" he asked.

Ira walked to his home office on the other side of the villa, wondering what would prompt Datz to call so late—or at all. It had to be something serious. Ira prepared himself to deal with whatever problem it was and spare Sara Jane the worry.

He waited for Sara Jane to hang up in the bedroom before assuring the rabbi that they would not be over-heard.

"I have been trying to reach you for hours," Mike said. "I have terrible news."

He told Ira to sit down. Ira's heart sped up. He dropped to his chair as requested. He heard the rabbi take a deep breath.

"Donnah was murdered."

"Can you please repeat that?"

"Donnah was murdered."

Ira felt his shirt dampen with sweat. His hands were clammy. He absentmindedly switched the phone from one hand to the other. He was overwhelmed. How could he accept what the rabbi just said?

"Tell me how—what—please—"

Mike Datz was still struggling to grasp the situation himself. Breaking the news to the Dreschers was excruciatingly difficult. He told Ira what he knew about the intruder and Donnah's bizarre ride home from the airport.

"The man was apparently crazy. He somehow got into the house today. He beat her with a hammer."

Ira's entire body was convulsing.

"There's more," the rabbi said. "Mark shot and killed the driver."

Mark had had to kill a man! Ira could not absorb any of this. He bombarded Datz with questions, believing that somehow, if he knew exactly what had happened, it would make sense.

The rabbi patiently answered as well as he could. There were details he did not know: for example, how the intruder had gotten into the house. He assured Ira that Mark and Ruby were safe and with him. The rabbi said, a little apologetically, that he felt he had to hold a memorial service for Donnah on Thursday in Springfield. It would be inconvenient for the Dreschers, but the people in Springfield needed a way to say good-bye before Donnah's body was taken away for burial. Ira said he would make arrangements to fly the family and friends there the next day. They agreed to meet at the rabbi's home.

Ira was paralyzed. He could handle the travel plans, no matter how complex, but first he would have to do the most difficult thing of his life: tell Sara Jane. How could he do that? He begged the young rabbi for advice.

"Stay as calm as possible," Rabbi Mike said. "Take whatever time you need to recoup. You know Sara Jane. Do it the best way you know how."

Ira hung up, trembling and crying. Heeding the rabbi's advice, he sat alone in the dimly lit room for a good ten minutes, attempting to regain his composure. No matter what he did and how he did it, Sara Jane's life would never be the same. He was overcome with dread.

When Ira walked back to the bedroom, he was sopping wet with sweat. He stood by the door. Sara Jane, reading without her glasses, could not make out his face from that distance.

"Everything okay?" she asked casually.

Ira walked slowly towards her and stopped by his side of the bed. He did not respond. Sara Jane repeated the question. Ira stood like a statue. Sara Jane put on her glasses and saw that the color had drained from his face.

"Ira, what's wrong?"

Sara Jane's heart raced. She moved to Ira's side of the bed. She had never seen Ira behave like this. He was scaring her.

"Honey, what's wrong? Tell me."

"I can't," Ira said. "I can't tell you."

Ira kept shaking his head. Sara Jane crawled over and sat directly in front on him on her knees. She grabbed his hands.

"Ira, you have to tell me. Tell me. Whatever it is, we will deal with it."

Sara Jane saw tears fall from Ira's eyes.

"You've got to tell me!" she said, squeezing his hands hard. "What happened?"

"It's terrible. It's so terrible. How am I going to tell you?"

Sara Jane was beside herself. Ira had no choice but to tell her. Like Rabbi Datz, he was straightforward.

"Donnah was murdered this afternoon," he whispered.

Sara Jane collapsed in Ira's arms and screamed. For the next half hour they held each other, rocking, wailing, and sobbing.

"Loud screams and then quiet. Again and again until there was nothing left," she later wrote in her notes.

6

Glorious Days

Sara Jane's last days with Donnah had been glorious ones. It was the happiest time of Donnah's life.

There was that beautiful spring morning when Sara Jane videotaped baby Ruby's arrival. This was her first grandchild, the culmination of Donnah's unrelenting efforts to have the family she longed for. That ideal day—with trees in full bloom and birds bursting with song—was one of the best in her life.

"She's going to have such a wonderful, wonderful home here," Sara Jane gushed, narrating the video. "What a lucky little girl!"

Less than two months later, in mid-July, when Mark went to a training seminar in Chattanooga, Donnah took the baby to Florida. She spent eight whirlwind days there, showing off Ruby to family, friends, and everyone else she met. She snapped roll after roll of photos.

"My other daughters were here," Sara Jane later told Richard Schlesinger. "So we just spent lots of time together. Just 'cause we wanted to be together."

Donnah's sisters showered their newborn niece with affection and presents.

In August, when Mark went back to Chattanooga to finish his training, Donnah returned to her mother's home.

"I could see Donnah's face as she was walking from the plane, holding this beautiful child," Sara Jane said. "We all felt the blessing of this child."

They spent another week cooing over the baby and watching her grow before their eyes. Time passed quickly. Early in the morning on Wednesday, August 23, Donnah and Sara Jane slipped into the master bedroom to wake Ira. They were about to leave for the airport and it was time for another good-bye.

When Ira opened his eyes, he saw Donnah flash a big smile. Ruby was next to him, on his pillow, at eye level.

"Hi, Pop-I," Donnah said, using her affectionate name for Ira. "Good morning! Look who's here!"

They giggled, hugged, and kissed good-bye, just as they had done a few weeks earlier. Ira was sure he and Sara Jane would be going to Springfield in the near future. It never crossed his mind that this would be the last time he would see Donnah.

Donnah and Sara Jane talked all the way to the airport, mostly about Ruby.

"I am never very good at good-byes," Sara Jane later explained. "But what I always did with my girls was tell them . . . when I kiss them goodbye, the last thing I always said is: 'Tell the pilot to drive carefully.'

So I kissed Donnah right on the curb and said, 'Tell the pilot to drive carefully.'"

Donnah called her mother to let her know that she got home safely. They chatted, as always, before saying good night. They looked forward to their next time together, but that would never happen.

The third shift was on duty when Detective Charlie Cox returned to the station after leaving Westview Drive. He found a report that Donnah's friend DeAnn Shultz had called in when she was staying with Donnah. Just as Mark Winger had said, Donnah had been frightened by the man who drove her home from the airport.

"Schultz said Donnah Winger is very trusting and she fears the man will take advantage of the fact that he knows where Winger lives," the report said.

DeAnn's call generated a "premise check," meaning the officers on duty in patrol cars drove by once in a while to see if anything seemed out of the ordinary.

Cox ran a background check on Roger Harrington. Just as he thought, their paths had crossed before. Cox had once managed a mobile home park and had rented a trailer to Harrington and his wife. One day Cox heard a lot of shouting and smashing glass coming from that trailer. He went to check and ended up physically throwing Harrington out on the street.

"He was beating her," Cox said. "He had her bent over the couch and was getting ready to hit her again when I grabbed him."

Cox said he wanted to nail the lowlife, but Harrington's wife refused to press charges.

Cox also learned that Harrington had spent time in a mental health facility. All in all, Cox thought, he seemed to be capable of doing exactly what Mark Winger had said he'd done.

Mark Winger's reputation, by contrast, was untarnished. Just about every neighbor the cops spoke with praised the Wingers. They were a great couple who were thrilled to finally have a child. The timing of the crime could not be more tragic.

Charlie Cox echoed that sentiment in his written report. Winger, he wrote, was "genuinely hurt and it is very apparent that he and his wife were very much in love and that this should have never happened."

Sangamon County State's Attorney Patrick Kelley spelled it out in a press conference arranged hastily before the eleven o'clock news.

"Mr. Winger acted in self-defense when he shot Mr. Harrington, and so therefore no charges will be filed against him," Kelley said. "I anticipate that there will never be any charges filed against Mr. Winger."

Sara Jane and Ira Drescher spent the night breaking the awful news to Donnah's sisters and other relatives.

"I had to hurt my daughters, rip them to pieces," Sara Jane said later. "I don't know where I got the strength to lift up the phone and dial. I don't know the words I used."

The next day the family flew to St. Louis and made the long drive to Springfield, retracing Donnah's journey. When they arrived at the Datz home, there were cars parked up and down the street. The house had become a gathering place for mourners.

Mark and Ruby spent the night there, as did DeAnn Schultz. DeAnn, an experienced mother of two, took care of the baby, making use of the nursery Jo Datz had set up for her expected child. Throughout the morning, friends and family trickled in, hugging each other in shock and grief.

Mark's family was there when the Dreschers arrived. Mark's mother, Sallie, embraced Sara Jane. Sallie said that Mark felt horrible and was afraid that Sara Jane would hate him.

Sara Jane wanted to assure Mark that she did not blame him. He was in a back room with DeAnn, talking with detectives. Mike Datz explained to the Dreschers that, because there had been a double homicide, the police had an obligation to wrap up any loose ends. They understood Mark was under stress.

When Mark emerged, Sara Jane went right to him. She could feel the eyes of everyone in the room focus on her, and heard whispers. She embraced Mark and they cried together, oblivious to everything else.

"I am sorry," he repeated over and over.

"Mark," Sara Jane said, looking straight at him and composing herself, "I know you did the best you could. And I love you very much."

They hugged. It was so hard to get the words

out, but Sara Jane had to communicate that thought.
She buried herself in Mark's arms, paying no attention to the din of voices around her. She was in a
nightmare, she thought, or an out-of-body experience. She heard someone mention Ruby's name and
looked up.

DeAnn Schultz was there, with the baby in her
arms. She slowly handed her to Sara Jane. Sara Jane
cradled her precious granddaughter and kissed her
face. She was so innocently unaware of the loss she
had just suffered. DeAnn said she would take care of
Ruby as long as she was needed. Sara Jane was grateful that Donnah had good, caring friends.

So many friends and neighbors came to Sara Jane
and expressed their love for Donnah. People from the
temple brought armloads of food. Everyone was eager
to give whatever comfort they could.

Sara Jane asked Rabbi Mike for counsel. There was
so much she did not understand.

"Why would anyone want to kill Donnah?" she
asked. "Tell me, what happened?"

The rabbi sat with Sara Jane in a quiet corner of the
living room and held her hands. He patiently told her
what he knew about Roger Harrington's background
and the strange phone calls. Harrington must have
fixated on Donnah, he said, and Donnah had been
frightened.

Sara Jane was puzzled. Why didn't Donnah mention any of this to her? She thought hard and remembered that Donnah had said something. She said

the driver who took her home was a little . . . nuts? Was that the word she had used? Yes, she had said "nuts." She mentioned that DeAnn was staying with her until Mark returned, and did seem a little concerned. But she was not really frightened or alarmed.

Sara Jane told the rabbi what she had told her daughter.

"I said, 'You know, Donnah, there are all types of people in this world. You're home now. You're safe.'"

Sara Jane had not been the least bit worried for her daughter. Their conversation moved on and they talked about Jo Datz's upcoming baby shower. The ride home from the airport never came up again. How did Donnah's brief encounter with the driver lead to her murder? Why would he want to kill her? She still could not understand.

Sara Jane listened as the rabbi told her as many details as she could bear. When she could not take any more, she ran to the bathroom. She felt nauseous but had not eaten: there was no food to throw up. She came back to the living room, and a doctor who knew Donnah asked if she wanted medication to help her through the next few days. Sara Jane thanked him but declined his offer. People brought her food and urged her to eat. She did not feel like eating, but she knew she would need strength.

"There would be decisions to be made and if I allowed myself to get weak, I would not be able to make those decisions," she wrote later.

She did not want other people to make those decisions for her. She had given birth to Donnah. It was her responsibility to bury her.

She picked up a fork and took a bite of something. After a while, she took another bite.

"It was the beginning of my journey to survival," she said.

7

Ceremonies

When Ira went to console Mark, Mark hugged him hard. Ira felt his son-in-law's body tremble. Mark had never looked so terrible. Ira could not imagine what he was going through: Mark had been forced to take a life and it was in vain. If only Mark had come up those stairs a little sooner or turned left into the dining room instead of right towards the bedroom! The precious seconds saved might have been enough to save Donnah. Like everyone else, Ira worried that Mark would be consumed by unwarranted guilt.

Ira later told *48 Hours* that, several hours after he got to the Datz home, Mark told him that he was going back to Westview house to get some things he needed in the next few days. DeAnn's husband, John Schultz, was going with him. Sara Jane asked Ira to go along and pick out a dress for Donnah's burial.

The three men piled into Mark's bright red pickup truck. Mark insisted on driving. Shortly after leaving,

Mark spontaneously began talking about his encounter with the intruder. He painted a vivid picture, but his words were solemn.

Ira's heart ached for him. Mark had done what he had to do.

"He had to see his beautiful wife get her head crushed and he held her in his lap, trying to tell her to hang in there," Ira said later. "I told him he was incredible."

Ira had lots of questions, but he kept his curiosity in check and refrained from asking any of them. The last thing he wanted was to add to Mark's pain. John Schultz also kept quiet. Mark kept talking.

Nothing Mark said prepared Ira for what he saw when he walked into the house. He immediately felt physically ill. The room that Donnah had lovingly decorated reeked of gore. It was like a scene from a horror movie, with bloodstains streaked across the ceiling and walls. Two large sections of carpet had been removed, but the blood had soaked through to the floor. Donnah's homey touches—the quilts, the framed photos, Ruby's colorful plastic toys—seemed grotesque in this context.

To Ira's surprise, Mark walked to one of the stains in the floor and pointed out the bullet hole. He showed where he was standing when he fired the shot at Roger Harrington. None of it seemed real to Ira. He wondered if he had the guts to do what Mark had done.

Ira had a lot of affection for Mark. The two men had bonded in a male kind of way, over home improvement projects and sports talk. Mark, originally from Cleveland, was a loyal Indians fan. Ira cheered for the Marlins. They reveled in their rivalry.

Ira saw some of himself in Mark, but considered himself more "hip." Mark lived up to his geeky reputation. Ira remembered how excited Mark was a few months earlier when his father gave him a book for his birthday.

"I open it up; all it had was chemical equations," Ira later told *48 Hours* correspondent Richard Schlesinger. "He was bonkers because he thought this was fantastic."

Sara Jane joked that she wanted to read it after Mark did.

"Just don't give away the ending," she told him.

It all seemed so trivial now. Ira realized how much he had grown to love Mark. He wondered if he would ever be the same.

While John Schultz helped Mark gather his belongings, Ira said he took the time to conduct a quick survey. Everything appeared normal in the basement. The workout area and Mark's workshop seemed undisturbed. Ira peeked in the garage: nothing was out of place there, either. For a fleeting moment, he thought about Stonewall, Mark and Donnah's 180-pound mastiff. Stonewall spent most of his time in the garage, where there was a doggy door that gave him access to the yard. He was nowhere to be seen. Ira remembered how Donnah loved to rub him and scratch behind his ear. She babied the giant canine by wiping his drooling snout with a dishcloth. That dog had loved Donnah, as everyone had.

Ira went to the master bedroom closet and rummaged through Donnah's summer dresses. She had been a skilled shopper; each dress was prettier than the last. Ira's first priority was Sara Jane, but he also felt a profound sense of personal loss. He would never see Donnah smile again or argue with her about a boxing match.

Her death had been so brutal. What kind of human being bashes in another person's head with a steel hammer? What had motivated that driver to commit such a cruel act? Donnah was a pussycat; she could have never angered anyone that much. Ira wondered if Harrington had made sexual advances that she resisted.

Mark and John were ready to leave. Under pressure, Ira chose Donnah's blue flowered dress; she always looked cute in that. He was glad to get out of the house.

"Do you think she suffered?" Sara Jane asked when Ira returned.

Ira was unprepared for the question. His mind flashed to the bloody mess he had seen.

"I don't think she felt a thing after she was hit the first time."

It felt like the right thing to say.

That night in their Springfield hotel room, Sara Jane Drescher absentmindedly turned on the news. Donnah's murder was the lead story. Sara Jane saw the yellow tape around the house and the crowd gathered outside. She saw the gurney carrying Donnah being wheeled to the ambulance. She would later learn that Donnah was still alive at that point.

The next day was equally difficult. Ira, Sara Jane, Mark, and Mark's brother, Greg, went to the funeral home to make arrangements for Donnah's body to be flown to Florida. Sara Jane was grateful that Mark had agreed to have her buried there.

The funeral director asked them if they wanted to see Donnah one last time before he closed the casket. Sara Jane cried.

"I can't, I just can't."

Mark steadied his jaw and said he would see her. Ira wanted to go with him but would not leave Sara Jane alone. Greg Winger accompanied his brother to the basement and Donnah's casket.

"Mark just collapsed," Greg later told *48 Hours*. "He absolutely collapsed to his knees on the floor, holding her hand, crying. He asked God to take his life and give hers back."

When the brothers returned, Ira asked Mark how Donnah looked.

"Like she was sleeping," Mark said.

Sara Jane's friends later assured her that she had made the right decision. It was better to remember Donnah alive, not as she looked after the assault. Maybe so. The image she carried was Donnah's "radiant smile and laughing eyes." But she had misgivings about not seeing her daughter that one last time. Ira unequivocally said he had made a mistake.

"I'm real sorry for that," he said. "It's my biggest regret."

The Springfield memorial was held on the last day of August, in a hot chapel packed with horrified people. The Dreschers sat in the front row, behind Donnah's casket. Sara Jane visualized her daughter sleeping inside. She was astonished by how many people told her that Donnah had touched their lives.

"Some mentioned how much they loved her, others how much they respected her."

Attorney Michael Metnick sat quietly in the back. He had come out of compassion, but also, he later admitted, curiosity. This was an unusual case, even by the standards of a defense attorney. There seemed to be so little motive for so much violence.

The bushy-haired young rabbi poured his heart and soul into the thirty-minute eulogy. He was struck by the raw injustice. No one deserved to die the way Donnah did, but in her case it was especially senseless. She had been a good person whose life was at its peak. Her young daughter, who depended on her, would be deprived of her forever.

"It was hard not to let those feelings permeate the eulogy," Mike Datz said.

Datz's goal was to get through the service without breaking down himself. He succeeded, but many other mourners did not.

The rabbi's wife, Jo, thought about how Donnah blossomed when she became a mother. She was always caring and full of life, but after the baby came home, there was another dimension to her. Jo had looked forward to experiencing the same profound change.

Sara Jane remembered being a twenty-two-year-old who cherished her unborn baby. That baby was the fulfillment of her childhood dream.

"I wanted this baby more than life itself," she said. And baby Donnah was even more beautiful than she had imagined.

"Her coloring was a soft pink that glowed even in the dimmest of light."

Sara Jane thought about holding that infant in her arms. How could she know the future? How could she know how short that baby's life was to be?

Sara Jane was the last person to leave the room after the service. She was standing alone by the coffin when Ira came to tell her they were ready to take Donnah to Florida. Sara Jane kissed the casket and told her daughter how much she loved her.

"Tell the pilot to drive carefully," she said.

The funeral was held the following day in Florida. That morning Sara Jane cried through her shower, then sat at her dressing table and stared at the mirror. She decided to put on makeup and get dressed. It was impossible to keep her eyes from tearing, but she was resolute. She would be there for Donnah.

It was hot and humid, with almost no breeze to

mitigate the stickiness. The chapel was crowded with friends and family. Mike and Jo Datz and DeAnn and John Schultz flew in from Springfield. Sara Jane was numb but went through the motions, hugging and kissing the dozens of people desperate to comfort her.

"I don't know how I got through those first couple of days," she said later. "I remember very little of it. I think that there's a higher being that comes and focuses in on you. I think you go into a mode of shock."

Mark walked around grief-stricken, carrying Ruby everywhere he went. Her tiny fingers gripped his shirt tightly.

"We hurt terribly for him," Ira said later. "He was left alone with his baby."

The Dreschers watched as Mark, baby in arms, bent down and kissed Donnah's casket. They silently vowed to embrace him as a son, no matter what his future held.

The service was officiated by the same rabbi who had married Donnah and Mark. Then the casket was taken to the grave site. There were more prayers, then it was time for the casket to be lowered. Sara Jane rushed forward and fell on it, sobbing and screaming.

"'No' was all I could say over and over," she remembered. "I could not leave Donnah alone. She would be afraid."

Ira and other family members gently coaxed her back to the car. They drove home in silence. Once there, Sara Jane retreated to her bedroom. She lay on her bed, hoping to die.

8

Case Closed

The double homicide alarmed the Wingers' neighbors. The police went to great pains to reassure them that there was no imminent danger. This was not a random crime; the killer had specifically targeted Donnah Winger.

The press covered the case more as a heartbreaking drama than a mystery. Donnah and Mark were undeserving victims of unexpected violence. Roger Harrington's dilapidated car became a creepy backdrop for television reporters who interviewed bewildered people on the street.

"They were very good neighbors," said a man in his forties, shaking his head. "I watched their dog."

When Sara Jane returned to Florida, she summoned the courage to say a few words to the press herself.

"Donnah was the most caring human being I ever met," she said, adding that she found solace in "knowing that my daughter died at the happiest point in her life."

There was speculation about the circumstances of

the crime. Roger Harrington emerged as a menacing figure. The question was: what drove him off the edge?

People who knew Harrington were contacted, but they seemed oblivious to his dark side. The media turned to court records.

"Harrington was committed by court order to a mental health facility," Springfield's *State Journal-Register* reported. "He was depressed and delusional at the time."

"Not surprisingly, Harrington had a dark, troubled past," a television anchor stated. "Court records paint a picture of a very disturbed individual," said a reporter standing in front of the courthouse.

There was the "lessons to be learned" angle, an attempt to put a positive spin on the tale of senseless brutality. How could crimes like this be prevented?

"Donnah Winger met her killer on a shuttle bus ride," one reporter said. "In Illinois, neither private nor public shuttle companies are required to do background criminal checks on potential employees."

A state official charged with transportation oversight promised to rectify that.

In mid-September, barely two weeks after the crime, the county coroner assembled a jury to examine the circumstances of Roger Harrington's death. It was, more or less, a legal formality. The autopsies revealed grim details—Donnah had been hit with the hammer seven times—but no real surprises. Harrington's two gunshot wounds and the bruises on his chest were consistent with Mark Winger's statements.

Detective Charlie Cox testified that Harrington believed he was guided by a demonic spirit named Dahm. Cox told the jurors that Donnah's friend had stayed with her until Mark Winger returned from his business trip. That friend answered an ominous phone call from an unidentified male. It made her apprehensive enough to notify the police. Sadly, that did not avert the tragedy.

The record showed that Mark Winger called Harrington's boss, Ray Duffey, to complain. Duffey called Harrington to let him know he was suspended from work until the problem was cleared up. On the morning of the murder, Winger spoke with Harrington directly. Winger tried to reason with him, but Harrington was talking with an imaginary third party. The man was clearly deranged.

"There is nothing to indicate anything other than what the husband described," Cox testified. "Everything fit perfectly with the evidence at the scene."

The coroner's jury acted swiftly, ruling that Mark Winger was justified when he shot Roger Harrington in the head. The case of the bizarre double homicide was officially closed.

9

Decisions

Mark Winger's legal problems were behind him, but he faced a cruel new reality. He had a tough decision to make: was he prepared to be a single, working father? Ruby's adoption was not yet finalized. The Wingers had met all of their obligations, but the requisite amount of time had not passed. Mark was crazy about the baby, but under the circumstances it would not be unreasonable for him to turn her back to the state.

Mark took a leave from work and retreated to his parents' home in a suburb of Cleveland. He had to re-evaluate his position. There was a lot to digest.

"I was overwhelmed by shock," Mark said years later. "I was fearful of losing my daughter as much as I was fearful of being a single parent. I was besieged by confusion and loneliness. I blamed myself for Donnah's death for having complained about Roger Harrington."

Mark's parents, Jerry and Sallie, were also bereft. They had adored Donnah. Donnah called her mother-in-law at least once a week and Sallie was energized by their conversations. She already missed Donnah's cheery "Hi, Mom!" and her breathless chatter. Neither Sallie nor Jerry could fathom the grief their son felt.

"He took Donnah's death extremely hard," Sallie said.

In an interview with *48 Hours* correspondent Richard Schlesinger, the Wingers said their family had always been close-knit. Mark had never given them any problems at any age.

"He was really a wonderful child," Sallie said.

Mark was a high achiever, she said. He had excelled in school while still managing to have an active social life. He graduated from the Virginia Military Institute with a degree in its grueling physics program. After leaving active duty in the army, he joined the reserves, rising to the rank of captain.

"We were extremely proud of Mark," Sallie said.

"He was a good military man: he did things by the numbers," Jerry said. It was good training.

But, the Wingers said, nothing in Mark's past had prepared him for what happened the day Donnah was killed.

"He was very, very distraught that he had to take a human being's life," Sallie told Schlesinger. "He is a loving, warm human being."

Mark's brother, Greg, agreed.

"He told me it was very difficult—even though the guy was attacking his wife. He said, 'I just can't seem to cope with that part of it.'"

Mark returned to Springfield in late September. He went back to work and took temporary refuge in his boss's home at night. He accepted a generous offer from one of Donnah's friends, who said Ruby could stay at his home. Ruby's grandmothers took turns helping to take care of the baby.

Mark's boss's wife made sure her houseguest sat down for meals. She worried that he was not eating well and had lost too much weight. As she saw it, he was consumed with concern about how to keep his daughter safe.

Mark's friends were eager to help him. Rabbi Mike Datz referred him to a psychiatrist. Mark had a few sessions with her but chose not to continue. He seemed determined to find his own path to recovery.

Mark decided to keep his job and continue living in Springfield. He had his house cleaned and refurbished. He took the necessary steps to finalize Ruby's adoption, which breezed through the courts. He contacted a nanny school and hired a twenty-one-year-old graduate to help with parenting chores. By mid-autumn, he and Ruby moved back to their Westview home.

Mark wrote a letter to the *State Journal-Register* expressing his gratitude to Springfield's citizens for helping him in his days of distress.

It was published on October 15, 1995—less than two months after Donnah and Roger Harrington were killed. Mark began by stating that he and his wife were strangers to the community when they first arrived but had met "many wonderful people" over the years. He said he was overwhelmed by the compassion everyone showed him after Donnah was murdered. He remembered Donnah as a "caring and decent" person whose life was "suddenly and needlessly ended." On behalf of himself, his daughter, and his wife's family, he assured the community that he would long remember its kindness.

While the community mourned Donnah Winger and rallied behind her heroic husband, one family stood bitterly alone. Ralph and Helen Harrington knew that their son Roger had his share of all problems, as all kids did. But they were damn sure he was no psychotic killer.

The Harringtons were salt of the earth: They worked hard and expected little in return. Ralph had been a trucker for most of his life. Helen was a clerk in a state government office. They lived in a small single-story house on the north side of town, just down the block from the state fairgrounds. It was the same house their children were raised in.

Ralph and Helen adopted Roger and his younger sister, Barbara, from Helen's cousin. Both children were infants when the Harringtons took them in, and they were close growing up.

On the evening of August 29, 1995, Helen stepped out on the porch to feed the cats that had grown accustomed to hanging out there. The hot day was cooling down. She came back inside and prepared her husband's dinner. He was working late, in the stockroom of a large food distribution company. It was heavy work, but his years in trucking had prepared him for it.

Ralph got home a little before 8:00 p.m. He and Helen sat down to a late meal together. Neither of them had any idea that their son had died three hours earlier. Just as they began eating, the telephone rang. Helen took the call. A woman asked if she knew Roger Harrington.

"Yes," Helen said. "He's my son."

The woman would not identify herself by name but said that she worked at Memorial Hospital. Something had happened and the Harringtons should get there as soon as possible. Helen, panicked, asked for more information. She was worried because, a few hours earlier, she had heard Roger's license number run on a police scanner. The woman on the phone refused to give specifics.

"Just get down here," she said curtly.

At the hospital, Ralph and Helen were taken to a room to meet with the coroner and police. The coroner bluntly told them that Roger had been caught in the act of beating a woman with a hammer and the woman's husband shot and killed him. It was a home invasion, he said, and the woman died. The Harringtons could not believe their ears. Roger broke into a home? He was *dead*? He had *killed* someone? Nothing made sense.

"Roger was a happy-go-lucky guy," Ralph told *48 Hours.*

Helen asked if the murdered woman's husband was injured. Where was he? He was with his rabbi, the coroner said. Helen envied that. Her brother-in-law was a minister and she wished he were there with her now. She badly needed some guidance to make sense of the nightmare she found herself in. No one at the hospital was concerned about comforting her at the moment, however.

The Harringtons had no idea where to turn. They were with the authorities, and they seemed to have no doubt that Roger had been shot in self-defense. They were convinced that he was a crazed killer.

"They treated us like crap," Helen said.

She recalled that one detective, who said he was helping out on the case, stood with his foot propped against the wall, casually taking notes on a pad every time she said something. She felt his disdain as he bombarded Ralph and her with questions.

Helen told the detective that she had spoken with Roger the previous night. When asked if he had expressed any problems or troubles, she gave an emphatic "No!" The detective asked if Roger had been having trouble at work. No, Helen and Ralph said. Roger had been working for Bootheel Area Rapid Transportation (BART) for six months and was very happy.

The detective asked about Roger's mental health issues. The Harringtons said they did not know of any. The detective said he already knew that their son had been hospitalized. The Harringtons said they had vague memories of Roger voluntarily checking himself in for a brief stay four or five years earlier. It had been nothing serious.

The questions were relentless. Helen's head was spinning. She told the detective that Roger had moved out of their home earlier that month and moved in with his friend, Susan Collins, who rented a trailer outside of town. Collins needed money and Roger paid her two hundred dollars a month for a room. Helen gave the detective Collins's phone number. She was called and asked to come to the hospital.

"The interview at this point with the Harringtons was concluded, as they were in no emotional condition to continue," the detective wrote in his report. He noted that the Harringtons "seemed somewhat defensive in their protection of any background information on their son."

The detective would hand over his report to Cox and Williamson, but he was certain that the Harringtons had nothing useful to add to the investigation. This was not a complicated case.

10

Discrepancies

Roger Harrington's sister, Barbara Howell, rushed to the hospital still clinging to the hope that there was a terrible misunderstanding. How could her kid brother be dead? She had seen him just a few days before and he was fine. He dropped by to pick up some baby clothes for a friend who was running low on money.

"He slid me twenty dollars and said he'd see me later," Barbara told *48 Hours* correspondent Richard Schlesinger.

When she got to the hospital, Barbara only had to look at her parents to know that the horrible news was true. She grabbed her mother and held her tightly. Helen's whole body shook, Barbara says, as if her very insides were shivering.

"My parents are good, honest, decent people," Barbara said.

Barbara was proud of her upbringing. Her parents had given their children a loving home. They were taught good values. There was pizza every Friday night, but it had to be takeout. Helen did not want her children to eat in a place where alcohol was served.

Barbara had no idea that her family had had less than others. There was always food on the table and the kids had plenty of clothes. They went on lots of camping and fishing trips. She loved being with her kid brother. When she got her driver's license, he was her first passenger.

Barbara was convinced that the cops were wrong. She knew her brother better than anyone making accusations against him. Sure, he had talked weird and had some silly ideas. Yes, his brief marriage was a bad one: his wife brought out the worst in him. But Roger was incapable of real violence. Barbara hated it that no one questioned Mark Winger's story. They took his word and accepted that her parents had raised a psychotic killer.

In the days after Roger was killed, the Harringtons scraped together money to bury him. Helen asked her sister to write the check, fearing someone might recognize her name if she wrote it herself. There was a simple service—nothing as elaborate as Donnah's memorial—but Helen and Ralph had the support of a few loyal friends and relatives.

"They knew better," Helen said.

Afterward, the small group gathered in the Harrington living room and cried together. Helen and Ralph were grateful to be heard. Getting the authorities to listen was impossible.

"I felt branded," Helen later told Richard Schlesinger. "How would you feel if your son was called a murderer and you didn't have a chance to do anything about it?"

It wasn't as if the Harringtons didn't try. Barbara Howell was determined to talk with Detective Charlie Cox.

"I'm sorry to bother you," she said when she finally reached him by phone, "but you have this so wrong."

"No, ma'am, we don't."

"I never knew Roger to be angry," she said. "He was mellow, a happy-go-lucky guy. There's got to be more to the story."

Cox lost his patience. Relatives of murderers had an enormous capacity to deny reality, no matter how strong the evidence.

"Ma'am, any time you want to know how your kid brother walked in that home, snapped, and killed that woman, come to my office and I'll show you step by step."

Cox had told Barbara's mother the same thing when she called.

Barbara was stung by the rude treatment. She felt horrible—and, worse, helpless. She could do nothing to make them investigate further. Ironically, she had known one of the detectives, Doug Williamson, in high school. He had visited her home. How could he be so dismissive of her family?

The detectives were not only ignoring her family's feelings, they were paying little attention to an impor-tant witness. Roger's roommate, Susan Collins, told Barbara that Roger had an appointment to meet with a customer. If Winger knew he was coming, then he was not an intruder, as Winger claimed.

Helen Harrington was convinced that the cops did not look beyond the addresses of the victims. Everything her family said was brushed aside.

"We don't have a $72,000-a-year job. We're not nuclear engineers," she said. "And we don't live in a brick house that has concrete walls that you have to drive nails into to hang up a hat rack."

With their son officially declared a murderer, Ralph and Helen kept to themselves. They put in fewer hours at work. They stopped their newspaper delivery because they could not bear to read what was written about the case. They no longer sat on their porch because they hated watching the cars slow down as they passed.

"You go to the store and think everybody is watching you," Helen said.

They had no idea why Roger had been killed, only that Mark Winger had lied to the police. They turned to each other and shared their memories.

They remembered the sound of Roger sprinting up the porch steps when he came to pay a visit. He always had a smile on his face when he swung the door open.

They remembered how sensitive he had been. When he was a child, his dog ran into the street and was hit by a car. Ralph and Roger buried their pet in the yard the next morning. Roger's tears ran down the shovel handle.

They remembered how Roger had tried following in Ralph's footsteps and become a trucker. He was not cut out for it. Then he got the job with BART and everything changed. He was proud of his work and kept his van clean inside and out. He loved interacting with his customers.

Now he was gone, just like that.

The Harringtons' home became their sanctuary. Their world was unlike the one outside. But they were not as isolated as they thought they were. Someone else doubted Mark Winger's heroic and heartbreaking story—someone close to the investigation.

The Winger case was a welcome no-brainer for the Springfield police department, which was inundated by an inexplicable spike in homicides in August 1995. The same day that Donnah Winger died, a nineteen-year-old boy was shot to death on the north side of town. That, plus four unrelated murders earlier that month, nearly doubled the tally for the year. Mark Winger was a godsend: a reliable witness who gave police a lucid and logical account of the crime.

Detective Doug Williamson was not buying a word of it.

"Mark Winger is very convincing," he said. "But I am not convinced."

Williamson had expressed his doubts to his partner the very first day. He sensed something fishy. Detective Charlie Cox vehemently disagreed. He felt that Winger's pain was raw and real.

Williamson pointed out the problems he saw. With no signs of forced entry, someone had to have let Harrington into the house. Who would that be— Donnah?

"Why on earth would she open the door to someone she supposedly feared?" Williamson asked. "And even if she did, she definitely would not have left the baby alone on the bed when she went to the door."

Cox shrugged it off. He was emotionally drained by Winger's ordeal.

"Why would Harrington park right in front of the house?" Williamson continued. "The wrong way, no less." That was hardly the method of a stealthy killer.

Cox knew that, unlike in television dramas, real-life crimes were never tidy. It was the totality of evidence that mattered, and in this case there was more right than wrong with Winger's story.

"There are things in every homicide that don't fit," Cox later explained to Richard Schlesinger. Yes, he was bothered by the questions Williamson had raised, but most of the evidence he saw matched up.

"What did you do with those things that bothered you?" Schlesinger asked.

"Let them bother me. Like they always do."

What troubled Williamson most was that crumpled piece of paper he had seen on the front seat of Roger Harrington's car. It turned out to have Mark Winger's name and address written on it, and, most perplexing, a time: "4:30."

Winger had told the police he did not know who the man who was beating his wife was. He said he had never met Roger Harrington in person. He said nothing about having an appointment with him. Yet, here was a piece of paper that indicated that a time and place had been set.

Cox agreed that the note was disturbing, but he guessed there was a logical explanation he simply did not know at the moment. Crazy people do crazy things for crazy reasons. Roger Harrington was not in his right mind when he attacked Donnah.

The morning after the homicides, there was a meeting at police headquarters attended by Cox, Williamson, the other major case squad detectives helping them, and their supervisors. Everyone stated his position and the supervisors weighed the evidence. They would ultimately decide how the case would be handled.

Cox was confident that the case was solved. Williamson urged them to keep it open.

"I was argumentative," he said. "I pointed out red flags, pieces that don't seem to fit, all over the place."

One of the detectives who interviewed the Harringtons at the hospital sided with Cox.

"He told me he'd been working homicide for ten years," Williamson told *48 Hours*. The implication was that Williamson was too green to know what he was talking about. His request was turned down.

"They discounted everything I had to say. They

just didn't listen. They had no answers for what I was saying, but they said the case is going to be closed and that was that."

Williamson felt belittled. He was fuming. He did not give up.

"I asked for something very basic, which was to subpoena phone records from the residences of Roger Harrington and Mark Winger. I also wanted to get the records from the hotel where Mark had been staying in Tennessee."

That might reveal there was more going on than they knew about, he said.

The answer was still no. Williamson's more seasoned colleagues prevailed. Mark Winger had killed Roger Harrington in self-defense, they stated flatly. The supervisors did not want to do anything that would embarrass the department or cause the nuclear engineer further grief. This was a simple case and there was no need to complicate it. Williamson was ordered to drop it.

The young detective bristled at the dismissive treatment. True, he was new to the job, but he thought things through and felt that the investigation had fallen short. Phone records were sought routinely, even in far less serious cases. It was entirely possible that Mark Winger would be proven to be the distraught victim he said he was. It was just good police work to check.

He left the room in a huff. There was no choice but to follow orders. He would do so—reluctantly.

* * *

Charlie Cox felt he owed his defeated partner the courtesy of hearing him out in the privacy of their workspace. They wheeled their chairs out from their adjoining cubicles and talked. Williamson's large frame spilled over his seat and his resonant voice boomed, even when he tried to restrain it. He argued his case passionately as his partner politely listened. He kept at it for days, then weeks, then months.

The more Williamson learned about the circumstances, the less sense Winger's story made. For one thing, the crime scene techs found a blackjack—a tire iron fashioned as a weapon—-underneath the front seat of Roger Harrington's car. They also found a small knife in a sheath inside an overnight bag.

"The guy has two weapons with him but decides to leave them in the car and rely on using a weapon in the house that he didn't know was there. Does that sound right to you?" Williamson asked.

"He was a nut," Cox countered. "He wasn't always logical."

This was a man who spoke to some sort of demon-god. Maybe he hadn't gone to Winger's house with murder on his mind, Cox said. Maybe he just wanted to intimidate the Wingers and he snapped.

Williamson insisted that the note in Harrington's car indicated there was a meeting. He had no idea why Winger would invite him to his home. All he knew was that there were missing pieces and further investigation was needed. Maybe Winger and Harrington were working together somehow and something went wrong.

"So you think Winger might have wanted his wife dead?" Cox asked.

Everyone, without exception, said that the Wingers had a rock-solid marriage that was strengthened by their baby. Even Mark's in-laws had nothing but praise for him. He had no motive to want his wife dead. Williamson was overthinking the case, Cox believed. His experience taught him that simple answers were often the right answers.

How would a nuclear engineer be connected to a mentally deranged man who happened to drive his wife home from the airport? A man who happened to beat his own wife? A man who happened to make harassing phone calls to the Winger home?

Williamson admitted he had no idea why Winger would have any reason to be involved in any way.

"I just think he lied about having a meeting with Harrington. That's where the evidence leads."

Williamson reminded Cox about the interview they had conducted with Mark Winger and DeAnn Schultz at Rabbi Datz's home the morning after the murder. Williamson asked Winger if he had noticed anything in his house that was unfamiliar. Winger said he remembered seeing a large plastic mug and a pack of Marlboros on the dining room table. They weren't his.

Williamson later went back to the Westview house to retrieve those items. A professional cleaning crew had already begun its work and thrown them away. Williamson fished the mug and cigarettes from a garbage bag at the curb and checked them into the evidence room.

"Don't you find it strange," he later asked Cox, "that Harrington would walk into the house with his coffee mug and cigarettes? Doesn't that sound like he was expecting to have a chat?"

Cox nodded. Another good point. Another discrepancy.

Williamson was on a roll. It seemed clear, he said, that Harrington had an appointment.

In that same interview at the rabbi's house, Williamson continued, DeAnn talked about the hang-up phone calls that supposedly came from Harrington. She mentioned that she had a background in psychiatric nursing and was experienced with mental patients. She started to say something about Harrington's condition and the way people like him communicate when Winger cut her off, steering the conversation elsewhere.

"I'm sure he wanted to shut her up," Williamson said. "And it's not like she was making all that much sense, anyway."

Cox was puzzled. What did that mean?

Williamson had no idea. He just found it odd.

In early January 1996, out of the blue, Detective Cox got a phone call from Mark Winger. He asked to have his gun back. The request surprised Cox; most people would not want any reminder of a such a traumatic day. But, the detective knew, everyone deals with grief in his own way. Releasing the gun was easy to arrange; the case was closed and the evidence was slated to be destroyed.

When Winger came to the station, Cox told him again that he thought he was a hero. He wondered why he wanted the gun back. Winger reminded him that it was a gift from his father.

Cox nodded. He handed Winger the weapon, wished him well, and turned to leave. Winger kept talking, giving the detective an update on his life.

For the next half hour or so, Winger told Cox about his boss opening his home to him, going back to work, hiring a nanny to take care of his baby, and spending time with his parents, and how he was still close with Donnah's family. They were really going out of their way for him.

Cox found the details mind-numbing—and Winger's apparent need to recite them curious. The families of victims sometimes did get attached to cops, but usually during lengthy, difficult investigations. Cox had dealt with Winger for little more than a few hours. Why was the man being so chummy?

"How are things going with you?" Winger asked.

"Fine. We've been busy."

"How's the case going?"

"How's it going?"

Winger casually asked if there was anything new. Cox's antennae were up.

"As far as I was concerned, he should have just accepted that the case was closed," he said.

He assured Winger that nothing was new and sent him on his way, waving good-bye as the elevator doors closed. For the first time Cox believed his partner had been right all along. Winger had not been straight with them.

11

Healing

After Donnah's murder, Ira and Sara Jane Drescher remained close with Mark Winger. Sara Jane took on babysitting duties without hesitation when Mark moved in with his boss. Being with Donnah's child helped Sara Jane escape her pain.

From her vantage point in Springfield, however, Sara Jane became concerned for Mark. He was not himself. He rarely visited his daughter. Sara Jane repeatedly asked him to come by after work for dinner or even after dinner. It was all to no avail.

"I told him he had to help me take care of the baby," she wrote later in her notes. He needed to learn how to handle his daughter's wants and needs.

Sara Jane felt that Mark was avoiding her. It was part of his way of coping with his grief, she told herself. He could not handle seeing Ruby. The baby reminded him of the idyllic life he had lost. He would have to overcome that.

She also noticed that Mark was drinking a lot. It

was probably mostly beer, but it was too much. That was not healthy, either.

Sara Jane chided herself for those thoughts. How could she be so hard on Mark? He clearly needed help he was not getting. But it was equally clear that he needed to spend time with his daughter. Sara Jane wondered how she could take care of Mark and Ruby when she could barely take care of herself.

In the weeks after the crime, Ira replayed it over and over in his mind. Donnah's head had been pounded seven times. Why did Roger Harrington harbor such rage for her? It made no sense that it was because Winger caused him trouble at a job he had had for only six months.

Early one morning, for a fleeting moment, Ira thought about other circumstances that made little sense. How did Mark hear a 110-pound woman fall on a carpet while he was running on a noisy treadmill? Ira was pretty sure Mark listened to music when he worked out too. Even more puzzling was what Mark did when he came upstairs. Why didn't he go immediately to the room he had heard the noise come from? Instead he turned the opposite way—through the master bathroom, all the way to the back bedroom, far from where Donnah was being attacked. Ira expressed his thoughts to Sara Jane that morning, then let them go. Donnah was dead and things had happened the way they did whether it made sense or not.

Sara Jane was Ira's top priority. Her healing would

be a long, uphill battle. Ira decided to sell his business.

"It didn't matter very much anymore," he said later.

He wanted to make him self available full-time to Sara Jane.

"I was her sounding board."

The Dreschers drove forty-five minutes to Coral Gables to meet with a support group called, chillingly, Parents of Murdered Children. They walked into a darkened church, down a narrow staircase, and into a room where they sat in a circle with twenty or so other people. Each person took a turn telling his or her harrowing tale. The grief therapist in charge saw Sara Jane tremble. She was not ready for this. The therapist took the Dreschers to a private room in the back. She asked what she could do to help.

"I don't want the man who murdered my daughter to murder me," Sara Jane said, tears moistening her eyes. "Please help me find a way."

"We will find a way," the therapist assured her. Ira put his arm around Sara Jane. He would not be left out of the process.

Sara Jane would work with the therapist for years, but it was her own fortitude that allowed her to regain control. Her motto became "Think small." She would live one minute at a time and give herself credit for accomplishing tasks most people took for granted. She would force herself to "push through the invisible wall" every morning. She would get out of bed, take a shower, and get dressed. In time, she would go to the local market. She would overcome her fear of running into people she knew, and, worse, meeting new people who asked the dreaded question: "How many children do you have?"

Sara Jane wanted to be there for the people who needed her. She had two living daughters, a traumatized son-in-law, and a motherless granddaughter. She also resolved to live for Donnah. Donnah deserved that.

"My daughter was the victim. I am a representative. I think, as a mom, I sort of felt like Donnah's soul returned to me. And now I represent not only myself but her. Every day, every minute of my life, I lead for both of us. And I try to lead it in the best possible way that I can, honoring her memory and—trying to do things that—will help other people. Because that's what she was all about," Sara Jane later told Richard Schlesinger.

There would always be days when it was nearly impossible to push through that invisible wall in the morning. But Sara Jane refused to let it imprison her.

In December 1995, Sara Jane and Ira Drescher went to Springfield to help Mark Winger sort through Donnah's personal possessions. It was an emotionally charged task. The house had been thoroughly cleaned, but there was no escaping the reality of what had happened there. There were reminders of Donnah everywhere: her quilts in the living room, the dishes she picked out in the kitchen, her clothes in the closet. They were now being packed away.

Mark was the living link to Donnah. The Dreschers reminisced with him. They spoke about Donnah's penchant for shopping, her boundless energy, and her unabashed candor. They remembered her simple pleasures, like country music and romantic novels. They talked about her storybook wedding. And they remembered her transformation from a giddy girl to a woman when she became a mother. Her time with Ruby was brief, but she had realized her dream.

Sara Jane remembered Donnah sitting on the couch, feeding the baby.

"I've never known anything like this before," Donnah whispered. She lifted Ruby and pressed their cheeks together.

"Look at this gorgeous baby! Look at her! She's beautiful!"

Sara Jane's mind wandered further back in time, to when Donnah was a child. Before moving to Florida, Sara Jane, her first husband, and their three daughters lived in Newburgh, New York, a scenic town nestled in the Hudson River Valley. It was sixty miles north and a world away from New York City.

Their house sat on property once owned by Franklin Roosevelt's grandmother. It was a leafy paradise, full of old, exotic trees that Mrs. Delano had planted— a perfect playground for an exuberant child. Donnah and her friends had free run of the neighborhood and could end up eating dinner at any neighbor's house on any given night. They were all welcome everywhere.

Donnah had been a perfect child. She was popular with other children. She looked after her younger sisters. She excelled at sports.

Sara Jane's one concern was school. Donnah had been an eager student, but she was hamstrung by her learning disability. Sara Jane changed schools and monitored her education, but the disability persisted. Donnah struggled throughout high school. She did one semester at Santa Fe College in Gainesville, Florida. Then she gave up and quit.

Sara Jane had worried that her daughter had no sense of direction. Months later their family dentist came to the rescue, giving Donnah a job as his assistant. The patients loved her.

"She was young, beautiful, upbeat, sweet, kind, with a zest for life that emanated all around her," Sara Jane said.

Donnah found her calling. She had a passion for the medical profession. She ended up going back to school, determined to become an operating-room technician. She battled her way through exams, overcoming bouts of nausea and anxiety. Her sheer will ensured her success. Her mother and sisters were thrilled, but once Donnah was on the job, they instituted a new family rule: no shoptalk at the dinner table. No one but Donnah had the stomach for it.

"Life just kept getting better," Sara Jane said. "I

was told she was the best and was always requested by doctors in the hospital."

Donnah put her medical skills to use in 1992, during a family vacation. Donnah, Mark, the Dreschers, and Donnah's sisters were driving in a van down a dusty, desolate road on their way to the Grand Canyon. They came upon an accident scene and a badly injured man. Without hesitation, Donnah took charge, covering the man with their jackets. Her family tried to flag down help—cell phones were not common in those days—and Donnah stayed by the man's side, speaking calmly to him. His chest was crushed and she knew he needed to stay conscious.

The paramedics arrived two hours later, by helicopter. Until then, Donnah never left the man's side.

"She always could talk, about anything, and that day, for two hours, she talked and asked questions," Sara Jane said.

When the helicopter lifted off, Sara Jane saw just how stressed Donnah was. Through tears, Donnah told her that if the man went to sleep, he probably would never wake up. The paramedics credited her with saving his life. They suggested she get an AIDS test, as she had had contact with his blood.

"She looked at me and said, 'What else could I do Mom?'" Sara Jane recalled. "I put my arms around her and said, 'Donnah darling, you did what your heart and your experience told you to do. I am so proud of you.'"

Later that night, Donnah learned that the man had

made it to surgery. Back in Springfield, she tested negative for HIV. She would not suffer for her act of compassion.

Every item of Donnah's that Sara Jane packed away brought back memories. She decided to ship all the boxes back to Florida. Sara Jane would let her daughters take what they wanted and she would keep a few things for herself. The rest would be donated to Women in Distress, a organization that helped victims of domestic violence. It was a worthy charity. Donnah would be pleased.

Ruby Winger spent her first New Year's holiday in Florida with the Dreschers. Oblivious to the Christmas decorations that absurdly adorned the palm trees, she took to the balmy weather and basked in the attention that her grandparents bestowed on her. At seven months, she was recognizing and reacting to the people around her. She was a happy child with a sweet disposition who was, mercifully, unaware of the extraordinary circumstances of her young life. When Ruby was older, Sara Jane promised herself, she would tell her about her special mommy.

Sara Jane faced the sad prospect of a new year without Donnah. How could that be? she wondered. She made it her business to not let her pain show in Ruby's presence. She knew how sensitive babies were. She was grateful to Mark for allowing her to visit for the holidays.

The nanny Mark hired did not work out. He was hiring a replacement. Both Sara Jane and Mark's mother advised him that Ruby would be better off with an older, more mature woman, but Mark went ahead and hired another young woman fresh from nanny school.

Sara Jane embarked on the journey back to Springfield the morning after New Year's Day. It was an ordeal traveling by herself with the baby—and the luggage, the car seat, and the baby bag. Sara Jane prided herself on being fit, but the walk to the gate took forever. Fortunately, Ruby took it in stride.

As Sara Jane strapped herself into her seat on the plane, a flight attendant passed by and smiled at her. She told Sara Jane how beautiful Ruby was and how lucky the baby was to be traveling with her grandma. Sara Jane bit her lip. It was one of those inadvertent comments that made life so difficult. Lucky, my eye, she thought. Her daughter should be there with them. She should not be alone with this baby. This baby had no mother.

When they landed in St. Louis, it was snowing. Sara Jane felt her heart pound. She had not driven in snow for years. Would she remember how to do it? She flashed back to a wintry day in New York State when she was driving fifteen-year-old Donnah up Storm King, a hump-shaped mountain that loomed over the Hudson River. The family was about to move south.

"This is a winter wonderland and I don't want us to forget how the trees glisten with the ice on them and how pure the snow is on the ground," Sara Jane had told her daughter. "So white, so shiny—could anything be so magnificent?"

Donnah had pressed her face against the car window and stared. Her mother's words gave her new appreciation for the beauty she had taken for granted.

Sara Jane eyed the empty seat next to her on the plane. She wanted so much to share her memory with Donnah, but Donnah was not there. She looked down at the baby. She promised Ruby she would tell her all about the wonderland when she grew up. She would take her to all the places her mommy had lived.

On the ground, Sara Jane was jarred back to reality and the tasks at hand. She again struggled with Ruby and the luggage, switching arms frequently as she made her way to the rental car area. Along her way, people smiled at Ruby and remarked how beautiful she was. Sara Jane felt proud. This was her granddaughter. They were bonded for life.

Sara Jane dressed Ruby in her coat, hat, and gloves before going outside. The snow was coming down hard. She put the car seat in back, secured the baby, started the car, turned up the heat, and took a deep breath. She had made the trip many times. It was the same route Donnah and Roger Harrington took the night he had frightened her. The snow looked as if it could become a blizzard.

Sara Jane was on a mission and nothing was going to stop her. Several times she had to make the difficult decision whether to stop and feed the hungry baby or to push on. Once, after stopping, Ruby was reluctant to be strapped back in her seat again. Sara Jane felt guilty for not being more attentive to her, but she had to concentrate on reaching her destination. She talked to Ruby and sang silly songs. She concentrated on the road, careful to keep control. It was a nerve-racking drive, but she kept going. She knew Mark would be concerned if they were not at his house before dark.

When she finally got to Mark's house, she was surprised to find he was not there. Sara Jane trudged alone in the snow and got the baby inside. She needed attention but was otherwise fine. Mark did not come home until the evening. Sara Jane wondered where he had been all those hours, but he offered no explanation and she did not ask.

"I wanted to do as much for him as I could, as I knew he had been through so much," she later told *48 Hours*.

Sara Jane had agreed to stay in Springfield long enough to show the new nanny the routine. She did not have high hopes that the twenty-three-year-old would work out any better than nanny number one. To Sara Jane's pleasant surprise, the young woman quickly won her over.

Jessica Walters was attractive and charming. She was well-mannered and respectful. She had a dewy, fresh look about her but seemed smart and professional. She came from a religious family—her father was a minister—and was active in her church. Most important, Jessica was immediately smitten by Ruby.

She giggled when Ruby playfully tugged at her long, wavy hair. When Sara Jane gave instructions, Jessica listened attentively.

After dinner, Sara Jane took the time to unwind. She retired to catch up on her reading. Mark knocked on her door and asked for a favor.

"Would you mind watching the baby for the night?" he asked. He wanted to take Jessica out for a couple of beers.

A couple of beers! Sara Jane was unprepared for that—especially on Jessica's first night on the job. She reminded herself that everyone has a different way to deal with trauma. She should expect the unexpected. She should be patient and tolerant.

"No problem," she said. "No problem at all."

12

Changes

In the months after Donnah's death, Rabbi Mike Datz and his wife, Jo, realized that their relationship with Mark Winger had become strained. They had anticipated having long, soul-searching talks with him, but that never happened. They witnessed Mark break down only once, at their home. Through tears, he said it was unfair that Roger Harrington had taken his wife from him. It was a rare display of emotion.

Most of the time Mark was composed. During another visit Mark pulled out a copy of the letter he wrote to the newspaper and read it aloud. He seemed pleased with himself, humbly expressing his gratitude to the citizens of Springfield. Jo was a little miffed.

"We thought it was rather peculiar given that they'd never done anything for him but we and the Jewish community had and he never thanked any of us," she said later.

Sometimes Mark's behavior was odd and inappropriate. Once, Mark dropped by for dinner while Mike was working late. Jo remembered being alone with Mark at the table when he said, innocently enough, that he missed Donnah. Mark would probably deny this, Jo said, but he went on to tell her that, specifically, he missed having sex with Donnah. He missed being held by a woman.

"It felt like a proposition and made me very uncomfortable," Jo said.

The Datzes witnessed other lapses in Mark's judgment. Soon after Donnah died, he went on a spending spree, buying an expensive truck and a massive computer system. He fell into a bad habit of leaving Ruby with all-to-willing babysitters and neglecting to see her for long stretches of time. As new parents themselves—their son was born two months after Donnah's death—Mike and Jo found it incomprehensible.

Shortly after hiring Jessica, Mark told Mike and Jo that he planned to take a vacation in South Africa at the month of March. He asked what they thought about him taking a female coworker with him. The Datzes said—in no uncertain terms—that it was a terrible idea. The trip would be only six months after Donnah's death. He needed to let more time pass. He should not be away from Ruby for so long. Mark heeded their advice, at least partially. He went to South Africa but took his brother, Greg, with him instead of the woman from work. Jo happened to be in Johannesburg at the same time as Mark—she was visiting her family—but Mark never bothered to contact her.

Mike and Jo, like almost everyone else Mark knew, were inclined to give their bereft friend a free pass to do and say what he pleased. No one dared question him. No one could imagine how they would behave if they were in his shoes.

"I think it was our pity for a friend which fueled our excuse-making for Mark when his behavior just didn't seem right," Mike said later.

Even so, it got difficult to keep up the friendship they had had when Donnah was alive.

Mark Winger readily admitted that he did not handle himself well in the months after Donnah's murder. He said he tried to keep up appearances, but he was spiraling into despair. He had a hard time relating to his old friends. He drank too much and made off-putting comments. He said he hit bottom on a bitterly cold night, a week before the year's end.

"I checked into a hotel room with myself, a bottle of Jim Beam, and a handgun," he told *48 Hours* correspondent Richard Schlesinger. "I wrote a beautiful letter to my wife and to Ruby and actually had the gun in my mouth."

Across the room, he said, he saw his image reflected in the television.

"It was something more than that that made me stop, and I don't want to discuss that," he said, without elaborating further.

Mark said his situation improved greatly a week later, when his new nanny began working for him. She had compassion for the baby, and Ruby took to her right away. Once she took charge of the household, he said, everything changed.

Jessica did take control. She had been trained at one of the best schools in the country and she took her work seriously. She made certain that Ruby ate properly, that she had stimulating playtime, and that she was reaching all of her developmental criteria. She excitedly commemorated every milestone.

"Her taste buds are booming! She loves to try anything," Jessica proclaimed in a letter to Grandma Sara Jane. "Her favorite vegetable is peas and she loves bananas!"

Sara Jane felt that Ruby was safe in Jessica's arms. Whatever problems Mark Winger had, her grandchild was being well looked after.

Once Jessica settled in, Sara Jane Drescher's babysitting duties eased up. She and Ira monitored Ruby's progress from afar, thanks to nanny Jessica's detailed updates. They sent their grandchild plenty of presents, as Sara Jane had a hard time resisting any cute baby item she saw. But the Dreschers still worried about Mark. They feared he was not coping well with his grief.

Ira later told *48 Hours* about a phone call he got from Mark late one evening. Mark was sobbing. He said he was under the dining room table. He was afraid that someone was going to come into his house and kill him.

Ira was saddened that Mark was in such bad shape.

"I have news for you," Mark continued. "I'm converting to Christianity."

Ira did not anticipate *that*.

"Why?" he asked.

Mark said that the Jewish religion was not giving him what he wanted and needed in his time of crisis. He had been led to Christ.

"Have you told your father?"

Mark said that Ira was the only one he had told so far.

"Wow."

Ira was at a rare loss for words. He decided to keep Mark's secret—at least, for the moment.

"You have to do what you feel is right for you," he said.

Whatever spiritual crisis Mark Winger had, he traveled to Florida on May 25, 1996 for a Jewish ritual: the unveiling of Donnah's headstone. He brought Ruby, who was days away from turning one year old. Rabbi Mike Datz and his wife, Jo, also flew in.

The family and a few close friends gathered at Donnah's graveside. Everyone was crushed by emotion; the enormity of the injustice was still raw. Ira clutched a handful of balloons that each had a written message to Donnah inside. It was his attempt to mitigate the pain. His other arm was wrapped around Sara Jane, who was disconsolate.

The Florida rabbi recited a heartfelt prayer and the

headstone was uncovered. Mark chose the inscription: *Time Gives Memories to Our Lives; Love Gives Eternity to Time.*

Mark held Ruby in his arms during the entire service. When it ended, he knelt by Donnah's grave and whispered something to her. Ira's heart still ached for his son-in-law, but Mark was getting difficult to read.

Ira let go of the balloons. They rose high and drifted towards the ocean. Everyone watched until they were out of sight—except for Mark, who was still on his knees. When he got up to leave, he took his wedding ring off and put it on the corner of the headstone. He walked away without looking back.

"We were aghast," Jo Datz said later. "He intended to leave it there for who-knows to pick it up."

Sara Jane also saw what Mark did. She could not bear the thought of that ring being left out in the elements. When she was sure Mark was out of sight, she walked to the grave, recovered the ring, and slipped it into her pocket.

Mark and Ruby returned to Springfield the following day. His future was looking up. Jessica was a capable and tireless caretaker, attending to Ruby's every need. Ruby had grown attached to her and that was all right with him.

"I saw the potential for a mother for my daughter," he said later. "I also saw great potential for me."

It did not escape Mark that Jessica was young and attractive.

"What did I know?" Jessica asked later. "I was the twenty-three-year-old nanny."

With Ruby in good hands, Ira and Sara Jane rebuilt their own lives, socializing with friends and taking overseas vacations. They brought back numerous gifts for the baby and kept close tabs on her. They had less contact with Mark but knew him well enough to sense that, within months after Jessica's arrival, he was regarding her as someone more than a nanny. Sara Jane, motherly instincts intact, gingerly offered him advice in a letter.

"I hope that the love and respect we have nurtured over the years can withstand some loving input," she wrote. She told him about her own experience: how she had been tempted to remarry right after her divorce. Fate intervened and she remained single for four years. Then Ira came into her life.

"For the first time in four years of being alone, I was able to be in a relationship that time did not rush," she wrote. She said she was sharing her story because she wanted to encourage Mark to give his new relationship a similar test of time.

Sara Jane was worried that Mark did not have the necessary tools to work through his loss. He had refused all help. Sara Jane knew firsthand how crucial counseling was, how impossible it was to go it alone. Mark was too traumatized to see things clearly.

She closed her letter promising Mark "unconditional acceptance" of his decisions.

* * *

Less than six months later, in October 1996, Mark asked Ira and Sara Jane to watch Ruby while he took Jessica away for a week. He was coy about their plans. The Dreschers gladly accepted, as they had not seen their grandchild for a long time. To their delight, she was better than ever—a happy, well-adjusted child.

Before Mark and Jessica left, Mark offhandedly mentioned that he bought an old farmhouse in Pleasant Plains, a rural area on the outskirts of town. The house needed a lot of work, he said, but he planned to move there mid-December. Sara Jane felt a chill. Donnah dreamed of someday moving to a rambling country home, with a large family in tow. Mark would live at least part of that fantasy without her.

Ira wondered how Mark was financing the extensive renovations. One day, while Sara Jane was out with the baby, he decided to investigate. He rifled through the files in Mark's home office, rationalizing that, since he planned to keep Mark in his life, he had to make sure that Mark was being responsible with the baby's future. In truth, Ira had an insatiable curiosity and—without Donnah there to fill the Dreschers in—there was a lot going on in Mark's life that they knew nothing about.

Ira found what he was looking for—and more. Mark's new house sat on four and a half acres of land. He was doing a lot of the renovations himself, but, as Ira suspected, there were a lot of expenses. Part of that was likely being paid by money Mark had collected since the tragedy. There was more than $150,000 in life insurance paid by a company that insured military families. Mark also applied for—and received—$25,000 from a state victims' compensation fund. Ruby was entitled to dispensation from Social Security. Ira had concerns about how Mark was handling his money, but he knew he had no business saying anything about it.

When Mark and Jessica returned on October 15, they were giddy with excitement. They announced that they spent the week in Hawaii and had tied the knot. They showed the Dreschers a wedding photo with the happy couple decked out in colorful leis. The Dreschers were genuinely happy for Mark: he deserved another chance. Jessica, young as she was, already proved herself to be a terrific mother. She was bound to be a good wife. Still, it was hard to see Donnah being replaced. Especially so soon.

Like Donnah, Jessica was upbeat, intelligent, and energetic. Like Donnah, she came from a close-knit family and was extremely close to her mother, Karen and her older brothers, George and Albert. Karen was a self-proclaimed country gal who worked tirelessly for her community and church. Once, in a conversation with this author, she casually mentioned baking thirty-five dozen corn muffins for a charity event. But her most cherished role was that of mother. She was there whenever her children needed her.

Karen instilled in her children the same values she

had. Her son Albert taught special-needs kids. George would later work in a military hospital. The siblings developed an ability to read each other's mind and were quick to offer advice. Jessica's brothers were not thrilled when she accepted the job in Springfield, but they supported her when she made up her mind.

Jessica had had her choice of families to work for. She gave her decision thought and prayer. There were wealthier households, where the work would be shared, but she was deeply touched by Mark Winger's story. It was unfair that Ruby, after being adopted into a loving home, would grow up without a mother. Jessica wanted to help save them.

As Mark told it, the three of them fell in love.

"You could see Jessica falling in love with Ruby immediately," he said. "And that just kind of made me fall in love with her. And she saw the way I loved Ruby and that made her fall in love with me."

Mark showered Jessica with attention and ingratiated himself to her family and friends. He went to church with her and met her fellow parishioners. In a short time he joined the church himself.

"I remember a day when I was all alone by myself," he said. "And I knew that I needed Christ in my life."

Jessica's brother, George, believed that Mark had another reason for embracing Christianity. Mark knew that Jessica would not marry out of her religion. From the moment Jessica walked into Mark's life, George says, he had his sights set on her.

When Jessica talked with her family, she gushed

on and on about the baby but said little about her employer.

"She definitely fell in love with Ruby," Karen said.

The family knew Mark's sad story, of course, and they saw his letter to the newspaper thanking the citizens of Springfield. He seemed to treat Jessica well. Nevertheless, neither George nor Albert warmed to Mark and neither fully trusted him. His efforts to impress them failed.

The first time Albert met Mark face-to-face was in the summer of 1996. Albert was on his way home from a summer camp job in Colorado and his car broke down near St. Louis. Jessica was away, enjoying a few days with her school friends, but Mark offered to pick Albert up. They drove to Springfield together.

Not long into their ride, Mark, unprompted, recounted the story of Donnah's death.

"He tried to make the story as 'macho' as possible," Albert said later. "This was his chance to tell me what a man he was for killing Roger Harrington to protect Ruby and avenge Donnah. I didn't ask many questions. I just let him speak."

Albert was troubled by Mark's apparent lack of emotion. There were no tears; there was no anger. Mark recited the narrative as if he were describing a movie.

"He didn't even know me and he opened this whole thing to me in an unsettling way," Albert said.

By the time they pulled up to the house, Albert was creeped out. Here he was, about to spend the night at the "murder house," with the image of the crime freshly planted in his mind. His sister's employer, the "hero" of the story, was weird. Albert's brother, George, agreed.

George and Albert put up with Mark because none of the things that bothered them bothered their sister. But as time passed, Mark increasingly got on their nerves. Separately, they began to question his heroic history. Something was wrong. They shared their doubts with each other but dared not tell anyone else in the family—especially Jessica. After all, the police had examined all the evidence and cleared Mark Winger.

Jessica did not want to be treated like a child. She did want to be second-guessed. Her brothers stood by as she succumbed to Mark's charms. They had no idea how deeply involved she was until she confided her plans to her family in September 1996.

"She told us she was pregnant and that she was going to elope," Albert later told *48 Hours*. "I was shocked."

This was not the big wedding that Jessica's family had envisioned the girl in their brood would have. This was not the man they had imagined she would bring into their fold.

"If I tried to put a face on her groom, it would not have been Mark Winger," Albert said.

Jessica had been jetted off to Hawaii and she returned as Mrs. Winger. Her family had no choice but embrace her with open arms. She was a grown woman with a husband, a loving child, and a baby on the way. Karen looked at the bright side.

"There was every indication that Mark was going to be a good dad," she said. "Jessica fell in love with the idea of living happily ever after."

13

New Home

Mark and Jessica Winger's new home was, in ideal circumstances, a twenty-minute drive from downtown Springfield. The spacious two-story clapboard structure was near no others, on a corner where one lonely country road dead-ended into another. It was surrounded by fields and silos.

The Wingers moved there just days before Christmas. With the cornfields fallow, it seemed like the middle of nowhere. There was beauty in the isolation, in the sound of wind ripping across the land. The air was fresh and crisp. The sky was endless and on clear nights the stars shined brightly in the blackness.

Less than a month after the move, Jessica adopted Ruby, making her defacto motherhood official. Her other child was due in March.

Mark continued to break away from his past. He was no longer in contact with John and DeAnn Schultz nor any of the other friends he and Donnah had. The exception was Rabbi Mike Datz and his wife, Jo, whom Mark saw on rare occasions.

Sara Jane visited Mark's new home for the first time three months after Jessica's baby girl was born. Following Mark's directions from the airport, she drove the desolate country road past endless miles of cornfields.

"I could not imagine why he bought this house," she said. Why did he want to be so far away from everything?

When Sara Jane finally reached her destination, Mark greeted her at the door. A much-grown Ruby stood beside him. Ruby was her jubilant self; Donnah would be proud. Mark seemed distracted.

"He was distant and formal," Sara Jane said.

Sara Jane was surprised how lovely the house looked. Mark had done a wonderful job with it. It was freshly painted and tastefully restored. The detailed woodwork was beautiful. A large deck overlooked a pond in the back. Sara Jane thought about Mark working on the renovations and it gave her the chills.

"I thought to myself: How could he put a hammer in his hand after what he went through?"

Sara Jane enjoyed her time with Ruby as always, and Jessica made her feel welcome. The baby was adorable and Ruby loved having a little sister. Sara Jane did not see Mark very much until they went shopping one day. It had been a long time since they were alone together, and Sara Jane felt some tension. When they returned to the house, Mark pulled his shiny red pickup truck into the driveway and turned off the ignition. He leaned over the steering wheel and began to sob.

Sara Jane was startled.

"What's wrong?" she asked.

"I feel so guilty, I feel so guilty," Mark said softly.

"About Donnah's murder?"

"Yes. You don't know, you don't know."

Sara Jane knew that Mark considered it his duty to protect Donnah. The responsibility weighed heavily on him. She told Mark that she loved him, that what happened was not his fault, and that he had done everything he could. She gently suggested that he seek professional counseling.

Sara Jane was used to Mark rejecting the idea but she felt in her heart that he needed it. She could not understand his vehement resistance. Now that he was so distraught, he might finally be ready.

"Everyone who experiences trauma like that needs help," she told him.

Mark shook his head.

"I can't," he said. "I just can't."

"Why?"

"You don't understand," he turned away from her. "I just can't."

They sat together for a few minutes without talking or touching. The only sound was the wind rustling the corn. Then Mark abruptly left the vehicle and walked to the house.

Mike and Jo Datz had all but given up on offering Mark advice. Before he eloped with Jessica, Mark asked them how long he should wait before having another child. Mike told him not to rush. A few weeks later they found out that Jessica was already pregnant. Why did Mark pretend to seek counsel? Jo predicted that their days of friendship were numbered and she was right.

It came to a head on a stifling night in July 1997. The Datzes went to the Wingers' home for dinner. Jessica still arranged play dates for their children, but the couples rarely got together anymore. Mike and Jo knew they were in for a difficult time. Sara Jane had bought Mark a mezuzah——a decorative case containing a prayer that is hung in the front doorway of a Jewish home—as a housewarming gift. If Mark asked Mike to hang it, the rabbi would be in an awkward position. He heard that Mark had left the Jewish religion.

The evening began well enough. Ruby was happy to show off her baby sister. Mike and Jo complimented Mark on the work he had done on the house. It had a contemporary, roomy feel. The one thought Jo kept to herself was what came to mind when she saw the deck: It was something Donnah had always wanted. She had talked about it a number of times.

After dinner, there was amiable talk about the children. Then, as Mike feared, Mark asked the rabbi to hang the mezuzah. Mike politely refused. Mark bristled, accusing Mike of turning him down because Jessica was Christian. Mike countered that many of his congregants were intermarried and he had hung many a mezuzah in their homes.

"My difficulty was that I wasn't sure that Mark was Jewish any longer, and, if so, then it wasn't really a Jewish home in any meaningful sense because there were no Jews living there," he explained later.

He voiced his concern to Mark and Mark did not deny he had converted.

"He tried to do some dance about how he would always be Jewish in his heart because he'd been born Jewish," Mike said. "I tried to explain that if he'd taken active and formal steps to join another faith, then his Jewish status was in question and I couldn't do the mezuzah."

Mark was seething. The visit had become exceedingly uncomfortable for everyone. The two men stepped out on the deck to continue their conversation. They shouted to be heard above the crickets.

"Why didn't you tell me that you had doubts or a crisis of faith, if that's what it was?" Mike asked. "Why didn't you come to me?"

Mark mumbled something about doing things his own way, that Christianity was easier and more forgiving. Mike did not press him what he meant by that. He realized that Mark had long needed counseling and never gotten any.

"Why did you cut yourself off from the Jewish community?" he asked. "Everyone had been so kind to you."

Mark was no longer in the mood to justify his actions. He let Mike know that he was deeply offended. The visit was over and so was their friendship.

The following day, Mark called Jo Datz and let her have it.

"Don't think that I don't hear the innuendos you and Mike make," he said.

He accused Mike and Jo of blaming him for Donnah's death. They made it all too clear that they believed Donnah would still be alive had he not complained to Roger Harrington's boss. He felt guilty enough already. He did not need their judgment.

Jo protested, but to no avail. Mark continued his tirade and threatened to bring a lawsuit against the rabbi. In the subsequent days, the Datzes left several voice messages, hoping for reconciliation. Mark never returned their calls.

Shortly after the confrontation, Sara Jane Drescher received a letter from Mark. He noted that they were kindred spirits who had both been thrust into a tragic situation. But, he added bluntly, she need not worry about his well-being anymore.

"I've resurrected my life from the darkest of pits," he wrote.

Mark praised his new wife for her "loyalty and endless compassion."

His tone became harsh as he went on to address an issue that he said was straining his relationship with his former in-laws—the "issue of Mike and Jo." Mark spared no contempt for the Datzes, accusing them of harboring resentment toward his new family. They were liars, he said, and he would no longer tolerate their disrespect. For that reason, he could not continue to trust the Dreschers unless they severed their ties with Mike and Jo. Mark underscored his sentence demanding that, just in case the Dreschers missed his point.

"As a survivalist," he wrote, "my choices are brutally limited."

The Dreschers were stunned. They had developed a genuine friendship with Mike and Jo Datz and were not about to end it. The next time they visited Springfield, they met the Datzes at a pizza shop. They told them about the strange letter from Mark. Mike said there was no way to reason with him.

"He's determined to make a clean break from the past," he told the Dreschers. "I'm afraid one day it will be your turn too."

14

Civil Matters

Mark Winger did initiate a lawsuit, but not against his rabbi. Once he was cleared of criminal charges, Winger sued Roger Harrington's employer, BART. Michael Metnick, the attorney who was a member of Mark's temple, filed the suit December 29, 1995, four months after Donnah's death. He contended that Harrington had been unfit to drive for BART and the company should have conducted a better background check. Its negligence, Metnick argued, ultimately cost Donnah Winger her life.

Metnick was one of Springfield's top attorneys. He worked in an impressively furnished downtown office that had a spectacular view of the golden-stoned, red-domed old state capitol. That was where Abraham Lincoln had delivered his famed "house divided" speech and would later lie in state after being assassinated.

Metnick was frank with Winger. As a defense attorney, he represented people accused of deplorable crimes, including one charged with kidnapping and murdering a child. In light of what Winger had gone through, Metnick wanted to make sure he was comfortable working with him. Winger assured him he was. All that mattered was winning the case.

Metnick was optimistic. He himself had been to the memorial service Rabbi Datz conducted for Donnah. He saw how Mark's life was senselessly shattered. If Metnick could show that Roger Harrington's violent behavior could have been foreseen, then Winger deserved to be compensated for his loss.

BART was a family business that operated eighteen reservation-only vans that shuttled passengers door-to-door to and from Lambert Airport in St. Louis. Besides the drivers, a small staff worked from a small single-story building in Cape Girardeau, Missouri, a hundred miles south of the airport.

Owner and president Ray Duffey, an unassuming man with graying hair and a gentle face, sat in a modest office in the back. He had started the business from scratch with a partner in 1987. A few years later they realized there was not enough revenue to support two families and he bought his partner out.

On August 29, 1995, Ray Duffey was at home, lying back in his easy chair. He had just been released from the hospital after knee surgery. He took a call from a Springfield detective who said he had an urgent matter to discuss. Duffey was not prepared for what he was about to be told.

"It gets you out of anesthesia quickly," he later told Richard Schlesinger.

Duffey remembered taking Winger's complaint. His grievance was serious. It was also odd. Winger was adamant that he speak directly with the man who drove his wife home. In the past, dissatisfied customers preferred dealing with the boss.

Duffey was also surprised to hear any complaint about Harrington. He had always been cooperative and friendly.

"He was a go-with-the-flow kind of guy," Duffey said, a natural for a work schedule in a constant state of flux. "That's why this was so shocking."

Duffey could not imagine the easygoing driver beating anyone with a hammer, but that was precisely what the police said he had done. Duffey wondered how things could get so out of hand. He quickly issued a statement saying that the company was "shocked and deeply saddened" by the tragedy. He promised to fully cooperate in the investigation. When Winger sued, Duffey handed the case over to his insurers, who turned to attorney John Nolan.

Nolan took the position that BART did nothing improper in hiring Roger Harrington. He had had the necessary license and requirements. Nolan also disputed the money damages due Mark Winger for his loss. It was part of the process to coldly calculate the value of Donnah's life in dollars.

Mark Winger's lawsuit also named the "estate of Roger Harrington" as a defendant. It was good legal strategy. Unlike BART and its president, Roger Harrington was a citizen of Illinois. That made it easier for Winger's attorney to gain access to information he needed. Naming Harrington also eliminated hearsay problems down the road. The lawsuit was another burden for Roger's parents, Ralph and Helen, to bear. They said it cost them $1,200 in legal fees and they were angry. What kind of "estate" did Roger have? they asked.

"All Roger owned was the car he drove," Helen said.

Ralph had the car destroyed shortly after it was returned to them. It was too painful a reminder of their son's absence.

During the next three years the civil suit slowly wended its way to trial, with both sides filing numerous briefs and motions. Facts about Roger Harrington came to light. He earned $5.75 an hour. On his job application, he noted that he had "special skills" in "communications, computer knowledge, creative ideas, driving, manual labor, public relations, and problem solving." No previous complaints had been lodged against him.

The record showed that Harrington had been arrested for battery, for that episode when Cox caught him beating his wife. He also had a burglary arrest. In both cases, the charges were dismissed. Other records documented his brief hospitalization in a mental facility three years before BART hired him.

Metnick asked the police department for the evidence it had collected, thinking it might come in handy. The police gave him everything, including crime scene photographs, the hammer, Donnah's handwritten note, the items found in Harrington's car, shell casings from the bullets, and the clothing worn by Mark, Donnah, and Roger. Metnick was surprised how easy it was to get it all.

"My mother used to say, 'If you don't ask for something, you won't get it,'" he said.

Attorneys on both sides of Winger's lawsuit against BART geared up for a battle of experts with arcane knowledge of laws and regulations regarding negligent hiring. Metnick's position was that, in this case, the lives of the passengers were literally in the hands of the drivers BART hired. The company had an obligation to ensure that they were fit for the job.

Metnick's team also contended that Duffey handled Mark Winger's complaint badly.

"Rather than resolve the complaint personally, Ray Duffey had Roger Harrington speak directly with Mark Winger and apologize for his behavior," the lawsuit stated.

In other words, Duffey had set up an explosive situation.

Duffey felt terrible about what had happened but had no choice but to fight back. BART's attorney, John Nolan, found experts who said that the company complied with preemployment screening requirements. Harrington had never been convicted of a violent act. His mental health record did not indicate a predilection for violence.

Duffey was right to suspend Harrington and launch an investigation, the defense said. The statements Harrington allegedly made to Donnah Winger did not contain specific threats to harm her or anyone else. Harrington denied saying anything about killing people or planting car bombs, as Winger claimed.

Later, when Duffey spoke with Richard Schlesinger, he said that Harrington conceded that he was speeding. He had kept the cruise control at seventy-eight miles per hour, Duffey said, grimacing. But the driver seemed genuinely surprised that he had frightened Donnah. He talked to customers to keep them comfortable, he said.

"Then he chuckled and said, 'It increases your chances of getting a tip.'" Duffey said. Donnah tipped him well.

Ray Duffey was required to give a deposition. He went to the historic building that housed Michael Metnick's office. For three hours Duffey sat at a polished wood table in a conference room across from Mark Winger and answered his attorney's questions.

"He was nitpicking," Duffey said later. "It was frustrating."

Duffey tried to explain that it had been Winger's idea to talk directly with Roger Harrington, not his.

"He wanted to talk to Roger Harrington to tell him to leave him alone, his family alone, and that basically was it," Duffey testified. "He said, 'I am not going to be mean and yell at him, I just want to talk to him.'"

"Did Mark inform you in any way that Harrington can visit him at his house?" Metnick asked.

"That was not discussed."

"Did he inform you in any way that Harrington was welcome to make a telephone call to his house?"

"No."

Michael Metnick was optimistic that Duffey's deposition would help Winger's case. His client was on solid ground. Duffey found the experience highly unpleasant, but when he got up to leave, he reached across the table to offer his hand to Mark Winger. Winger hesitated before shaking it.

"I think he was surprised that I'd shake hands with him," Duffey said.

At the same time that BART's attorney, John Nolan, consulted with negligent-employment experts, he took the offensive on another front: he challenged the underlying basis of Mark Winger's lawsuit.

"The burden of proof was on Mark Winger to prove that Roger Harrington killed his wife," Nolan explained later.

Although that seemed evident, the case had never been fully vetted because it was closed so quickly. Roger Harrington never had his day in court. Nolan would force Winger's team to jump through a few legal hoops to meet its obligation.

On the afternoon of April 14, 1997, Mark Winger and the attorneys assembled in Michael Metnick's office. Winger gave his deposition. It was the first time he spoke on the record about Donnah's death since he was interviewed by the detectives the day of the crime. There were three lawyers present: John Nolan, representing BART; Michael Metnick, representing Mark Winger; and Alfred LaBarre, an appointed lawyer representing Roger Harrington's estate.

Nolan brought up Winger's marital status, thinking it might have an impact on any compensation Winger received for his loss. In his lawsuit, Winger claimed he had been deprived of Donnah's "means of support, service, society, and comfort." But he remarried quickly and Jessica provided some of that.

Winger admitted that Jessica was pregnant before they wed.

"After you began to have an intimate relationship with her, did her duties change?" Nolan asked. "Did she become more of a partner for you as opposed to just an employed nanny?"

"Well, yeah, but she was still an employed nanny. Just because we had a contract."

Metnick gave Winger the opportunity to talk about his loss.

"Is there ever a day that goes by that you don't think of Donnah?" he asked.

"Not a day."

"Explain that, as you have explained it to me."

"Donnah and I had a great relationship," Winger said. "There was a period of time where we were trying to have children, conceive a child, and we weren't able to, and during that time we became so close. When you think you can't get any closer to someone—then you adopt this little baby, and I never seen my wife so happy and we were at the top of our marriage. And I can't look at my daughter without thinking about how much Donnah loved her. . . . I always think of just how great it was. . . . [W]e just had it made."

Winger said that Ruby was adored and now had a "score" of loving grandparents—his parents, Donnah's, and Jessica's. Still, he insisted, Donnah's murder had taken a heavy toll on him.

"I lost about twenty-five pounds. I rarely slept. I lost a lot of friends. All my relationships have changed."

Winger admitted that he had not sought much counseling. He could not remember the name of the psychiatrist he briefly consulted. He never sought the help of any group. His rabbi was a close friend, he said, and he spoke with him.

When Winger was asked about what Donnah had told him about her ride from the airport, he said she told him she was okay but that something bad happened.

"The driver scared her to death," Mark said.

"Was there any specific threat of injury to you or your wife or your child prior to her death on that Tuesday?" Nolan asked.

"Well, no, other than driving at eighty-five miles an hour. That's pretty threatening."

Winger said that before he returned from Tennessee that Saturday, he did not know that Donnah's friend DeAnn Schultz had called the police to have a "premise check" put on his house. DeAnn answered one of the strange phone calls, he explained.

"My wife described this driver to DeAnn, the way he talked and sounded and looked and everything . . . and DeAnn felt that this was the guy by the way he was talking."

Attorney LaBarre said he was a little confused. He asked Winger what it was about the phone calls that made Winger so concerned. Winger did not know much about the calls. He was not even certain how many there were.

"I've just always kind of been under the understanding that there were several calls," he said.

"Were you at home when any of those calls came in?"

"No."

The caller basically hung up after being told Mrs. Winger wasn't there, Winger said. He and Donnah had never received calls like that before.

"I can't ever remember getting hang-ups or crank calls," he told the attorneys.

Winger said that Donnah's ride and the phone calls had bothered him enough that he called the police and the state's attorney's office but neither agency was helpful. For safety reasons, he moved his gun from the closet to his nightstand on Monday, the day before the homicides.

"I was worried of an intruder," he explained.

Winger said that he spoke to BART owner Ray Duffey three times.

At first, Winger said, "he seemed a little ambivalent about the whole thing." That motivated Winger to take charge. He felt he needed to say something that would get Duffey's attention.

"I basically told him a fib," Winger said. He told Duffey that an attorney advised him that he was in a good position to take action. He said he needed the driver's full name in order to file a police report. Duffey was reluctant to give him that before consulting his own attorneys.

"What was your intention after receiving that information? What were you going to do?" Nolan asked.

"Well, I was kind of spontaneous, because, the way Mr. Duffey was on the phone, I felt like I was gonna get the runaround."

Winger said that he never solicited Harrington's telephone number, just his name. He said Duffey told him that the driver was willing to talk with him and clear things up.

"Was that the first time that anyone had suggested that you talk with Roger Harrington?"

"Perhaps. I am not sure."

Mark said he called Harrington Tuesday morning with the intention "to just tell him that if he's the person that has been calling my house, to please stop and that my wife is not his friend."

Winger said he did not get very far because Harrington began talking to the third, nonexistent party.

"He said something about 'Yeah, I know your address.'"

Winger said he realized it was a mistake to contact Harrington, so he ended the conversation, making up the excuse he would be in meetings all day.

"At any time did you tell Roger Harrington that you wanted to meet with him personally to discuss this situation?" Nolan asked.

"Never."

Asked if he was aware of the note found in Harrington's car, Winger said yes, he was aware of it, but he never saw it. He never saw Donnah's handwritten note, either, he said, although he was the one who suggested that she write it.

Once more, Mark Winger gave his account of being on the treadmill, hearing a thump, and running upstairs.

"Did you hear your wife screaming?"

"I don't remember if I heard her scream," Winger said. At the time, he said, he did not know what he heard.

"I know now that it was the sound of a hammer going through someone's head."

His memory of Roger Harrington's death throes was equally graphic.

"The guy I shot was like a fountain of blood coming out of his mouth," he said. When the dying man moaned, Winger said, he "grabbed the hammer from him—and I started poundin' him in the chest and tellin' him to shut up."

Winger was asked to review Detective Charlie Cox's nine-page account of their interview and correct any mistakes. He made one change: Cox had reported that Winger told Harrington he would be in meetings until 3:30 p.m. That should be 5:30 p.m., Winger said.

"I didn't tell him the correct time that I was getting off work."

Everything else, he said, was accurate.

Attorney Michael Metnick believed the case would likely end with a generous settlement. If it was put in the hands of a jury sympathetic to Mark Winger, it could cost BART's insurers millions. Metnick wrote attorney John Nolan a letter spelling it out.

"Donnah Winger's death could have been prevented had BART exercised reasonable precautions in its hiring practices," he wrote. He said a conservative value of a potential jury verdict would be more than two million dollars. The Wingers were prepared to settle for a fraction of that—one million, two hundred thousand dollars.

Metnick felt well positioned to make the demand.

15

Something Stinks

Once Detective Charlie Cox began to have doubts about the Winger case, everything his partner Doug Williamson said made sense. The final straw came a year after the crime, when Winger paid Cox another visit. This time he had cheerful news: he was getting remarried.

"To his nanny!" Cox told his partner. Every bone in Cox's body told him he had been duped.

"Something stinks here," he said. "Big-time."

Williamson refrained from saying "I told you so." He was too relieved to finally have his partner's solid support.

"Everybody makes mistakes," Williamson later told Richard Schlesinger. "I've made some and he fixed mine."

Together the detectives went back to their superiors, this time as a united front. Something was wrong, they said. They needed to go back and check the phone records. They needed to send evidence to the lab for tests. They needed the resources to launch a full-scale investigation.

"This guy is a first-class actor," Cox said. "But my gut tells me he is in it up to his ears."

The detectives were turned down. Their bosses were not about to reopen a case on gut feelings, especially when the lead detective had came to the opposite conclusion before, using the same evidence. It was odd that Winger was marrying his nanny, but hardly proof of murder. It did not change the case. If the detectives wanted to investigate, they needed to come up with a better reason than that.

The detectives were caught in a classic catch-22. They needed more evidence but were denied the resources to get it. They could not seek out witnesses or do anything that would attract public attention.

"We were told to leave it alone," Williamson said. "They said they made their decision. This is what happened and we were wrong."

Williamson would not relent. He pointed out the note in Roger Harrington's car. It indicated there was a meeting arranged, but Winger denied this. He was told that even if there had been a meeting, it did not mean Winger was a killer. Maybe, after Harrington went berserk, Winger was afraid to admit that he had foolishly invited the driver into his home.

Williamson did not buy that theory.

"If there's a meeting, Harrington's sitting at table

and he gets angry. He's with Mark," the detective explained.

"Donnah was in the bedroom, we know that because that's where the baby was. How does she get to the dining room to get bludgeoned? How does Mark get the gun? And why doesn't Mark get hit at all?"

Williamson's arguments fell on deaf ears. The case was closed. The detectives' only hope was that Winger would let his guard down and make a mistake. Maybe he'd slip up and confide to someone. All they could do was quietly monitor him from afar.

In July 1997, Charlie Cox attended a homicide investigation class in Louisville, Kentucky. One of the teachers was a well-known blood spatter expert, Tom Bevel. Cox told him about the Winger situation. He said they had photographs taken by crime scene techs and physical evidence from the scene, including the clothing everyone wore. If they were ever able to re-open the case, he asked Bevel, how could that evidence help them?

Bevel assured him that the evidence would tell the story. Blood falls in telltale patterns. If Bevel ever got his hands on those items, he would know for sure which man was swinging the hammer that day.

At the same time that the detectives were spinning their wheels trying to re-open the case, Ira Drescher was orchestrating a project to honor Donnah's memory. He got word that a visitors' clubhouse was being built for families of patients at the Joe DiMaggio

Children's Hospital, which was near the Dreschers' Florida home. The clubhouse would have sixteen private sleeping rooms where families of ailing children could get free accommodation while visiting their relatives. Ira set out to raise the $25,000 necessary to dedicate the playroom in Donnah's name. Sara Jane was delighted. It was the perfect way to memorialize Donnah's love of life and passion for children.

Never having done anything like this before, the Dreschers began by writing letters to friends. Before they knew it, they had collected more than $42,000.

"Our response was absolutely incredible, what with the checks we received and the heart-wrenching letters accompanying them," Ira said. "Everything was simply overwhelming."

On September 17, 1997, the hospital hosted a dedication ceremony. One hundred and forty people showed up, including, to Ira's great delight, Joe DiMaggio himself. The local media were eager to cover a positive angle of the Donnah Winger tragedy.

Mark was not there, but when Ira spoke he assured the crowd that Donnah's beloved husband had been exonerated in the legal system. Choking up, Ira repeated the moving words Mark had chosen for Donnah's headstone: *Time Gives Memories to Our Lives; Love Gives Eternity to Time.* After long months of tribulation, Ira said, Mark was now remarried to a wonderful young lady.

Donnah's sisters took turns reading a heartfelt poem they wrote for the occasion:

We'll hear your voice, we'll see your smile,
Though blindly we may grope,
The memory of your helping hand
Will buoy us on with hope.

Sara Jane took the podium and talked about Donnah's life. She praised the "prince" her daughter had met and married.

"Her storybook wedding is never to be forgotten," Sara Jane proclaimed in a strong voice. "She was my princess and she will never be forgotten, because the people who knew and loved her would not let that happen."

The ceremony was a resounding success. More important, Donnah's Playroom was spacious, comfortable, and inviting. It was filled with brightly colored furniture and toys. Donnah would have been thrilled to see it.

Nearly six months after the dedication, Sara Jane and Ira returned to Springfield. They had not seen Mark and his new family for nearly a year. They booked themselves into a downtown hotel and made plans to visit friends, including Mike and Jo Datz. Sara Jane had come to feel Donnah's presence in Springfield. It was comforting to be in the city where her daughter lived.

"I see her walking with me into Target or asking me what plates she should buy in the party store," Sara Jane would later write in her notes. "I see her look up at the waiter with a big smile on her face as he hands her the chocolate milk shake she ordered at Steak 'n Shake. I see her car outside her home and watch her run in with her arms filled with groceries. Smiling, she was always smiling."

Jessica invited the Dreschers to lunch at the country house and Mark came home from work to join them. The meal was pleasant, but as the Dreschers were about to leave, it began snowing heavily. Jessica insisted they wait it out and stay for dinner. They spent the rest of the day reading and playing with three-year-old Ruby and her little sister. Before leaving, Ira invited Mark and Jessica to brunch on Sunday.

Mark responded quickly, saying they were unable to do that.

"Why can't we?" Jessica asked. "We can do that. We'll be free after church."

Mark had no further objections, so everyone gathered again on Sunday at a downtown restaurant. Everything went smoothly, except for one tense moment. Sara Jane was sitting next to Ruby, marveling at how grown-up she was. They were having real conversations. They giggled a lot and made each other laugh. At one point Ruby grabbed and played with a pendant dangling from Sara Jane's necklace. It was one of the pieces Sara Jane had kept from Donnah's jewelry collection: a gold profile of a female face. Mark recognized it and exploded.

"Would you mind putting that away?" he sneered. "Because that really bothers me."

Sara Jane tucked the pendant into her shirt. Everyone stopped eating and fell silent.

"I'm sorry, Mark," she said, turning her attention back to her grandchild, who seemed shaken by her father's outburst. Jessica murmured something to Ruby and the conversation resumed.

By the end of the meal, the mood had lightened considerably. The Dreschers were about to head back to Florida. The family lingered in the parking lot as they bid their farewells. Sara Jane embraced Ruby and promised to see her soon. Mark gave Ira a big hug and kissed him on the side of his neck.

"I love you, big guy," Mark said.

It would be their last social get-together.

Two weeks after returning from Springfield, Sara Jane got a letter from Mark. It sparked a series of responses that eventually led to the end of their relationship. The dispute centered, ostensibly, on the form of address that Ruby and her younger sister would use for Sara Jane in the future.

Mark's first letter expressed his belief that he had long "sacrificed" his own "healing process" to accommodate others. He told Sara Jane that his method of dealing with tragedy differed from hers. She sought the sympathy of others, he stated directly and critically, while he chose not to dwell on it. As a thirty-five-year-old with a family, he was ready to move on.

"It would be inappropriate for me to stand vigil

over a past that will never grow beyond what it was," he wrote.

Mark continued, matter-of-factly, proclaiming that it was not in Ruby's interest for her to know anything about Donnah, nor the brief time they had together. Therefore, he demanded, Sara Jane's relationship with Ruby would change. Mark's next words broke Sara Jane's heart.

"Ruby is not to refer to you as grandmother nor come to know you as her grandmother."

If Sara Jane wanted to have any relationship at all with his child, Mark said, it would be on his terms. The Dreschers would also be required to treat both of his children equally. To top it off, Mark demanded that the Dreschers stop using Ruby's name in their efforts to raise money for their charity, Donnah's Playhouse.

Sara Jane was devastated.

"I loved that baby," she told Richard Schlesinger. "She was my one link to Donnah and she was my first grandchild."

Sara Jane wrote back, assuring Mark that she had the utmost respect for Jessica, and that she would treat their children equally, as she always had. She would never do anything with either child that Mark and Jessica did not give permission to do. She agreed that, for now at least, it would be detrimental to tell Ruby about Donnah. The one request Sara Jane had was to keep her title, "Grandma Sara," even though

Ruby would soon realize she was not a blood relation.

Sara Jane also made a point of letting Mark know that she and Ira had resumed their active social lives and travel. They had chosen to go toward the future in a healthy way and were not wallowing in their sorrow. "But," she added, "losing a child is like an amputation. You can never replace that part which was taken from you; instead you learn to live without it." She thought about Donnah every day, and would always do so.

She explained how the Donnah Winger Family Fund helped the families of children staying at the Joe DiMaggio Children's Hospital. It enabled them to be with their loved ones while they were undergoing treatment. It was a worthy cause.

Sara Jane told Mark she understood that they would deal with Donnah's murder differently. He was young and deserved to establish a new life.

"Jessica, in my eyes, is a woman secure enough within herself to make me feel welcome and comfortable in her home," Sara Jane wrote, praising his young wife's sensitivity and wisdom.

Sara Jane closed her letter by promising Mark that she would never do anything to hurt his children. She wanted both Ruby and her sister to call her "Grandma Sara" so that she could be a "very special lady" in their lives. She begged Mark to allow her the honor of that title.

Ira, ever his own man, wrote his own letter in his

own blunt manner. He told Mark that he feared he was "running away from the past." He hoped Mark would take his advice and face up to what had happened and deal with it. But the issue he really wanted to address, he said, was Sara Jane's title.

"She is someone important to your family and she would always like to be. We love you guys and your family and can only hope that your compassion is great enough as to include us in your family," Ira wrote.

Mark would not budge. His position was non-negotiable, and he said so in a letter addressed to both Sara Jane and Ira. He also said he would grieve in whatever way he saw fit.

"You received the horrible news of Donnah's death in a comparatively compassionate and sanitized manner," he stated. "I, on the other hand, witnessed the destruction of a soul."

The images he saw that day could "never be amputated," he told them.

Mark firmly restated that the only way the Dreschers would see his children at all would be on his terms. The decision was his. Sara Jane was not "Grandma Sara" and that was that.

In another response, Sara Jane held her ground, taking the high road. She let Mark know that she was not comparing their emotions to see which was greater; she was merely acknowledging that they were different. She, too, had mental images of what happened that awful day. But her final image of Donnah was one that Mark had given her in the funeral home when he said Donnah had looked like she was sleeping.

In addressing the situation with Ruby, Sara Jane wrote, "No matter how you try to hide it or bury it, there would never be a Ruby in your life if it weren't for Donnah and her persistence."

She wished her former son-in-law a long, healthy, happy life.

Ira also wrote one more letter.

"I simply don't see how the word 'Grandma' is so difficult for you to accept," he wrote. It was a simple term of affection, he said, one that Sara Jane had earned. He chided Mark for being "callous" and "insensitive," but said he held out hope that he would someday come around and see the error of his ways.

Mark did not respond. As furious as Ira was, he was saddened that his relationship with Mark was severed. He had become somewhat of a father figure to Mark over the years. He had taken Mark and Donnah on vacations and given them guidance. He got pleasure out of helping them out and they were comfortable confiding to him. He liked engaging Mark in the kind of macho banter he had with his own kids. Even after Donnah died, Ira felt he had Mark's respect. He realized that Mark needed help he was not getting, but how had he drifted so far away?

Sara Jane felt she had gone as far as she could go. She had given Mark all the leeway he needed. She was there for him whenever he called. She accepted unconditionally every decision he made, including getting remarried so soon. This time he had crossed a line.

"Mark told me that I could not be a grandmother to Ruby. And I begged him not to take that privilege away from me because Donnah left me as Grandma," Sara Jane later told Richard Schlesinger. "And he said that it was not up for discussion."

With matters as they were, there was no chance for reconciliation. Sara Jane was torn from her granddaughter, her one living link to Donnah. Ruby would grow up without knowing her or how much love Sara Jane gave her when she was a baby. She would know nothing about the mother who wanted her more than anything in the world.

When Roger Harrington set foot in the Westview home on that hot August day, he set off a chain of tragic events whose repercussions were still being felt. Now alienated from Donnah's beloved husband, Sara Jane wondered if the ripple effect would ever end.

16

Lucky Breaks

Mark Winger's new family continued to grow. Jessica gave birth to another baby girl in 1998. A few months later, on a Friday night, the Wingers celebrated the end of the work week at Gabatoni's, a popular downtown Springfield restaurant. Ruby was helping her little sister manage a piece of pizza when Doug Williamson, his wife, and two other cop couples came in and sat at the table next to them.

"Mark Winger looked at me and acted like I wasn't there," Williamson later told *48 Hours*.

Williamson could not respond in kind. He could not keep his eyes off of the man he believed had gotten away with murder. Two murders. While his wife and friends engaged in lively conversation, Williamson heard nothing but the din of voices. He pushed some pasta around on his plate but barely touched it. Normally he would be digging into the generous portions, but that night he had no appetite. Here was Mark Winger, free to go wherever he wanted to and enjoy whatever he pleased.

"It eats at you," Williamson said. "Any unsolved homicide does. But this one especially because I felt we were shortchanged by our supervision when we were not allowed to investigate."

If he could not work the case, Williamson was still determined to monitor Winger's life.

"We were keeping track of him for two reasons," Williamson said. "One, we believed at some point we would be able to work this case. Two, we wondered, if Mark Winger did what he did to Donnah, would he do it to his new wife too?"

If Mark Winger sensed the detective's disdain, he did not show it. He was in high spirits. He was back in charge of his life, the head of a thriving household. He was now the father of three daughters and husband to a beautiful, dedicated wife. He also got a promotion at work. He now headed the Department of Nuclear Safety's remote monitoring section. Moreover, he was on the verge of collecting a large sum of money from Roger Harrington's employer, BART. A trial date had finally been set and Winger's attorney was confident that BART would settle the matter rather than take its chances with a jury.

BART owner Mark Duffey later told *48 Hours* that he was "pretty far along" in negotiating a settlement. But it was not yet a foregone conclusion. Somewhere, deep in the bureaucracy of the insurance company, there was yet another person who questioned Mark Winger's heartbreaking story. The circumstances were suspicious. There were no signs of forced entry. The only adult survivor of the incident was unscathed. The police had taken everything he said at face value. The situation warranted further investigation. The settlement could wait a little longer.

Some former friends of Mark Winger also harbored doubts about him—at least privately. Rabbi Mike Datz and his wife, Jo, had no idea that there were detectives itching to reopen the case or that the civil suit was stalled. They only knew that they shared a queasy feeling that Mark Winger had not told the truth.

Jo could not shake a niggling memory of a conversation she had had with Donnah at her baby shower, three days before Donnah was killed. It was the same day that Mark drove home from Chattanooga. Donnah came to the shower with their friend, DeAnn Schultz, Jo remembered, and left Ruby at home with DeAnn's teenage daughter. She would not have done that if she feared that someone was out to harm them.

"She told me the story about the ride from the airport but she was not terribly concerned; it was more an interesting story," Jo said.

She distinctly remembered Donnah saying that she was not going to tell Mark about the crazy driver until he got home. Mark later claimed that Donnah had told him while he was away. He called the driver's boss on Friday, the day before he came back. Jo wondered how Mark had found out about the ride and why he lied.

Mark's behavior was also disturbing. The day Donnah was killed, when Mike and Jo made efforts to comfort their friend, Mark kept repeating, "I killed a man."

"I do remember feeling, even at the time, that it was odd that he said that and not 'My wife is dead' or 'He killed my wife,'" Jo said later.

"He was trained in the military. Why would killing the 'enemy' have upset him so?" Mike asked. "I know that, had I found myself in that situation, I wouldn't have had any qualms about taking the life of the man who was bludgeoning my wife."

There were plenty of other instances of strange behavior—not the least, the sexual advance Mark had made on Jo. There was his plan to take a female colleague with him to Africa a few months after Donnah was murdered. And he got his young nanny pregnant six months after she came to work for him. He left his wedding ring on Donnah's grave. Most disturbing was his uncalled-for hostility towards Mike and Jo and the way he cut himself off from people from his past.

"I accepted different ways of grieving, but his did not seem to be in the normal range," Jo said.

Mike and Jo suspected that Mark may have had something to do with the murder, but they kept that dark thought to themselves. There was nothing to be gained by causing Donnah's family any more pain than they already had. Besides, they reminded each other, Mark had been cleared by the police. Moreover, he and Donnah had been genuinely in love. If anything was wrong, Donnah would have said so. Mark had no reason to harm her.

Detectives Cox and Williamson were constrained, but both had faith that they would one day be able to launch a proper investigation. Someday, they believed, Mark Winger would slip up and do something rash. Someday other evidence would come to light. They had to be patient.

In early 1999, there was a change of supervision at police headquarters. Once again the detectives asked for permission to reopen the case. They were given approval to quietly submit a few items of evidence to be tested. But, just as they prepared to do that, they got the surprise of their lives. The case was about to be flung wide open.

"What changed?" Richard Schlesinger asked.

"We got a lucky break," Charlie Cox said with a broad smile.

BART president Ray Duffey was home with his family late one night in March 1999, when he got a phone call. The caller would not identify herself, but she said she was involved in the Winger case. She told Duffey that she was going to give the police information that might influence them to take another look at it.

"She simply suggested that if we were about to settle, we might want to wait just a little more," Duffey told Schlesinger.

He copied the number on his caller ID and passed it on to his attorney.

Around the same time, homicide detectives Doug Williamson and Charlie Cox also got a phone call out of the blue. The caller was an attorney who said that his client had information pertinent to the Winger case. The detectives recognized his client's name but had no idea what she had to say. They agreed to meet at the attorney's office the next day.

"I thought it was too good to be true," Doug Williamson said.

"Did you sleep well that night?" Schlesinger asked.

"No."

"You knew this was going to be big?"

"I knew it was going to be big," Williamson said.

The attorney led the detectives to a conference room. A few minutes later he returned with DeAnn Schultz, one of Donnah Winger's best friends. DeAnn took a seat across the table. From the looks of it, the past four years had not been kind to her. The petite brunette looked frail and drained of all energy. Her face was gaunt. Her sunken eyes darted nervously around the room.

They exchanged polite greetings. Then, in a hoarse, faltering voice, DeAnn told the detectives that she was having a lot of psychological problems dealing with her friend's death.

"She says, 'I've been through counseling. I can't sleep. I've lost a lot of weight. I'm on all these drugs,'"

Cox said later. "We asked her what was going on."

DeAnn turned to her attorney, who nodded, giving her permission to answer the question. Her voice became so soft that everyone sat stock-still so they could hear her. She said she had a secret she could no longer keep. She was not sure it would mean anything, but she thought the police should know what she knew about Mark Winger. His marriage had not been as perfect as everyone thought it was.

The detectives wondered what DeAnn knew. But they knew better than to interrupt her.

DeAnn talked about the close relationship that she and her husband, John, had had with Donnah and Mark. She and Donnah were especially close. Sometime in spring 1995, she confided to Donnah that she was having intimacy problems with John. Donnah apparently shared that information with Mark, DeAnn said, because later, in July, Mark called her from out of town.

DeAnn said Mark just chatted for a while, then told her he had heard about her problems and was calling to commiserate. She was uncomfortable at first, since she had not told anyone but Donnah about it and this was not something she wanted other people to know, especially John's friend. But Mark kept the conversation going and DeAnn said she opened up. She told him that she was thinking of moving out of state to be with an old boyfriend. Mark said he did not want her to leave. He treasured their friendship, he said. He always thought she was very attractive. Then he rephrased that and said he had always been attracted to her.

"It was nice to hear compliments," DeAnn told the detectives.

DeAnn said that she and Mark talked a little more and then he asked her if she would be interested in seeing him while he was on his business trip. DeAnn told him she would think about it. When Mark called back later, DeAnn said, she succumbed to his flattery. She told John that she needed a little time to herself and left their home on Saturday morning, July 22. She drove two hundred miles to the Comfort Inn in Mount Vernon, Indiana, and spent the weekend with Mark. They had sexual relations and began a secret affair.

"In your report you say that Winger and his wife were very much in love," Richard Schlesinger amicably reminded Charlie Cox.

"Yes."

"And now, DeAnn Schultz says, 'We were having an affair.'"

"Yes," Cox said.

"And what did you make of that, Detective?"

"I said, 'We got the evidence we need.'"

Schlesinger, a television reporter with a rare appreciation of understatement, smiled.

* * *

DeAnn Schultz needed little prompting. She seemed relieved to get her story out. On March 8, 1999, she gave the police a formal statement.

DeAnn said that her affair with Mark Winger began more than a month before Donnah died and continued several months afterward. Since Mark's work required frequent travel, they had ample opportunity for clandestine rendezvous. When he was out of town, they met at motels. In Springfield they met in parking lots.

DeAnn said that Mark told her he wanted out of his marriage. He hated that Donnah could not bear children. He feared that if they divorced, Donnah would take Ruby to Florida.

DeAnn told detectives that the relationship heated up quickly. She and Mark professed their love for each other. They talked about living together. That was incriminating enough, but DeAnn had more. Love was not all that was on Mark Winger's mind: he also harbored hate—and a chilling fantasy.

In early August, DeAnn said, she and her husband were at a cookout at the Winger home. She and Mark shared a stolen moment in the driveway, by the tailgate of his truck. They could see Donnah and John sitting on the front porch. Out of nowhere, she said, Mark's dissatisfaction with his marriage took on an ominous tone.

"It would be easier if Donnah just died," Mark told her.

DeAnn said she did not know how to react. She

thought Mark was attempting to make a sick joke. He persisted. He told her he had been thinking about it for a while. Maybe DeAnn could have a part in it. He'd be out of town, there would be an intruder, and DeAnn would come to the house and find Donnah's body.

"I said, 'That's crazy. That's crazy talk,'" DeAnn said. She said she told Mark emphatically that she would never be involved in anything like that. That, she thought, was the end of it. Mark was just talking. She did not take it seriously.

The next time the couples were with each other, DeAnn told the detectives, Mark brought up his morbid fantasy again. This time they were in DeAnn's kitchen. Their spouses were in the living room.

"It would be easier if Donnah just died," Mark said again. He said he did not want his child to be raised in hot, humid Florida.

DeAnn said she told him to stop: she didn't like talking about anyone dying. If anything like that happened, she told him, "I would cease to be a vital person." Both of them had to do what they had to do. She would get a divorce from John; he would have to break up with Donnah.

DeAnn said that later, when Mark found out about Donnah's harrowing ride home from the airport, he was irate. He was angry at the driver for putting Donnah and Ruby in harm's way. He insisted that Donnah write the note complaining about the ride.

"He said he wanted to get the driver in his house.

My impression was that he . . . was going to do what men do," DeAnn said. "Give him a hard time and make sure that he never messed with his family again."

When DeAnn heard that Donnah was killed, she said, for a moment she thought Mark may have been involved. But she quickly brushed that thought aside. When she saw Mark at the Datz home that evening, she said he told her it was "imperative" that she keep their affair a secret. The police spoke with her but did not ask probing questions. They seemed to believe Mark's story. They were the professionals. DeAnn said she accepted the sad event as a tragic coincidence.

"Did you believe DeAnn when she told you this?" Schlesinger asked Detective Cox.

"Yes."

"Why did you believe her?"

"You could tell by her emotional state. What she'd been going through. Donnah was her best friend. And it was eating her alive."

Cox said DeAnn also feared for her own safety.

"She was scared of Mark. She was afraid that—as I would have been if I were in her shoes—that I'm gonna be the next person. Because if he knows I'm talking, he's gonna want me out of the way."

DeAnn was apparently not afraid anymore. She was resolute. She told the detectives the exact date and place where she and Mark had consummated their affair. She gave them a list of all the weekends when they had met. She said that, if they checked, they would find records of her lengthy phone calls with Winger. She also said that, after Donnah died, she and Mark exchanged symbolic wedding rings. She still had hers.

"We were pretty excited about it all," Charlie Cox said. "But we didn't jump up and down in the office. We held it back till we high-fived each other back at our desks."

Doug Williamson, for the most part, kept his excitement under wraps. Inside, he felt the exhilaration of knowing that his rookie instincts had been right after all. He knew there was a missing piece to the puzzle, and he finally found it. To the outside world he was a seasoned detective calmly embarking on an investigation.

DeAnn had given the detectives a lot of ammunition, but Williamson did not know how much of it they could trust. They would have to verify what she had said. Richard Schlesinger pointed out that it made no sense for Winger to plot an intricate murder and then reveal his plans to DeAnn.

"He needed some help, I believe," Williamson explained. "DeAnn Schultz provided cover. She stayed with Donnah. She called the police to have the house put under a premise check. She gave us a statement about the phone call that came from someone who sounded psychotic. At the time she said that, I thought it was unusual that she could come to that conclusion so quickly."

Now it all added up.

Williamson methodically reviewed what DeAnn had said. The affair was juicy and it was proof that Mark Winger had lied. But adultery did not necessarily add up to murder. Winger's dark fantasy about Donnah's death was creepy, and possible evidence of a motive. But DeAnn's most salient revelation was that Mark had told her that he had to get the driver into his house.

"What did that mean?" Schlesinger asked the detective.

"That meant that he set it up and he killed them both," Williamson said. It was evidence there was an appointment.

"DeAnn Schultz didn't know about the note on the front seat of Roger Harrington's car that had an address and time on it," Williamson said. "We did."

Williamson put the pieces together. Mark Winger had wanted Donnah dead. He was thinking about killing her and pinning the blame on an intruder. The perfect patsy, Roger Harrington, came into his life at the opportune moment. Winger lured Harrington to his house, then killed both him and Donnah. Winger then staged the scene to make it look like he had tried to save his wife from a madman.

"This is a man who is an upstanding member of the community, a religious fellow," Schlesinger said. "And you think he was capable of planning something like that?"

"Yes."

"That's diabolical."

"Yes, it is."

It was the worst of the worst, Williamson thought. This was not a crime committed in the heat of the moment. It was carefully planned, brutally carried out, and coldly covered up with another murder. It was the most evil plot he had seen yet. Now all he had to do was prove that it had happened.

17
Coming Clean

DeAnn Schultz cooperated fully with the police. She gave them a wedding band and phone bills documenting calls she had made to Mark Winger while he was away. She also gave them two pocket calendars in which she marked the dates and times of her secret meetings with Mark. She told them about a disturbing comment Mark made on the morning of the day that Donnah was killed.

"He asked me if I would love him no matter what."

She did not think anything of it at the time, DeAnn said, but that comment haunted her ever since. She also said that in the weeks after the murder, Mark feared the police were watching him.

"He talked about feeling afraid to speak openly in his vehicle, that possibly it was bugged, that he was afraid to talk out loud to himself in his home," she said.

"We will be interviewing Schultz again because of the stress level she attained during this interview,"

Doug Williamson wrote in his report. "Two and a half hours was enough at this time."

DeAnn also agreed to meet with BART attorney John Nolan, who called her after she unknowingly left her phone number on Ray Duffey's caller ID. She gave a deposition. Once again she recounted the story of her affair with Mark Winger.

"He wanted out of his marriage; he wanted to marry me," DeAnn testified.

She said her liaison with Mark ended abruptly when he returned from his trip to Africa in March 1996. She had not heard from him while he was away. After he came back, she left several messages, which for a long time went unanswered. When he finally called, he told her he was "in a fog," they could no longer be together, it was over. That was the last time she would speak with him for nearly three years, she said.

DeAnn suspected he had a new love interest.

"Who did you suspect that he was involved with?" Nolan asked.

"The nanny who was taking care of his adopted daughter, Ruby."

DeAnn said she tried to get on with her own life and put the past behind her. She told no one about her relationship with Mark or the disquieting comments he had made about Donnah. Her secret gnawed at her.

In November 1998, DeAnn was suffering from a

severe migraine. Her husband took her to a hospital emergency room. Mark Winger was there with his family at the same time. DeAnn says it was jarring to see him, although they had no opportunity to speak with each other. The chance encounter unleashed a lot of bottled-up emotions, she said. Her doubts about Mark's role in Donnah's death were rekindled. With a strong urge to put her own mind at ease, she called him at work.

"He sounded pleased to hear from me," she said.

DeAnn said Mark told her he missed her and said a lot of nice things about her. His flattery was reminiscent of that conversation they had had in July 1995, when he first suggested that they get together. Other telephone conversations followed.

DeAnn wanted to meet with Mark in person so that she could look him in the eye and confront him with her questions. Mark told her he was about to go out of town on a business trip and suggested they meet while he was away. DeAnn refused.

She said Mark told her he had to be discreet about being seen with her because he was involved in a civil case. He was suing the company that had hired Roger Harrington. Ruby stood to gain millions of dollars, he said. He seemed nervous that the police might be watching him again.

DeAnn said she told Mark that she had been having a lot of problems. Their secret was destroying her. She mentioned that she had thought of coming clean. Mark warned her not to.

"He told me if I told anybody, 'our gooses will be cooked,'" she said. "Those were his exact words."

A little while before her encounter with Mark, DeAnn told her psychiatrist that she had severe migraines and suicidal thoughts. He asked her if there was anything going on that could be causing that—anything that they did not talk about. DeAnn decided to let her secret out. Apologizing for not being honest in the past, DeAnn confided to him her sordid affair with her friend's husband and her suspicions that he had had a hand in her death. DeAnn said she was afraid the man might kill her. Her doctor encouraged her to tell someone. After talking with Mark, she finally found the courage to tell her husband.

DeAnn said she no longer felt intimidated by Mark. With her husband's help, she found an attorney and ended up talking with the police.

DeAnn provided a key element to both the civil case and the newly opened criminal investigation. If she was to be believed, Mark Winger felt trapped in a bad marriage. It also exposed him as a liar. He had always boasted that his marriage was one to be envied.

"At the time he gave us his deposition, everyone believed he had a flawless marriage," John Nolan said. "I never even thought of asking him if he cheated on his wife."

In retrospect, he said, it would have been a good question.

* * *

Mark Winger's new wife, Jessica, did not care for DeAnn Schultz. The two women had met a handful of times when Jessica was a nanny and DeAnn dropped by to visit. It was clear to Jessica that DeAnn had designs on Mark. She suspected something was going on between them. Once Mark began wooing Jessica, she minced no words about his woman friend.

"I told him either break it off or I go," Jessica said.

Mark cut off all contact with DeAnn. Jessica was the object of his affection now.

DeAnn barely crossed Jessica's mind again until November 1998, when they bumped into her in the hospital emergency room. Mark seemed worried, as if the chance encounter gave him a premonition that something bad might happen. Jessica took it in stride, too busy to be concerned. She was preparing for the holidays while tending to the everyday needs of three young children.

Springfield was not a large city. They were bound to run into DeAnn Schultz sooner or later. Maybe DeAnn conjured up bad memories, Jessica reasoned, but she did not matter anymore. She had no inkling of the havoc Donnah's old friend was about to wreak on her family.

Whatever shortcomings DeAnn had as a friend, she proved to be a valuable resource for the police. Using the meticulous records in her date book, the detectives were able to hunt down receipts from the motels

Donnah Winger at age sixteen.

Donnah Winger proudly showing off her baby.
(Ira and Sara Jane Drescher)

Donnah and Mark Winger were a striking couple.

Everyone loved Donnah's disarming smile.

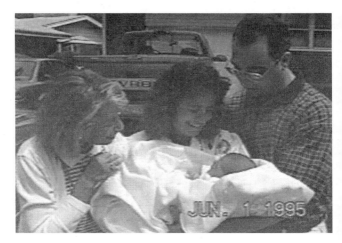

Sara Jane Drescher, Donnah, and Mark Winger on the day
that the baby arrived to the Winger home.

Donnah with her baby in the summer of 1995.
(Jo Datz)

Roger Harrington (center) with father, Ralph,
and sister, Barbara.

Roger Harrington's sister, Barbara, stood up
for her brother. (*48 Hours*)

Donnah and DeAnn Schultz, with Donnah's baby.

DeAnn Schultz, Donnah Winger's close friend,
had a secret. (*48 Hours*)

Sara Jane and Ira Drescher, Donnah's mother and
stepfather, were close to Donnah and her husband.
(*48 Hours*)

Rabbi Michael Datz and Mark Winger at a party for Mike in 1996, about nine months after Donnah died. (Jo Datz)

Rabbi Michael Datz and his wife, Jo. (Jo Datz)

LEFT Helen Harrington said that when she defended her son, she was treated like dirt. (*48 Hours*);
RIGHT Roger Harrington drove Donnah Winger and her baby home from the airport. (Helen and Ralph Harrington)

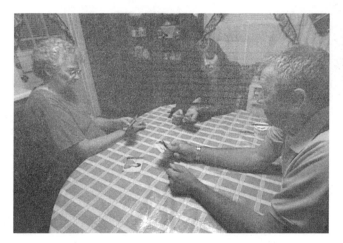

Roger Harrington's parents and sister look at photos of Roger. (*48 Hours*)

One of Dave Barringer's Polaroids,
showing where the victims fell.

Mark Winger's gun was found on the dining room table.
(Springfield Police Dept. crime scene video)

Roger Harrington's car was parked the wrong way
in front of the Winger home. (WICS-TV)

We entered ___ ___ and he introduced himself to me as Roger, after stopping for a coke, we proceded onto the highway. I asked him if he wanted to share a blueberry muffin that I had saved from the plane. He told me no thank you. He also told me he has this disease called anorexia. We talked about that for a period of time. Meanwhile, I felt as if we were speeding, so I peeked at the speedometer - we were going 75 miles per hour. It made me somewhat nervous that we were traveling that fast. Also, when Roger was wanting to pass another car, he would drive up very closely behind them, until the car moved over. I noticed him ___ his hands on the steering wheel acting nervously as if he was aggravated at wanting to pass another car. That, too made me feel uneasy.

Now, getting back to his eating disorder condition. He told me he's had this problem for many years. He said sometimes he doesn't eat for days. (3 days in a row.) We talked about many previous jobs that he has held (truck driving, phlebotomist.)

Somehow, he talked to me about being spiritual, and started telling me about his spirit, "Dahm." He told me that Dahm has been around for 10 years and has a vampire ___ (found out from a ouija board) although he looks like a dragon. ___ reveals himself as ___ in a form of a dragon. He told me things like Dahm makes him do things - some bad things - like sets car bombs + killing people. He said when this happens, he confides in his psychiatrist because it makes him mad. If he doesn't do these things, he said Dahm does bad things to his body. Ie. not eating. He also told me of some experiences when Dahm appears when he is driving. I was very nervous at this point. He said sometimes Dahm takes him out of his body when he's driving, and makes him fly above the tree tops when he's done with this to gets back into his body, and sometimes

Officer Dave Barringer snapped three Polaroids
before the victims were taken to the hospital. (*48 Hours*)

Officer Dave Barringer with his Polaroid camera. Thanks to
his good police work, the case got another look. (*48 Hours*)

Rookie Detective Doug Williamson had doubts
at the crime scene. (*48 Hours*)

Detective Jim Graham worked the case years
after it was closed. (*48 Hours*)

48 Hours correspondent Richard Schlesinger with
Officer Dave Barringer. (*48 Hours*)

Detective Charlie Cox (on the floor) explains how the case
was cracked to *48 Hours* correspondent Richard Schlesinger
at the Wingers' former home. (*48 Hours*)

Donnah Winger's lifelong dream was fulfilled
when she adopted her baby.

where she and Mark had met. There was little doubt that they had had an affair.

"She knew the exact weekends they met down in Mount Vernon," Detective Doug Williamson says. "She knew the exact date and time of Mark's first phone call."

The phone records showed that Mark and DeAnn had spoken to each other at length. He called her dozens of times while he was away. Williamson thought back to the interview Winger gave them the day of the murder. He denied knowing the phone number of his wife's friend, DeAnn. That was a lie too.

There was proof that Mark and DeAnn had spoken with each other, but it was impossible to verify what was said. DeAnn claimed that Mark wanted Donnah dead. There was nothing to back that up.

"Why did you take her word for it?" Schlesinger asked Detective Charlie Cox.

"Because, at this time, we're believing Mark is very devious," Cox replied. Besides, he added, DeAnn's statement fit the other evidence, especially that note in Harrington's car.

Nevertheless, DeAnn Schultz came with baggage. For one thing, she had kept quiet for more than three years. Why did she come forward now? She also admitted having an extensive psychiatric background. Maybe she was too unstable to be trusted. At the very least, she was not a very trustworthy friend. What proof did they have that Mark told her he wanted Donnah dead? Could that be nothing more than DeAnn's way of getting even with Mark Winger for breaking up with her? If the police did manage to build a case against Winger, DeAnn would be a key witness. And her credibility would certainly be challenged.

The detectives could not count on DeAnn Schultz's bombshell revelations to carry the case. They needed corroborating evidence, ideally physical evidence. They had a decent shot. The one thing the police did right on the day of the homicides was to photograph the crime scene and collect items from the house and from Roger Harrington's car. The science of forensics was growing exponentially. Prosecutors—and juries— liked nothing better than cold, hard science to bolster a case.

"Anyone who strikes someone in head with a hammer, throwing blood and tissue on four or five different walls and the ceiling, is going to get some on them," Williamson said.

Cox and Williamson were eager to see where those telltale bloodstains were. They planned to send the clothing and other items collected at the scene to the state lab and to Tom Bevel, the forensics expert who taught the homicide investigation class that Cox had attended. The detectives jubilantly sauntered to the evidence room. But when they tried to sign out the evidence, their glee came to an abrupt end.

"The case blew up in our faces again," Williamson said, shaking his head.

The evidence was gone. Unknown to the detectives until that moment, it had been handed over to Mark Winger's attorney, Michael Metnick, years before. At the time, Metnick thought he might need it for Winger's civil suit. Everything—the hammer; the clothing worn by Mark, Donnah, and Roger Harrington; the note found in Harrington's car; Donnah's handwritten narrative; the crime scene photos; Harrington's mug and cigarettes; the shell casings from the bullets; and more—was boxed up and given to him. He also had the gun, which had been returned to Winger earlier.

The detectives panicked. What if Metnick resisted giving it back? What if it was lost or, worse, destroyed? With trepidation, Doug Williamson called the attorney and, in a calm, professional voice, politely asked him to send the evidence back. He said, vaguely, that they were looking into "other aspects of the case." This time the detectives lucked out. Metnick readily agreed to send everything back. As his mother had said, all they had to do was ask. But it was another close call.

Cox and Williamson took some of the evidence and made the nine-hour drive to Norman, Oklahoma, to deliver it to forensics expert Tom Bevel. Bevel worked from an office and lab in his sprawling home. He promised to examine the items and see if the bloodstains corroborated or contradicted Mark Winger's story. He said he would also use the known circumstances to "reconstruct" the most likely course of events. Bevel's expertise came at a high price, but the Springfield police would share the costs with BART, the company Mark had sued for its "negligent hiring" of Roger Harrington.

Bevel told the detectives that the process would take several weeks. As confident as they were in their theory, they knew the results could go either way. There was a chance that the stains on the clothing would show that Mark Winger had told the truth. All they could do was wait. Meanwhile, there was plenty to keep them busy.

One unpleasant task was calling the victims' families. Williamson wanted to alert them that the case was active before word got out to the media. He knew it would open old wounds. Ralph and Helen Harrington had not been treated well by the authorities. They had buried their son as a murderer. If he was truly an innocent victim, the police had a lot to answer for. And there was also no guarantee that the new investigation would lead anywhere. Williamson steeled himself and made the call.

It went as exactly as he had anticipated.

"Of course Roger didn't do it. We always knew that," Helen said curtly.

She said she had no faith in the police. They had already declared the case solved. How could they prove otherwise now?

Williamson dreaded the call to Donnah Winger's family even more. Once a victim's relatives accept a theory of a crime, they usually do not want to rethink it under any circumstances. In this case, the Dreschers had even more reason to reject the new theory. They were close to their son-in-law, the man both detectives now believed had bludgeoned their daughter to death. They would not take it well.

Williamson planned to give the Dreschers general information and end the call quickly. He would simply say that there were unanswered questions and they were going to give the case another look.

"I soon learned that was not going to cut it with Ira Drescher," Williamson later said.

In September 1999, four years after Donnah died, Sara Jane and Ira Drescher were preparing to move to a new condo being built near the beach. The tenth-story unit had floor-to-ceiling windows with sweeping views of Hollywood and Miami. To the east was the ocean, to the west the Intracoastal Waterway with its seabirds and yachts.

It felt right to get a fresh start in a new home. Sara Jane had gone through the painful process of accepting that her daughter's life was cut short by a madman. Ira could not shake what he had seen at the Westview house from his mind, but he never shared that with Sara Jane. Rather than dwell on the horror, Ira and Sara Jane memorialized Donnah in a positive way, continuing to raise funds for the visitors' clubhouse and the playroom dedicated in Donnah's name.

The Dreschers had not heard from Mark since the

exchange of heated letters more than a year before. Ira was angry with him for hurting Sara Jane, but they both still had a soft spot for Mark, who was, after all, family. They were content to know that Mark's life was on track with his new wife and children. They missed Ruby terribly but knew that she had a good home and was surrounded by people who loved her: Mark, Jessica, her siblings, her grandparents, and Jessica's family. There was every reason to believe she would continue to be the happy, well-adjusted child she had always been.

In the afternoon of Monday, September 27, Ira and Sara Jane were at the condo. It was two months before moving day and they were supervising the installation of custom maple cabinets.

"I was making sure everything was done correctly," Ira said.

The Dreschers were standing by the living room window, watching gulls glide in the ocean breeze, when Ira took a phone call from a Springfield police detective named Doug Williamson. Williamson told Ira how sorry he felt for his family, then said he had news he wanted to share before it hit the papers. There were unanswered questions about the case, he said, so they were taking another look at it. Williamson began to say good-bye, but Ira cut him short.

"What unanswered questions?" he asked.

Williamson explained that he had been on the case since day one and some things always bothered him. That's why they needed to take a new look.

Ira's curiosity was piqued. The police investigation had been closed so quickly, he never fully understood their methods and procedures. He had no idea how they had evaluated the evidence or even what evidence they had considered, beyond what Mark had told them.

"What things bothered you?" he asked Williamson.

Williamson chose his words carefully. He did not want to reveal too much to a man he believed was still in touch with—and sympathetic to—Mark Winger.

"There were odd circumstances," he said.

"Like what?"

Williamson said there were no signs of forced entry. It seems unlikely that Donnah would have answered the door and left the baby on the bed. Harrington parked his car right in front of the house. He stopped himself before going further.

Ira told Williamson that was all very interesting. He mentioned that Mark had talked to him about the incident the day after it happened. He said that he and Sara Jane felt horribly for him and tried to help him, but last year they had a falling-out. They were no longer on speaking terms.

"Are you looking at anything else?" Ira asked.

Williamson said some new circumstances had just come to light.

"What circumstances?"

"We have a new witness." Williamson paused, knowing full well he would have to elaborate. He took a deep breath and said that a woman had come forward to say that she was having an affair with Mark when Donnah was killed.

Ira was speechless. Mark was having an affair? How could that be? Mark and Donnah had a perfect marriage.

"Who is she?" Ira asked, trying not to betray his shock to the detective.

Williamson parsed out more information. The woman was a close friend of Donnah's, someone who had had problems with her husband. Ira's mind was in overdrive. He remembered Donnah saying that her friend DeAnn was unhappy in her marriage.

"It has to be DeAnn Schultz," he said aloud, stunned by the thought of Mark cheating on Donnah with her best friend.

"That's up to you," Williamson said.

Ira was reeling. How could DeAnn do that to her best friend? How could Mark be so devious?

Williamson said the woman is credible. What she told them confirmed suspicions they had before she came forward. He took a deep breath and went all the way. It was bound to come out sooner or later.

"That's why I think Mark did it," he said. "That's why I believe Mark killed Donnah and Roger Harrington."

"Wow."

It was all Ira could muster. Mark had *killed* Donnah? This was impossible. Roger Harrington was the killer. Mark was the hero. Mark and Donnah had been crazy about each other. At least, Donnah had been crazy about Mark. Of course, from what Ira knew now, Mark had been cheating on her. He was not the loving husband he had seemed to be.

Ira had Sara Jane pick up the phone. He was concerned about her, because—despite her remarkable progress—she sometimes seemed to be physically affected by her pain. But this was something she had to hear herself. He could not protect her from this.

Sara Jane was astonished to hear about the new witness. Like Ira, she correctly guessed that the other woman was DeAnn Schultz. She was certain Donnah had known nothing about the affair. Donnah told Sara Jane absolutely everything. If Donnah suspected for one minute that Mark was sneaking around with anyone, let alone her best friend, Sara Jane would know.

Listening to Williamson talk about the unsettling circumstances of the case, Ira flashed back to thoughts he had banished long ago, when he was first coming to grips with the situation.

"There are some things that never made sense to me, either," Ira blurted out. "How did Mark hear a hundred-ten pound woman fall on a carpeted floor with the treadmill running? He usually listened to music when he ran."

If Mark did hear that thump, Ira continued, why didn't he go directly to the room where the noise came from? Why did he turn the other way and go to the bedroom on the other side of the house? Ira did not realize how disturbing these long-suppressed questions were until he heard himself ask them aloud.

Good points, Williamson told him. He was relieved that Mark Winger's in-laws were not likely to impede the investigation. It seemed that he had their cooperation.

"You have no idea how good a feeling that was," he said.

Williamson warned the Dreschers that the police would do their best, but the case might go nowhere. They were analyzing the physical evidence and tracking down witnesses. Williamson asked the Dreschers to be discreet; it would be best to keep everything as low profile as possible for now.

That was fine, Ira said, as long as he was kept in the loop. He was not about to let them go about their business without him.

18

A New Theory

After talking with detective Doug Williamson, Ira and Sara Jane Drescher sat together in their new living room, in the rosy glow of the afternoon sun. For a while they sat without talking, listening to the waves crash on the beach below. Ira clasped his wife's hands. He admired her strength but wondered if she could bear any more pain.

Sara Jane was bewildered. She had accepted that her daughter was murdered by a deranged stranger in a freak incident. The new possibility was so much worse. It was unthinkable that a man they had loved and welcomed into their family could carry out such a cold-blooded act of betrayal. Yet, that is what the detectives thought happened.

The questions that Ira had pushed aside long ago now ran through his mind over and over. There was no way around it: What Mark told him made no sense. Anyone familiar with the layout of the Westview house would realize that. Maybe Detective Williamson was onto something. Mark had kept at least one nasty secret from them: DeAnn Schultz.

Sara Jane remembered DeAnn as pleasant if not particularly engaging.

"She was Donnah's friend and they seemed to have a nice relationship," she later told *48 Hours*.

In retrospect, she thought, DeAnn seemed a little jealous of Donnah, even of Donnah's relationships with other friends, like Jo Datz. Donnah once brought DeAnn to Florida with her and DeAnn required a considerable amount of her attention.

"She sort of wanted Donnah on her own on a one-to-one basis," Sara Jane said.

"I thought DeAnn was nice but a little flaky," Ira said.

Both Ira and Sara Jane remembered that Donnah spoke openly about the intimacy problems DeAnn was having with her husband. Donnah said that Mark was trying to help them, listening to each of them separately. Maybe that was Mark's way of having time alone with DeAnn. As shocking as that was, it was a long way from plotting Donnah's murder.

"Sara Jane and I were nervous and uptight," Ira recalled, when asked about that day that Williamson called him. "We had cared about Mark as if he were a son."

Sara Jane thought about some of the odd things Mark did after Donnah died. She once caught a glimpse of him, alone in their guest room, drinking beer and watching the movie *Pulp Fiction*. Sara Jane wondered how he could stand the fake violence so soon after witnessing the real thing. But she never brought it up.

The Dreschers felt they had no choice but to tell their immediate relatives about Detective Doug Williamson's suspicions. To their surprise, some of them said they privately questioned Mark's story themselves. Taking the lead, Ira insisted that everyone give Mark the benefit of doubt.

"Innocent until proven guilty," he told them.

The police were professionals and they knew how to evaluate the evidence. Some of it was already at a forensics lab. They were tracking down witnesses. The family had to let the investigation go wherever the evidence led.

It was about to explode.

Four years after Mark Winger initiated his lawsuit against Roger Harrington's employer, BART, the court file was thick with documents. Most were mind-numbing briefs regarding arcane negligent hiring issues. The motion filed by BART attorney John Nolan on December 1, 1999, was different. Written in legalese, it called for Mark Winger to be held in contempt of court because he had "abused the discovery process." The way Winger abused it, Nolan stated, was to lie in his deposition when he said that he and Donnah had had a "great relationship." Winger lied again when he said he saw Roger Harrington kill Donnah.

Those statements, Nolan said, contradicted evidence that had since come to light. He attached two exhibits to support his claim.

One exhibit was an eight-page report by forensic expert Tom Bevel. The report disputed Charlie Cox's early claim that "there is nothing to indicate anything other than what the husband had described."

Bevel concluded that "the physical evidence is . . . consistent with a staged, domestic homicide by the husband, Mark Winger," and that Roger Harrington's murder "was used to explain Donnah's death." Winger lured Harrington to his home, Bevel said, to make it look like an intruder killed his wife. In reality, Winger killed both victims.

The second exhibit Nolan attached to his motion was a sworn statement from DeAnn Schultz. Her name was redacted to protect her privacy, but the facts, as she told them, were there. She stated that she and Winger were in the midst of an extramarital affair when Donnah was killed. Winger told her he wished Donnah would die. He even hinted at a scheme in which DeAnn would "find" her friend's body.

Nolan contended that this statement "diminishes completely" Winger's claims of injury "for the loss of companionship, society and support of his wife." Nolan's purpose was to show that Winger did not deserve the money he was seeking from BART. But the papers Nolan filed also implicated Winger in a double homicide.

"This is certainly not the kind of thing you see every

day as a civil defense lawyer," Nolan told stunned reporters.

The story made the front page of Springfield's newspaper, the *State Journal-Register*. The man the police had hailed as a hero was being accused of murder.

That same day another attorney, representing Roger Harrington's parents, filed a wrongful death suit against Winger. They demanded that Winger reimburse the family for its loss and to cover funeral and medical expenses. The Harringtons shied away from the media, but their lawyer gave a statement.

"As you can imagine, this has been a nightmare since the first reports came out four years ago. They've always known their son was innocent."

The Harringtons were skeptical they would ever collect a penny. Nothing would bring back Roger or end their pain. But this was a chance to clear their son's name, to prove once and for all that he was an innocent bystander, not a psychotic killer.

Mark Winger's attorney, Michael Metnick, was unprepared for any of it.

"I was blindsided, hit over the head, sucker punched, whatever cliché you like."

Metnick never thought of the Winger case as a whodunit. He thought the key issue was the reasonable steps an employer was obligated to take when vetting a prospective employee. Out of nowhere, Metnick's respectable client, the nerdy middle-class nuclear engineer, was being pegged as a man who got away with murder. This was a man Metnick had played golf with, a man he had invited to dinner with their families.

When reporters besieged him with the inevitable questions, Metnick said he gave "emotional, babbling responses." At the time, he was a strong contender in an upcoming race for state's attorney. He speculated aloud that the unexpected revelations could be a political move to harm him. He defended his client on the spur of the moment by questioning why it took the "other woman" four years to come forward. He also made it clear that he would have never filed the lawsuit had the police investigation left any shred of doubt about Mark Winger's innocence.

Metnick advised Mark Winger to drop his lawsuit. Winger complied, knowing he had a more pressing problem. If he were to be formally charged with the crime, he could end up spending the rest of his life in prison. Metnick referred Winger to Thomas Breen, a top Chicago attorney, who signed on to handle any future criminal charges.

In hindsight, Metnick said there were signs something was wrong all along. He never gave much thought to the note found in Roger Harrington's car. Mark Winger did not want to have Donnah's friend, DeAnn Schultz, as a witness, even though she was with Donnah the day after her harrowing ride. He was relieved to be off the case.

Thanks to the civil suit, the allegations against Mark Winger were out in the open. The police were on the hot seat, with the public demanding to know what they planned to do. The commander, who was not there in 1995, spun the situation as best he could.

"The detectives on the case have never been satisfied with the way it was concluded," he told the press. He said that the case was active again but would not say whether or not Mark Winger was considered a suspect.

Getting Mark Winger to drop his lawsuit was one thing, but charging him with murder was another matter. All that is needed to win a civil suit is a "preponderance of evidence." Criminal cases have tougher standards. The state would have to prove Mark Winger was guilty "beyond a reasonable doubt." That could be difficult, in light of the fact that the police had already investigated the case and come to the opposite conclusion.

"We don't know if there will be charges in this case," the commander conceded.

Detectives Cox and Williamson were determined to proceed but there was still resistance from within the department. At best, the case would bring embarrassing mistakes to light. There could be political repercussions and unwarranted criticism in unrelated cases. Some insiders thought it would be best to let the publicity simmer down and wither away.

"They don't like to admit mistakes," Charlie Cox said later. "If it was hard for them, imagine what it was like for me. I was the lead detective on the case. I was the one who messed up."

Still, he said, once he realized his error, he was not about to let go. Neither was Doug Williamson.

Ira and Sara Jane Drescher read about BART's accusations against Mark in the newspaper. They remembered giving Mark their blessing when he told them he was going to sue.

"We were so angry that this company could have hired somebody who would do such a horrendous thing," Sara Jane said. "Let's make them pay. Go ahead and sue."

State Journal-Register reporter Sarah Antonacci called the Dreschers for a reaction. Ira politely told her they could not say very much. Restraint did not come easily to him, but he kept his word to Detective Williamson that he would be discreet.

"We're just devastated to read an article like this. It's extremely distressing," he offered. He wanted to add—but did not—that they were even more disturbed by a phone call they did *not* get. Sara Jane later explained.

"I thought we would get a call and Mark would say, 'Mom, I want you to know I know what's happening, I know the police think that I killed Donnah. But I want you to know that I did not do it and I will prove that to you as time goes on.'"

That call never came.

When Mark Winger first told his heartbreaking story about the murderous intruder, the media—taking their cue from the police—virtually reported it as fact. Now that there was speculation that the upstanding citizen might be a conniving, cold-blooded killer, the press clamored for the case to be reopened. Sarah Antonacci, the reporter from the *State Journal-Register*, pried what she could from her sources. Reporter Linda Rockey began preparing a lengthy feature for the *Chicago Tribune*. Television newsmagazine producers descended on Springfield.

48 Hours was in good hands, represented by Doug Longhini. Longhini was a well-known Chicago producer who, for three decades, broke stories on station WMAQ and headed its investigative unit. He had earned a formidable reputation, exposing crooked politicians, unscrupulous businesses, and public safety dangers.

Longhini was more low-key than most investigative producers. He spoke in a slow, deliberative manner that made him seem a little distracted. But he had a knack for getting people to talk and for finding enlightening tidbits of information buried in mountains of documents. One colleague compared him to the TV detective Lieutenant Columbo.

Longhini first heard about Mark Winger while copying crime scene photos from an unrelated case in the office of a private investigator who worked with attorney Michael Metnick. The more Longhini heard, the more he was intrigued. Did the mild-mannered nuclear engineer get away with murder? Was he being victimized a second time, perhaps by overzealous investigators defending the company he was suing? Were the police really going to resurrect a case that was bound to bring them an onslaught of criticism?

If *48 Hours* was going to thoroughly investigate the case, Longhini needed the commitment of the management team in New York. There would be considerable expenses and no guarantee that the case would ever make it to trial. They would have to battle the competition. Unable to resist covering the compelling case, executive producer Susan Zirinsky gave it a green light and a team of producers.

Correspondent Richard Schlesinger, a veteran reporter and exceptional writer, was assigned to the team. Longhini would also get help from Ian Paisley, a talented young producer, and from this author. We had a lot of documents to get through and people to track down, but the case had only two possibilities: either Roger Harrington or Mark Winger was the killer. The other man was innocent. We vowed to keep open minds.

When the allegations against Mark Winger became public in December 1999, he was firmly entrenched in his new life. The congregants of his church embraced him, including him in family-oriented events and activities. Jessica was a devoted wife with three lively young girls. She was expecting a fourth child early in the new year.

Jessica's brothers, George and Albert, spent Christmas in Springfield that year. Happily reunited for the holiday, the three siblings fell into their usual patter, making the most of precious time. Jessica's girls delighted their uncles—they could not get enough of each other—but her husband was not growing on them at all.

Mark came across as more self-satisfied than ever. He seemed smugly aware that Jessica—and her mother—found him charming. George and Albert did not.

"Everything was bull," George later told *48 Hours*.

Both brothers sensed that Mark had been less than candid about exactly what happened the day his first wife died.

"I'm a preacher's son," George said. "I know lying when I see it."

For whatever reason, Mark brought up the horrifying incident again and again. He drew little diagrams to demonstrate what happened. Strangely, he said little else about Donnah. The brothers heard far more about her gruesome death than they did about her life.

Neither George nor Albert spoke openly about their queasy feelings, especially since the case was closed. Once the accusations against Mark became public, however, they gave it more thought. Maybe they should be having family discussions about Mark. True to form, Mark himself brought up the matter. He warned his brothers-in-law that things might get worse. There was "a girl" out there telling lies about him, he said. She was out to get him.

Mark said the woman was irrational and vengeful. No one in his right mind would believe a word she said. Soon everyone would know how crazy she was. Mark insisted he had always told the truth. George and Albert exchanged a knowing glance. Mark was trying to sell them.

"I kept saying 'Uh-huh, uh-huh,'" George said. "I just let him talk. He thought I believed him."

The more Mark talked, the less his story made sense. But Jessica saw it differently. She believed that her husband was being unfairly hounded and her mind was made up. When her brothers tried to broach the subject, she became defensive and cut them off. The situation was bad enough without them adding to it.

George and Albert could push their sister only so far. They did not want to risk allowing Mark Winger to alienate her from them. They had to keep communication open, play along, and accept Mark as part of their family. Frustrated and angry, they vented to each other, hiding their growing anxiety from everyone else.

The Christmas visit lasted longer than anyone anticipated, thanks to an unexpected snowstorm that halted traffic. Everyone was trapped indoors. George and Albert made the most of their extra time with their very pregnant sister and energetic nieces. They were losing patience with Mark.

George later remembered an evening when he and Albert were alone with Mark in his basement. There was no beer left and Mark was showing off his wine collection.

"We were cornered," George said later.

Mark reached for a bottle, cradled it in his arms, and began a long-winded tale about how he had come upon that particular treasure.

"I think he said it came from Africa—or somewhere," George said. "There was some kind of big story about it."

Mark boasted that he paid two hundred dollars for the bottle and had always intended to save it for a special occasion. He would share it with his son—whenever he finally had a son.

"With the way things are now, I don't know if I will ever see that day," George recalled Mark saying. "Who knows what the new year will bring?"

Ceremoniously, Mark popped the cork. He slowly poured the wine into three glasses, taking the time to savor its bouquet. They toasted Jessica, then each man took a sip.

Mark closed his eyes in dramatic rapture. George's eyes opened wide. He turned to his brother, who, like him, was unsuccessfully masking a grimace. It was the worst wine they had ever tasted.

19

Blood Trail

By dropping his lawsuit against BART, Mark Winger silenced one potentially damaging witness against him: himself. He would not be forced to give a second deposition to BART's attorneys, who would undoubtedly ask more probing questions than they did the first time. But Winger not only went after BART, he had also sued Roger Harrington's estate, and because of that he was the target in a wrongful-death suit. Winger's new attorney, Thomas Breen, moved to make sure that Winger would not be made to testify in that case, either.

Breen filed a motion requesting that the Harrington suit be put on hold, pending the outcome of a criminal investigation. He argued that if Winger had to answer questions in the Harrington case, it would give the police access to testimony that infringed on Winger's right to avoid self-incrimination. The court ruled in Winger's favor and the Harrington case was sidelined. Once again Roger Harrington's family was on the losing end of a legal procedure.

Mark Winger was not required to utter another word, but the detectives did have notes from the interview he gave the police on the day of the homicides. Forensic expert Tom Bevel used that interview to help him perform a full crime-scene reconstruction of the case. Bevel made a chart comparing and contrasting the known circumstances and evidence to what Mark Winger had told police and stated in his deposition.

Bevel noted the same odd circumstances that initially bothered Detective Doug Williamson. Harrington drove his own car and parked it conspicuously in front of the Winger home. He left weapons in the car but carried a plastic mug and pack of cigarettes into the house. He put those items on the dining room table (as they were seen in the photos), which was consistent with someone expecting to sit and chat. The note in Harrington's car indicated there was a planned meeting.

Bevel also questioned why Donnah would open the door to a man she supposedly feared. Why didn't she go downstairs and get her husband? Mark said he came upstairs because he feared his daughter was in danger. Yet, after seeing that the baby was fine, he grabbed his gun and ran to the other room.

Bevel's specialty was analyzing bloodstain patterns and spatter. Blood can be transferred from one surface to another by contact. It can also be projected through space after impact with a weapon. Sometimes it is cast off the weapon, as in this case, when the blood was flung from the hammer. Each droplet hits a surface in a particular place at a unique angle. Each droplet comes from a specific direction.

Bevel concluded that the blood spatter on the ceiling, floor, and walls belied Winger's version of the events. Winger claimed that Harrington was kneeling over Donnah, but Bevel believed she was struck from the other direction. Moreover, Bevel noted, none of Donnah's blood was on Harrington's clothes or shoes.

Bevel also claimed he found revealing bloodstains on Mark Winger's shirt. There were several large stains where the blood had soaked through the fabric, which were consistent with Mark holding his wounded wife, as he said he had. But two smaller stains, examined microscopically, were more incriminating. Those stains were spattered, not smeared.

"Bloodstain #7 on Mr. Winger's shirt is consistent with an elongated cast off stain," the report stated. "Bloodstain #8 is consistent with blood spatter from an impact into a blood source that was then projected onto the shirt and driven into the weave."

That pattern was typically produced during beatings, when blood is flung through the air. In simple terms, Bevel believed that those two stains indicated that the person who wore that shirt—Mark Winger—was the person who wielded the hammer.

Bevel said that Winger's story was also contradicted by the bloodstain where Roger Harrington fell and by a bullet that went through his head and lodged in the floor. There were two distinct pools of blood there, an indication that Harrington was rolled over before he was shot the second time, Bevel said. The bullet—discovered by paramedics under Harrington's head—showed that he was supine when shot. This conflicted with Winger's story that Harrington was kneeling over Donnah, he looked up, Winger shot him, he rolled off of Donnah but started to get up again, and Winger fired the second shot.

"The bullet exit and impact into the carpet is not consistent with this movement," Bevel stated.

Bevel spelled out what he believed really happened on August 29, 1995. Mark Winger lured Roger Harrington to his house with the promise that he would give Harrington a chance to apologize and save his job. Harrington entered the home, expecting to have a talk. At some point Winger pulled his gun and forced the driver to his knees. Winger shot him point-blank, then picked up the hammer.

"Upon hearing the shots, Donnah ran into the living room, leaving the child on the bed," Bevel's report stated.

Winger's plan worked: Donnah was exactly where he wanted her to be. Winger pounded his wife with the hammer—seven times—and she fell to the floor. He then hammered Harrington in the chest and called for help.

Tom Bevel had impeccable credentials. He literally wrote the book on bloodstain-pattern analysis. But as reputable as he was, there was bound to be another expert who would dispute him. Blood spatter is notoriously open to interpretation, especially in a bloodbath like this, with two gunshots and multiple hammer blows. It is like those ink blot tests psychiatrists once gave patients: that is, subjective. If Mark Winger were ever brought to trial, the case could easily become a battle of the experts. "Reasonable doubt" would probably favor Winger.

The detectives already had one strike against them. Bevel reviewed the same autopsy report and crime scene photos that that authorities used when they ruled that Winger shot Harrington in self-defense. Why would a jury believe that they got it right this time?

While Tom Bevel was analyzing the initial items given to him, Detectives Williamson and Cox sorted out the rest of the evidence that attorney Michael Metnick handed back to the police. Most of the boxes had been untouched for years, and when they were opened, the detectives winced at the fetid smell. Inside were the grim mementos they expected: pieces of bloody carpet, Harrington's mug, Donnah's handwritten narrative, the bloody hammer. But one envelope contained something neither detective had ever seen: the three Polaroids that Officer David Barringer took before Donnah and Roger were taken to the hospital.

The detectives were transfixed. There, starkly depicted, was the awful scene they walked in on four years earlier. There were the victims in their last moments of life. The images brought back the feelings of helplessness they felt that day. Only, that day Roger Harrington seemed out of place there, like the unwanted intruder they thought he was. It was striking, in retrospect, how vulnerable and similar the two victims looked now, lying side by side. Both had fatal head wounds. Both wore denim shorts and were flat on their backs, with their legs facing towards the kitchen. The detectives stared at the pictures in sad silence until, suddenly and simultaneously, they realized the significance of what they held in their hands.

"Oh, my God," Williamson said. "Do you see what I see?"

Cox nodded, unable to take his eyes off the picture of Roger Harrington. Cox was back in detective mode, blocking out the human tragedy and looking at the bodies as cold, hard pieces of evidence.

"It was the smoking gun," Williamson said later. "The placement of Roger Harrington's body blew Mark Winger's story out of the water. His story was done because of those photographs."

The pictures showed that Harrington's head was closer to Donnah than his feet were.

"Roger Harrington's head and feet were facing the opposite way of how they would have been, according to what Mark told us," Williamson said.

Winger told the detectives that he shot Harrington from the hallway. He said that Harrington was kneeling over Donnah and looked up just before the bullet hit his head. If that were the case, the detectives reasoned, Harrington's feet would be closer to his alleged victim.

"When you are shot in the head like that, you fall immediately. You don't move," Williamson explained. "So if you take Roger where he lay and stand him up on his feet, that's where he was standing when he took that first shot."

Roger Harrington's feet were less than five feet from the refrigerator in the kitchen, a long way from Donnah Winger. This, Williamson believed, was the evidence they needed to clinch their case.

The detectives remembered that David Barringer was his usual proficient self that day. They recalled that the officer took the crying baby out of the bedroom. They knew that he helped secure the crime scene, called the rabbi, and rode in the ambulance with Roger Harrington. But they had no idea that he had the presence of mind to get his own camera and photograph the scene before the victims were taken away. His pictures showed that Mark Winger had lied, and they strongly suggested what really might have happened.

"Mark Winger may have been showing Harrington Donnah's note that was hanging on the refrigerator," Williamson said. "And then Harrington was forced to his knees."

The *48 Hours* team spent way too many hours attempting to reenact the scene in our offices. We tried to imagine how the bodies ended up as they did, but it was hard because our small rooms did not resemble the Winger home at all. We knew it would be a challenge making this point clear on television, which requires simple, preferably visual explanations.

Charlie Cox eventually demonstrated it for us in Winger's old home. The Westview house was completely refurbished by its new owner, a woman with meticulous housekeeping habits and a lot of breakables on display. Although it looked very different from the way it had when the Wingers lived there, it was a solemn—and creepy—feeling being in a room where so much violence had taken place. Having studied the photographs, we knew where the blood had stained the walls, floor, and ceiling. We could vaguely make out ghostly traces of it—although that may have been in our minds.

With the camera rolling, correspondent Richard Schlesinger politely asked Cox to show us what happened. Cox, dressed casually in jeans and a white T-shirt, walked to the hallway, Winger's supposed vantage point. The producers peered through a crack in the bedroom door, careful as always to stay out of the camera's range.

"Right here, he sees Mr. Harrington raise his head up with the hammer in his hand and that's where he shoots him, " Cox said, reiterating Winger's story.

He spoke clearly, but Schlesinger wanted him to physically demonstrate his point. He asked Cox to show him exactly where Winger said Donnah was. Cox walked to the dining area.

"She was approximately in this position here," Cox said, getting down on all fours.

"Where am I if I am Harrington?" Schlesinger asked.

"You would have been on this side, kneeling."

"Like this?" Schlesinger asked, hovering over him.

"Like that. Getting ready to strike again. Winger shoots from the hallway, continues running, gets right over him, and shoots again."

It was time to switch roles.

"Show me how Harrington would have ended up if Winger was telling the truth."

Cox fell straight to the floor, lying on his back, his head towards the kitchen, his feet towards the hallway.

"He would have fallen backwards and landed down here," he said, looking up at the camera.

"And how was he really found?"

Cox bent his knees and pivoted his body without getting up.

"He was actually, completely, 180 degrees in a different direction."

When the detective stood, Schlesinger asked him to demonstrate how Harrington's body would have had to turn if he were shot from the hallway and ended up as he did. It was a critical point.

"There's no way that could have happened," Cox said, still tolerant, despite having explained it to Schlesinger umpteen times.

"Show me," Schlesinger insisted. "What would he have to have done—"

"He would have had to have done a complete back-flip."

"Can you show me?"

"I'm not agile enough to do a backflip," Cox protested. There was a moment of awkward silence, then Cox complied as best he could. He knelt on the floor.

"He looks up, he gets shot in the head, he would have had to completely turn"—the detective rose to his feet and turned, a bit like slow-motion ballet, twisting his body—"and land over here like this."

He was back on the floor, his feet close to the re-frigerator, just as in the photo. It was clearly an im-possible maneuver. Cox had made his point well, even by television standards. Schlesinger could stop testing his patience. Later, someone in Winger's camp was bound to have an explanation for how Roger Har-rington's body ended up as it had, but for now the photos seemed like damning evidence. We were grate-ful to walk out into the fresh air and leave.

The more the detectives studied Officer Barringer's photos, the more they saw. Charlie Cox pointed out that even if Harrington did somehow stagger to a dif-ferent part of the room, he would have left a trail of blood. No such trail was found.

"The absence of that led us to believe that whatever happened to Mr. Harrington happened near the kitchen," he said.

Doug Williamson noticed another detail. Looking closely at Roger's right hand, Williamson could not detect any sign of blood on it. Nor did there seem to be blood on Roger's watch and ring. Roger was right-handed. If he had just struck Donnah seven times with a hammer, his hand should be dripping with blood.

The three Polaroids undoubtedly bolstered their case. But they also presented a problem. The detectives would have to explain why no one bothered to look at them until four years after the crime. They were stuck with the embarrassing truth.

"We didn't know they existed," Detective Charlie Cox said.

They knew there were photographs taken by the crime scene techs who worked the scene after the victims were rushed to the hospital. That was part of the routine. Officer David Barringer had taken his own initiative. He followed procedure properly and handed the photos over to the evidence room when he got back to the station. The problem was that the case was closed so quickly, no one ever went there to go through everything that was checked in.

Worse for the two detectives, they themselves were in the house before the victims were taken away. They were live witnesses to the scene Barringer photographed. Cox had even reached into Roger Harrington's pocket and grabbed his wallet. Why didn't he notice the body positions then and there? Why did he believe Winger when he demonstrated what happened if he knew how the bodies ended up?

Cox said there was simply too much going on that day. The detectives were distracted by the commotion. He admitted he was so wrapped up in Winger's story that he missed the obvious evidence right there at his feet. As the more experienced detective, he said, he should have been more alert.

"Being a former crime scene man, I should have noticed the body positions. But my mind-set was, let me grab this identification before they pick him up and haul him outta here. I was formulating in my mind the questions I was going to ask Mark Winger. I didn't think about the body positions."

"How does that happen?" Schlesinger asked.

"It just happens."

"We blew it," Doug Williamson said.

As skeptical as Williamson had been that day, he, too, did not think about the body positions. All the more reason he had to work the case now and make up for the past.

20

Sad Anniversary

As the police tried to build a case against Mark Winger, Ira Drescher wanted to evaluate every piece of evidence himself. Reversing roles, he bombarded the detectives with questions, never accepting evasive or incomplete answers. He read books and articles about forensics. He quizzed his local district attorney—an acquaintance of his—about police procedure and expert witnesses.

Sara Jane wanted to know the truth but did not share her husband's desire to delve into the details. Ira agreed not to drag her in. He carefully avoided saying anything in front of her but spoke at length with anyone else who would listen. He also kept copious notes, both handwritten and on his computer, tracking the progress of the case, along with his grief, pain, anger, frustration, impatience, and doubts (with liberal use of capital letters, large print, and exclamation points).

Thanks to Ira Drescher and his hundreds of pages of documents and scraps of paper, this author had access to invaluable inside material. His notes also gave me a rare glimpse into what it is like to be besieged by the media. It was not pleasant.

No matter how much the Dreschers were badgered, they complied with Detective Williamson's request that they keep a low profile. They did not want to do anything to jeopardize the potential case. Once in a while Ira gave the local newspaper a vague, short quote, but for the most part the papers had to pursue other people who knew Donnah Winger.

Despite repeated rejections, *48 Hours* producer Doug Longhini kept trying to get Ira Drescher to talk with him. Sensing Ira's thirst for information, Longhini paid a visit to Ira's attorney and dropped off documents he thought Ira might want to see.

"I had to give him something," Longhini explained with a hint of the exasperation he felt at the time.

The documents were copies of the motel and phone receipts that DeAnn Schultz handed to the investigators. They were on file in the civil suit records. Ira was riveted.

"They were sooo revealing!" he wrote in his notes.

In the week when Donnah was visiting the Dreschers in Florida, Mark was at his class in Tennessee. He apparently had lots of time to chat. He talked with DeAnn at her home or at work twenty-two separate times for more than seven hours total. He called Donnah only eight times for a total time of about an hour.

"Mark would call Donnah at our house for three

and a half minutes and within a minute, he would call DeAnn and talk to her for 55 minutes!" Ira wrote.

The detectives told Ira that DeAnn was continuing to cooperate. Ira understood her importance to the case but sensed that she knew more than she was telling. DeAnn had talked about the "strange" call she took from a man who was later assumed to be Roger Harrington. As it turned out, there were only two alleged calls: the one DeAnn took, and another answered by DeAnn's teenage daughter while DeAnn and Donnah were at Jo Datz's baby shower. In both cases the caller allegedly asked for Mrs. Winger and, after being told she was not home, hung up. Ira wondered why DeAnn—and Mark—made such a big deal about the calls. Were they really so menacing that Mark felt the need to take his gun out of his closet and put it on his night table?

Williamson told Ira that they were keeping an eye on Mark. They followed him when he left his house in the morning. They watched him drop his kids at day care and go to work. They knew when he came home. The detectives did not want him to slip away before they were ready to make an arrest. Ira asked what they were waiting for. Williamson asked him to be patient. They needed to go over every aspect of the case.

Ira realized that, if Mark was guilty, he had deceived not only his family but also the police, including the lead detective. That, Ira wrote in his notes, had to be "VERY EMBARRASSING." He wondered if that was impeding the new investigation.

* * *

On August 29, 2000, Donnah's family gathered at the cemetery, as always, to mark the anniversary of her death. Five years had passed. Friends and relatives remembered her spirited disposition, how she lived every moment of her short life to the fullest. Ira thought about the man she loved and trusted. He wanted the case against Mark Winger to proceed so that he and Sara Jane would have an answer one way or the other. He feared they would never know for certain whether or not Mark took Donnah's life.

"The case is in limbo," he wrote.

One challenge in any case that lingers too long is the inevitable shifts in personnel. Just a few months after DeAnn Schultz came forward, Charlie Cox—the man who declared Mark Winger a hero and then pushed to have the case reopened—became a sergeant and transferred out of the major case unit. Doug Williamson was also promoted to sergeant but remained in the unit. With other homicide investigations now under his belt, Williamson took the helm of the case he had begged to keep open from the get-go.

Rookie detective Jim Graham joined the team. Twenty-eight years old, with a slight build and unimposing manner, Graham had spent seven years on patrol, mostly dealing with street-level narcotics. Graham had developed a passion for his work and a tendency to use colorful language when talking about it. He was friends with and a protégé of Doug

Williamson, so when his mentor became a sergeant, Graham leaped at the opportunity to take his place on the major case squad. The Winger case was his first assignment.

Graham immersed himself, going over every document in the thick files. He picked the brain of every cop who was involved in any way. He listened repeatedly to Mark Winger's 911 call. Winger sounded panicked and sincere, but Williamson pointed out a telling moment when Winger hesitated for a moment and there was a moaning sound in the background. Then Winger said his baby was crying and hung up. Williamson believed that was the moment that Winger realized the driver was still alive. He hung up so he could shoot Harrington the second time.

Graham also studied statements made by Donnah's close friend Jo Datz. Jo said that Donnah never censored what she said, so she was certain that Donnah had known nothing about Mark's affair with DeAnn. Once Jo learned about the affair, she said, everything fell into place for her.

"The last vestige of doubt was removed and I knew he'd done it," she said. "It confirmed my worst fears."

Jo was not fond of DeAnn Schultz. She met her through Donnah and sensed this was someone she did not want to get close to.

"She was a troubled person and I didn't want to get sucked in," Jo said.

They were friendly because they were both close to Donnah. But Jo felt that DeAnn was envious of Donnah's marriage and she told Donnah that. DeAnn was also too demanding of Donnah's time. Jo said that shortly before Donnah died, she was losing patience with DeAnn because she had become so suffocating.

"Their relationship was one of Donnah constantly rescuing and counseling a troubled and unhappy DeAnn," she said.

Jo told the police that she did not feel that Donnah was particularly frightened by her fateful ride home from the airport.

"She said that DeAnn insisted on staying with her the night after she got home. She was a bit irritated and bemused by that. I think she was just humoring DeAnn; she really did not feel threatened."

Jo said that when she and her husband found out that the police were launching an investigation against Mark Winger, they were not surprised. They had privately harbored doubts about their former friend for a long time. They wanted the case to go forward. Donnah deserved justice, they felt, and so did Roger Harrington. But Jo feared for Jessica and her children. Mark had already killed two people.

The detectives shared Jo Datz's concern. It was one of the reasons Williamson and Cox—who still attended meetings about the case—kept pushing to have charges brought as quickly as possible. If something went awry in Mark's life, Jessica could become his third victim. Who knew what could set him off? Meanwhile, they kept close tabs on him.

Detective Graham took on the task of surveilling

him. Graham parked his car by a silo near a cornfield and watched Winger through binoculars. He kept his distance but wondered if Winger was getting nervous. From Graham's vantage point, it did not seem that way. Winger followed the pattern of a typical family man. He shuttled between work and home and church, without much other activity.

Graham was also put in charge of keeping contact with witnesses. That meant tracking down people who were not easy to find and others who had reason to be hostile to the police. Graham also became the liaison with Ira Drescher, which kept him on his toes.

"Ira questions everything," he said. "He'll question whether the sun comes up."

Graham put up with Ira's incessant questions because Donnah's father-in-law was a good source of information. After all, Ira once knew Mark very well.

"Did you ever see anything about his behavior that was violent?" Graham asked.

Ira racked his brain but came up with nothing significant.

"He did some things that were kind of odd, but anyone could do that. Nothing sticks out in my mind that showed poor or violent behavior."

Ira had gone over it in his one mind again and again. He never suspected anything. Even now, he was not fully convinced that Mark was a killer.

"If Mark is guilty—" he began to explain.

Graham cut him off.

"If? Ira, I live and breathe and talk about the case

every day and night. I have absolutely no doubt that Mark is guilty."

Ira fell silent. If the evidence was so good, he thought, why didn't they file charges yet? He heard that the cops had incriminating crime scene photos, but he hadn't seen them himself. There were two sides to every story. He still could not visualize Mark beating Donnah with a hammer. Maybe the police were not acting because the evidence against Mark wasn't so great after all.

21

In Full Color

In mid-November 2000, one year after the case was revived, Detective Jim Graham planned to meet a gunshot wound expert in southern Florida. Ira Drescher invited him to stay at their condo, figuring that the money saved could be used elsewhere to speed the case along. Ira and Sara Jane also wanted to meet the detective in person, to get a better sense of him.

Graham agreed, seizing the opportunity to explain to the Dreschers what was happening. The victim's family deserved to know the status of the case. Graham wanted to let them know that the delays in bringing charges had nothing to do with questions of Mark Winger's innocence: they felt certain that he was guilty. It was more a matter of making sure they had everything covered. No case comes with guarantees that justice will be served, especially a case with the complications that this one had.

"It sounds tacky, but I truly wanted to help them through the grieving process," Jim said later.

Ira's invitation came with door-to-door service from

the airport. He was surprised when a light-haired young man wearing a backward-facing baseball cap walked from the gate and introduced himself.

"He surely doesn't look like a detective," Ira wrote in his notes.

"I was a lamb going into the wolf den," Jim said later. He was quick to add, "Ira is a smart man with a heart of gold. He would do anything to get at the truth."

The Dreschers' condo was unlike anything Jim Graham had ever seen. It was open and airy, with high ceilings with recessed lights. The floors in the hall were made of white stone and a there was an impressive collection of abstract paintings. In the living room, Graham sat across from the Dreschers on an oversize white sofa that was surprisingly comfortable. The furnishings and art were extraordinary, but the room's real showpiece was the view. Looking down on the palm trees, Graham saw an endless stretch of waves lapping at the shore below them.

Sara Jane and Ira were impeccably groomed and wore casual, stylish summer attire. They were gracious hosts. Graham accepted a soft drink and nibbled on the snacks they gave him. The Dreschers clearly led active and privileged lives, but their grief was palpable.

"I was greeted by two lovely people who are deeply scarred by Donnah being ripped from their lives," Graham said.

He took responsibility for an investigation he had

nothing to do with, apologizing that the police had not looked harder at the evidence they had from the beginning.

He told them what they found out about Mark's background. There were no known instances of violence, but there was at least one incident of questionable behavior in his military records. When Mark was in Korea, he led his men on a mock maneuver that, thanks to his recklessness and cockiness, was disastrous and costly. He was deemed unfit for leadership. It was not proof of murder, but it did show that Winger might not have been what he seemed to be.

More important, Graham said, was the hard scientific evidence. Tom Bevel's report was strong, but the medical examiner on duty the day of the homicides went along with Detective Cox's original statement that Winger had told the truth. They needed to find other experts who could explain why that had happened. Graham said that he brought the crime scene photos to show to the man he was meeting with in Florida.

Graham also told the Dreschers that he had personally met with DeAnn Schultz a number of times at a Cracker Barrel. She was nervous but her story was consistent. She was an important and credible witness.

Crying softly, Sara Jane listened to everything the detective said. If Mark was guilty, then she would have to accept an even crueler reality than the one she had lived with for the past four years. She and Ira told the detective they would do what they could to help.

They wanted to know the truth. They gave him names and numbers of some of Mark and Donnah's friends.

Ira showed Graham to the guest bedroom and, with Sara Jane out of earshot, asked to see the photographs. Ira wanted to see them for their evidentiary value, but he also had a personal reason. He was haunted by his decision not to view Donnah's body at the funeral home.

"I asked Mark how she looked and he said she seemed to be sleeping," Ira told the detective. "To this day, I feel that something is lacking in her finality for me."

Jim hesitated. He warned Ira that the pictures were graphic.

"I know." Ira remembered all too well the bloody aftermath he had seen at the house.

The detective took an envelope from his briefcase and sat next to Ira on the bed. He pulled out the photos taken by the crime scene techs after the victims had been taken away. He explained as best he could the significance of the blood spatter. Ira nodded, asked questions, and made a few observations of his own. Like the detectives, he was learning to separate his feelings from the analysis of the scene. Graham reached into his briefcase again and took out copies of Officer Barringer's Polaroids. Without speaking, he handed them to Ira.

Ira stared, his heart pounding. There was Donnah lying wounded on the floor. He wanted so badly to go back in time and change it so that moment never happened. He looked at the other two photos and his heart went out to Roger Harrington too. The man was clearly mortally wounded. But as much as Ira was succumbing to emotion, he could also see why the Polaroids were so valuable. For the first time he was certain that the story Mark had told was a lie. Roger Harrington was facing the wrong direction, just as the detectives said. He was too far away from Donnah. Moreover, his hand looked clean. There seemed to be no blood on it at all. How could that be if he had struck Donnah seven times?

Ira examined the photos more closely, one by one. The proof was there, before his eyes. Whatever doubts he harbored about Mark were obliterated. His ex–son-in-law was guilty.

Ira did not get a good night's sleep. Lying awake, he kept thinking about those images he had seen. Shortly after 5 a.m., he noticed that the predawn light was brightening the sky. There was no point staying in bed any longer.

Tiptoeing around the hall, he had an idea. He doubted that his houseguest, Detective Jim Graham, had ever seen the sun rise on the ocean. He did not want him to miss the opportunity.

Ira tapped on the guestroom door. He heard the detective stir.

"I want to show you something you won't see in Springfield," Ira said in a loud whisper. "But you got to come here right now."

Seconds later the bleary-eyed detective emerged. For a moment he wished he had stayed at a motel. He followed Ira to the living room.

"Have you ever seen the sun rise on the ocean?"

The two men stood by the giant window. The sky was getting bluer and brighter by the second. Graham was coming to. The impossibly bright orange dot peeking out from the back of the ocean was worth getting up to see. It grew larger and larger. A flock of gulls lined up on the sand to watch the spectacle.

The world outside was coming alive. A pair of joggers ran by the water's edge. The seabirds were crying out. The waves caught the light as they crashed and receded. Within minutes the giant orb was sitting on the ocean.

"Cool," Jim said.

"You never get tired of looking at that," Ira told him. "It's going to be a beautiful day. Absolutely clear skies."

After a quick breakfast, Ira got back to business. He gave Jim a copy of the motel receipts that Doug Longhini had given him, along with pages of his own breakdown of the phone calls. He also gave Graham a list of more people he thought the police should talk to. One was a family friend who visited Mark after Donnah was killed. Maybe Mark said something to someone that would be helpful to the police.

Later that day Graham returned to the condo. Sara Jane was out. Graham told Ira about his meeting with the gunshot wound expert, which seemed to be another step in the right direction. Then Ira took the detective to his den and showed him something that would inspire him to work the case even harder: the video from the glorious day when Ruby arrived at the Winger home. Graham was mesmerized to see Donnah come to life, her sheer joy permeating the room.

Donnah was handed her newborn and she snuggled against her husband.

"Oh, sweet!" she said, choking back happy tears.

Later, Donnah fed the baby, then handed her to Sara Jane, who sat next to her on the couch. Donnah could not take her eyes off her daughter.

"She's so perfect!"

Homicide detectives are not able to meet the victims at the heart of their cases. With Ira's help, Graham was getting to know Donnah not just as someone whose life was cut short but as a fleshed-out human being. She was beautiful and vivacious, compassionate and compelling. Graham would never forget the image of her tending her baby or the sweet sound of her voice.

As the year 2000 drew to a close, Springfield's *State Journal-Register* printed a story chronicling the history and status of the case. There was mention that some of Donnah's relatives were growing impatient with the pace of the investigation. A few days later, the paper published a letter from Roger Harrington's sister,

Barbara Howell, who noted that her family had been frustrated far longer.

Barbara said that her family knew all along that the murder did not happen the way the police assumed it did. She wrote about the last time she saw her brother alive, when he gave her the twenty dollars and picked up baby clothes for a friend. The next time she saw him, she said, he was in a casket.

Barbara assured Donnah's relatives that the truth would prevail. They should not lose hope.

Helen Harrington did not allow anyone to finish the question she had been asked too many times: No, she said, she never had any shred of doubt that her son, Roger, was completely innocent. She was sure from the moment she heard about his alleged intrusion into someone else's home. Her conviction was reinforced several weeks later, in the middle of the night.

"I was wakened from a deep sleep," she said in a moment of quiet reflection. "Roger was standing there in the room. He was so real. He was there."

In the comfort of her son's presence, Helen was at peace. She asked him if he had harmed anyone. He assured her he had not. She never saw him again.

Like Donnah Winger's family, the Harringtons spent years struggling to come to grips with their loss. Unlike Donnah's family, they were subjected to the scorn of strangers. They gave up on getting the authorities to listen to them. Years after the crime, Helen mimicked Charlie Cox's sneering comment to her.

"He said, 'If you want to know how he snapped and killed that woman, come here and I'll show you.'"

"The Harringtons hated Cox," Doug Williamson told *48 Hours.*

The Harringtons did not hold any of the police in high regard. But when the case was reopened, Williamson had a duty to update them on developments. They deserved the deference granted all victims' families. Although they had been less than genial to him when he first called, Williamson decided to visit in person.

Williamson had grown up on the north side of town, not far from the Harrington home. Driving past the fairgrounds, turning onto their block, he felt a pang of nostalgia. Everything looked familiar—sort of. The trees had grown in, providing more shade than he remembered. Children played in the street as he had. The small houses were a little shabbier than he recalled. Several were in need of paint jobs, as they always were.

The sense of familiarity was still there when Williamson mounted the steps to the Harringtons' porch and rang the bell. He steeled himself for a chilly reception, and that was what he got. Helen told him she had nothing to say, but Williamson said he had information she would want to hear.

Helen allowed him to take a few steps into her house. Neither she nor Ralph was in a talkative mood. Williamson apologized for the way the case had been handled and explained that they were on a new track.

He slumped down a little, in a futile attempt to not tower over the couple.

"I think your son was lured to the house," he explained.

This was not news to the Harringtons. They had little reaction as Williamson recited the circumstances that were obvious to them from the beginning. Williamson's eyes darted around the room. The sense of familiarity was, strangely, growing. He stopped mid-sentence to interrupt himself.

"I've been here before," he said.

Ralph had no reaction. Helen shrugged. She had no memory of that and did not care.

"Really—I've been here before."

Williamson suddenly understood his déjà vu. Roger's sister, Barbara, had dated Williamson's best friend in high school. His memory was streaming back to him. He remembered hanging out at the Harrington house with some friends. He remembered Barbara and vaguely remembered her kid brother. That brother grew up to be the man the police falsely accused of murder. It was a small world.

The Harringtons had no desire to conjure lost memories. Nevertheless, Williamson felt worse than ever that the case had been bungled so badly. All he could do now was make sure that it made it to court.

Detective Jim Graham handled the subsequent meetings with the Harringtons. Like Doug Williamson, he had a hard time getting his foot in the door.

"The first time I went to the house, they were sitting on the porch," he said. "If a shotgun had been in front of the house, it might have been pulled out."

Graham introduced himself and told them that the murder of their son was being actively pursued. He would be their liaison. They clearly did not want him on the porch.

"I remember a big dish with cat food in it," he said. "There were a lot of cats there."

"The police have been nothing but bad to us from the start," Helen told him. She asked him to leave.

Like Williamson, Jim had grown up in the area. The Harringtons reminded him of his own family. He related to their hardships. He was determined to convince them that the police were their allies. He told them he would make up for past mistakes.

"They had been mistreated for so long. I just laid down my sword and told them we messed up. We were trying to make it better."

On Graham's second visit, he was allowed into the house. He spoke to the Harringtons about their lives. Helen was still putting in long hours, but Ralph could hardly work at all. His health was failing. He had breathing problems and the doctors were considering putting him on oxygen.

Many visits later Jim Graham sat at the kitchen table, eating chicken and potatoes. The smells whetted his appetite; it reminded him of the home-cooked meals he ate growing up. Everything was delicious, he said, chowing down.

Ralph and Helen opened up. They talked about their thirty-seven-year marriage and the good times they had had with their children. They took out a cardboard box that held Roger's childhood photos. The pictures were worn around the edges from being handled so much. Another box was filled with mementos of Roger: Boy Scout badges, church camp certificates, notes that Roger had written to his parents.

"He was always scribbling little notes," Helen said.

Ralph and Helen said that Roger came back to live with them when his short-lived marriage fell apart. They had nothing nice to say about his ex-wife. Roger never had problems with anyone else, they told him.

At Graham's request, the Harringtons showed him the watch and ring that Roger wore the day he died. Graham asked if they had ever had the jewelry cleaned. No, they said: when they police signed it out to them, they put it away. This was the first time they looked at it since then.

"This could be important evidence," Jim told them.

The Harringtons agreed to give the watch and ring back to the police. They allowed themselves to believe that, this time, maybe the case would be truly investigated and Roger's name would finally be cleared. When a reporter called on the fifth anniversary of the crime, Helen said she did not want to discuss the case publicly. She did say that, for the first time, her family put a memoriam in the newspaper.

"I know the boy didn't do it and I figure, why should I be ashamed?" she said.

Roger Harrington's relatives were not the only people ignored by investigators in August 1995. They also wrote off Roger's roommate, Susan Collins. Collins was one of the last people to see Roger Harrington alive. In most cases, she would be considered a valuable witness. In this case, she was barely considered at all.

Susan Collins had not led an easy life. She and her husband had worked on road crews around the country. She would hold up the STOP and DRIVE SLOW signs to guide traffic around him. In the summer of 1995, she was living outside Springfield in a rented trailer she shared with her daughter, son-in-law, and grandchild. Her husband had moved out, and she found herself short on money. Her friend Roger Harrington came to the rescue, offering to rent a room from her for two hundred dollars a month.

Susan had met Roger through a neighbor three years earlier. He did odd jobs for her, like cutting the grass and minor repairs. They became fast friends and eventually worked together cleaning swimming pools. They talked about starting up their own pool-cleaning company someday, but that never got past the fantasy stage.

On the evening of August 29, 1995, just after it turned dark, Susan got a phone call from a cop. He told her he was at Memorial Hospital and something serious had happened.

"Can you come meet me here?" he asked.

"What is this about?"

Susan was worried because Roger had been expected home hours before. His mother called a while ago, concerned because she heard his license plate run on a police scanner. Was Roger in some sort of trouble? The detective's response did nothing to ease her nerves.

"We can't talk about this over the phone. I need you to come to Memorial Hospital."

Susan got a friend to drive her there immediately. She ran into the building and was met by the cop, who told her, bluntly, that Roger had attacked somebody and was shot in the head and killed. She burst into tears. Across the room she saw Roger's relatives huddled in grief.

Susan's head was spinning. How could Roger be dead just like that? The story she was being told made no sense at all.

She asked to see the body but was told she could not because she was too distraught. She agreed to go to a private room with two homicide detectives—the same detectives who would argue, a few hours later, that the case should be closed. She could feel their contempt but was eager to tell them what she knew.

Susan Collins told her story slowly and carefully, going over every detail she could remember. She answered all of the detectives' questions and added information she thought they should have. One of them took notes as she spoke.

Doug Williamson flagged that report the next day,

citing it as further reason to keep the case open. But he was overruled and told that the other detectives had more experience than he did. They were better able to judge which witness was telling the truth.

When the case was revived years later, Williamson dug out the report and gave it to Jim Graham. It was imperative, he said, that the young detective track down Susan Collins and establish a relationship with her. Graham understood why.

"She is the most glaring red flag of truth in the case," Jim said. "She told it like it was from day one and she was right on the money. Roger was baited to the Winger house." Susan Collins had said so that very first day.

22

Elusive Witness

When Susan Collins spoke with detectives on the night of August 29, 1995, she told them that she last saw Roger around 3:20 p.m. He told her he was going to meet with the husband of a woman who had complained about a ride home from the airport. Roger wanted to straighten things out because he was concerned about losing his job. His boss told him he had to clear up the problem if he wanted more work.

Asked to explain what kind of trouble Roger had with the woman, Susan said that Roger was "confused about this situation." He remembered the ride. The woman and her baby were his only passengers. He had a long conversation with her and they eventually talked about their experiences with Ouija boards. He also told her about his guardian angel, Dahm. He had no idea he offended her and, in fact, he thought that "everything went along real well."

The detective asked Susan to tell him more about Dahm.

Susan said Roger thought of Dahm as a "spiritual guide that kept watch over him," but in reality "Dahm is nothing more than a Halloween mask of a dragon that he keeps in his bedroom on a chair." Roger talked about Dahm, she said, but in a fun way. She denied the detective's suggestion that it was an "obsession."

Susan said Roger told her about the complaint against him a few days earlier. Just that morning, she said, Roger took a phone call from the woman's husband. While he was on the phone, he asked Susan for something to write on and she gave him a bank deposit slip. She saw him write down a name and address. She gave the detectives her bank account number. (The note found in Roger's car was written on a deposit slip for that account.) She told the detectives that she had caller ID and the man's phone number would still be on it.

Susan said Roger told her he arranged to meet the man at 4:30. His house was less than a half hour away, but Roger did not want to run the risk of being late, so he left around 3:20. He expected to resolve the problem quickly and said he would come right back and take Susan food shopping.

Susan was asked if she knew of any "emotional or mental disorder" that Roger had. She vaguely remembered that he had seen a psychiatrist a few times in the past but said that she was "more of a counselor than anything else." Asked about hospitalization, she said that Roger may have been to a hospital briefly, but she assured the detectives that he was "a very gentle and friendly person." Asked about substance abuse, she admitted that she smoked marijuana with Roger on occasion but said he was not into or addicted to any hard drugs that she knew of.

Susan agreed to let the detectives go back to her trailer with her. They searched Roger's room, taking pictures of the Halloween mask that was on the chair, exactly where she said it was. The detectives picked up two prescription medicine bottles. One was partially filled with penicillin, the other with Motrin. Susan told them that Roger recently had a toothache.

Susan reminded the detectives to look at her caller ID. (The number on it was later confirmed to be Mark Winger's work number.) They asked her again to elaborate on Roger's reaction to the prospect of losing his job. She restated that he was on the phone with his boss for about ten minutes and was told he would not get more work until the problem was cleared up.

In retrospect, it seemed clear that the detectives who interviewed Susan Collins had already made up their minds and were fishing for information to confirm their theory. They kept grilling her about Roger's reaction to losing work—the supposed trigger for his violence—and pushed aside everything she said about the arranged meeting. Susan was unequivocal: Roger had plans to meet someone. He wrote a note with the name and address. Her caller ID had the man's number. The appointment was set for 4:30. He promised to return after that.

Like Charlie Cox, the detectives already knew what the respectable nuclear engineer had said. They were not about to be swayed by a hard-luck, pot-smoking woman living in a trailer. She was one more element of Roger Harrington's unsavory world and had nothing to add to their case.

"They believed she was covering for Roger Harrington somehow," Doug Williamson said.

That was why the report downplayed her insistence that there was a prearranged meeting and played up her answers to questions about Roger Harrington's alleged motive and mental health problems. Williamson was not surprised.

"The report supports what they assumed to be the facts," he said.

By the time Detective Jim Graham tried to contact Susan Collins, she was long gone from the trailer. She had left no forwarding address. Graham found her daughter, who said that her mother moved around a lot, sometimes with her husband, sometimes without him. She called in every so often. The daughter promised to pass Graham's number on to her.

A few weeks later Susan Collins returned the call.

"Roger didn't do it," she said. She insisted that he was not an intruder. He went to the man's house for a meeting.

Susan told Jim Graham the same story he read in the report. She was relieved that they were giving the case another look but angry that no one listened to her. She did everything she could to be heard. She even had a television reporter in her home, who showed her caller ID on the news.

Graham took an immediate liking to Susan Collins. She was honest, simple, and outspoken. The trouble was, she did not stay put very long.

"I tracked that crazy woman all over the country," Graham said, laughing.

He was quick to add that he had deep respect for her and never stopped liking her.

"I drank beer with Susan," he said. "She was a rough woman with a hard life, but a good person. She always told the truth. And she was a good insight into Roger's life."

Susan gave a formal two-page statement to the police on January 11, 2001. She told her story about answering the phone, hearing Roger make the appointment, and watching him leave. Around 6 p.m., worried that Roger was not back, she felt that something was wrong. When she found out he was killed, she was "very upset and sobbing." Nevertheless, she agreed to talk to the detectives and took them back to her trailer.

Susan Collins resumed her nomadic lifestyle. She had a weakness for animals, and her pet ferrets went wherever she did. She took hardship in stride, but was sometimes overwhelmed. A few times she was arrested for writing bad checks.

"Susan's not a criminal in my mind," Graham said.

All the same, Graham and Williamson had a way to make Susan stay in town if they had to. She could always be held on a warrant.

"There were important dates we needed her to be here," Williamson said, smiling.

When Susan did disappear, Graham said, she called and checked in from time to time.

"I gave her an ear to vent about her life," he said. "It's part of being a detective. And she deserved it. She was a real person, not a phony."

Thanks to Susan Collins and the Harringtons, Jim Graham got to know another victim he had never met: Roger Harrington. Roger worked hard enough to get by. He enjoyed simple pleasures like fishing and playing Nintendo. He liked to laugh and, for relaxation, liked to get high. He also enjoyed talking with people, which was one reason he was happy working for BART.

Graham understood why Roger went so willingly to the Westview home that hot August day in 1995. Winger's complaint made no sense to him. He was confident that Winger would like him and he would clear their misunderstanding up quickly. Then he would get more work.

"He didn't smell a rat until he was on his hands and knees with a gun pointed at his head," Graham said. "He never saw it coming."

* * *

When the new year 2001 was rung in, Detective Jim Graham's cramped cubicle was piled high with Winger case documents and scraps of paper reminding him of tasks to be done. A photo of Donnah Winger flashing a characteristically engaging smile was tacked to the wall, directly in Graham's line of sight.

"I look at her every day and just keep working, just keep plugging away," he said.

Graham's boss, Sergeant Doug Williamson, also had a photo of Donnah Winger on his desk. Williamson was miffed that after all the hours he and his men put in, Mark Winger was still a free man.

Williamson felt there was enough evidence to make an arrest. Even if the significance of David Barringer's Polaroids eluded the jurors, there was clear evidence that Winger had lied: about his supposedly rock-solid marriage and, more important, about setting up a meeting with Roger Harrington. The note in Harrington's car was proof of that. So were Susan Collins' statements.

Williamson was heading the case, but even in his new position he could not force the case to court. It was up to the state's attorney to seek an indictment, and the state's attorney was not ready to go to a grand jury. Too much of the evidence was there all along, he believed, but it was overlooked. The prosecutors wanted to make sure that this time no stone was left unturned.

Williamson had to concede, grudgingly, that there

was some cause for concern. Two crucial witnesses, DeAnn Schultz and Susan Collins, would both face rigorous questioning by the defense team. Their credibility would be challenged. All Mark Winger needed was for a jury to find reasonable doubt and he would be free forever.

"This was a circumstantial case," Williamson explained. "There were no eyewitnesses. There were no surveillance tapes. We had to make sure every item was in place. We didn't want any surprises."

The police went on a lot of wild-goose chases but found a handful of witnesses to bolster their case. A neighbor reported seeing Harrington's dilapidated brown car—which stuck out like a sore thumb—at 3:50 p.m. That fit with Susan Collins's statement that Roger left at 3:20. It also meant that Roger was likely there before Winger got home.

Ira Drescher continued to contribute, largely by offering the police insights into Mark Winger's lifestyle, habits, and interests. But the stalemate was making Ira increasingly edgy. Obsessed with the investigation, he spent hours writing lists of evidence and possible motives Mark might have. He sent the lists to the detectives and prosecutors.

On an unusually chilly Florida morning in February, Ira bolted awake at 5:15. It was pitch-dark outside, but he felt compelled to go to his computer and write. It dawned on him that Mark might never be charged with the crime. There would be a cloud of suspicion around him, but he would just go on with his life. Sara Jane would always be haunted by not knowing for certain whether or not Mark had murdered her daughter.

"The state's attorney doesn't want to charge Mark as it will show so much incompetence by the Springfield police higher ups, pathologist, etc, and politically this case could be very damaging to them if they lose and can't get Mark convicted," Ira wrote.

He sent an e-mail to his friends and family, venting his frustration: "SARA JANE MISSES DONNAH TERRIBLY AND HER SUNDAY MORNING CHATS!" Ira wrote, with tears in his eyes. "She's such a decent HUMAN BEING and for this to happen to her, is simply UNSPEAKABLE!! Life simply isn't fair . . . and if you think it is . . . DREAM ON!!"

23

Probable Cause

The seemingly glacial pace of the case against Mark Winger was a little deceptive. Behind the scenes, police and prosecutors went over every detail again and again. They set up a "war room" in which men and women from all relevant departments met and compared notes and strategy.

Assistant State's Attorney Steve Weinhoeft, one of the prosecutors handling the case, became another one of Ira Drescher's regular contacts. Weinhoeft pleaded for patience, explaining they had to get it right. Winger had one of the best attorneys in the state.

Ira liked Weinhoeft. He came from a law enforcement family. Like the detectives, he sounded dedicated to the case. Weinhoeft called one day to tell Ira that they had spoken with more witnesses who contradicted Mark's story.

"He's VERY EXCITED!" Ira wrote in his notes.

One witness was Laurelee Smith, Mark and Donnah's next-door neighbor. Laurelee said she pulled into her driveway on August 29, 1995, around 4:30 p.m.

Her two young children were in the backseat. She immediately noticed an odd unoccupied car in front of the Winger house that she had never seen before. She was in her driveway for about three or four minutes, gathering book bags and helping her youngest child out of the vehicle, when she heard a shot ring out from inside Winger's home. It took her at least another minute to walk the children her own house. Ten minutes after that, she heard the fire trucks. She knew that the Wingers had a large mastiff, Stonewall, and wondered why he wasn't barking in all the commotion.

When Weinhoeft read Laurelee's statement, he said, "A light bulb went off." Mark Winger claimed he fired two shots in rapid succession. Laurelee heard *one* shot, not two. The fire trucks arrived nine minutes after the 911 call, so she must have heard the second shot. The first one would have had to have been fired at least three to four minutes before that, before Laurelee was there. It fit the theory that Winger shot Harrington, killed Donnah, called 9-1-1, and then, realizing that Harrington was alive, shot him again.

John Schultz, DeAnn's now-divorced husband and Mark's onetime friend, also gave the police a statement. Schultz said that he was out of town when Donnah was killed. He went to Rabbi Datz's home at 11:00 that night and spoke with Mark in the den. Mark told him that he saw a man pummeling Donnah with a hammer, just as he told the police. After that, the story differed, according to Schultz. He said Mark told him that he shot Harrington once, ran to Donnah and held her, and realized "there was nothing left of her." In his rage, he picked up his gun and shot it a second time.

Schultz went back to the house with Mark the following day and to Donnah's funeral in Florida the week after that. In Florida he discreetly asked Mark if they could talk about the incident, since something seemed odd about the pools of blood he saw at the house.

Schultz stated that Mark "immediately whisked me to the back patio to talk to me.

"Mark said that what he told the police and what he initially told me is not what really happened. Mark said now that I was asking questions, there is actually some variations of the facts that really happened. Mark said when he came upstairs from the basement instead of turning right, he actually turned left." When he saw Donnah being beaten, he said, "He beat the guy senseless." He then cradled Donnah and saw the man twitching on the floor. He went to his bedroom, got his gun, and shot the guy "execution style."

Amy Jaffe, a family friend whose name was given to the police by the Dreschers, claimed she heard yet another version of Mark Winger's story. Amy said she saw Mark a few days after the funeral. When she asked him what happened, he said he got some hang-up calls after he returned from a business trip. He said he called the shuttle driver to set up a meeting but then had second thoughts and told the man not to come. Mark said that after he came upstairs and got his gun from the bedroom, he found Donnah lying dead in another room. He then went back to the bedroom, where his baby was, and saw a man there. He shot him and called the police.

Amy said that when she spoke with Mark again he told her that he yearned to "make love to Donnah one more time." He told her he "needed to find someone to fill the void." Amy said she did not take the bait.

Police and prosecutors believed that conversation fit a familiar pattern. Winger inappropriately came on to a woman he knew, looking for sympathy. He was also "selling" his story, as he did ever since he called 911. In most emergencies, callers are most concerned with getting help quickly. They repeat the address and give explicit descriptions of the house. They run outside and wave down fire trucks and police cars. Mark Winger was more concerned with laying out the details in his narrative, telling the operator exactly what had happened. He did that again when he spoke with the detectives.

Unbeknownst to the investigators, Winger was also "selling" his story to Jessica's family, drawing little diagrams to illustrate his points. Sara Jane Drescher came to believe that Mark's efforts to ingratiate himself to Jessica and her family were part of the charade he played. He needed a wife and children so the world would continue to see him as a respectable family man.

"He camouflaged his life and married a very innocent young lady," Sara Jane said. "He had three more
children right away. He moved out to the country
where there were no neighbors. Just cornfields and
barns and silos."

Mark Winger was apparently accustomed to the status quo. He knew there was an investigation, but it
did not seem to be going anywhere. He had no idea
what evidence the police had, but the more time
passed, the more he felt it was not enough to charge
him. Off the record, someone familiar with the investigation (not named or mentioned elsewhere else in
this book) told this author that he had a chance meeting with Mark Winger around this time. Winger,
seeking reassurance, made the comment, "If anything
was going to happen, it would have happened by
now—wouldn't it have?" Mark's confidant knew
about the "war room" dedicated to the case but chose
not to tell him. Winger had no idea that the authorities were finally ready to pounce.

In the summer of 2001, Ira Drescher was let in on a
secret: The state's attorney was taking the case against
Mark Winger to a grand jury on August 23—just
a few days shy of the sixth anniversary of Donnah's
death. If the grand jury issued an indictment, Mark
would be arrested within hours and would probably
be arraigned in open court the following day. Ira and
Sara Jane decided to go to Springfield to witness that.

They left on a Sunday, after Ira pitched a double-header.

"We both feel anxiety and just thinking about what we will see gives me sweaty palms," Ira wrote before leaving, "BUT WE MUST HANG IN THERE!!"

In Springfield, Sara Jane again felt the solace of Donnah's presence. She understood why Donnah liked the place. She also enjoyed seeing Donnah's friends. The first night there, they had dinner at the home of Rabbi Mike Datz and his wife, Jo. The Datzes were as charming as ever and they now had two young, spirited boys.

The Dreschers spent the next day with police and prosecutors. Assistant State's Attorney Steve Weinhoeft looked exactly as they expected him to: thirtyish with a crew cut and suspenders—straight out of *Law & Order*. Sergeant Doug Williamson had a commanding stature that made it hard to imagine how his fellow detectives were so dismissive of him at the onset of the case.

John Schmidt, the state's attorney, graciously invited the Dreschers into his office behind the sea of cubicles. Elected to his post only two years earlier, he was the politician in the group. Impeccably dressed and rotund, his unyielding self-confidence was belied only by his fingernails, which were bitten to the nubs.

Schmidt told the Dreschers that they had a say in how the case would be handled. He said he expected the grand jury to return an indictment right away.

238 • Invitation to a Murder

It would take another year or so for the case to get to trial. If there was a conviction, Schmidt said, he thought it best to ask for life without parole. He could ask for the death penalty, but he felt it might be difficult to get a jury to go along with that.

"What do you think?" he asked.

Ira spoke up.

"I don't want Mark to simply fall asleep and get it over with the easy way, as if he's going for a colonoscopy," Ira said. "I want him to tough it out with all the other mean bastards for the rest of his life."

Sara Jane said she supported Schmidt's decision too.

Schmidt sat back in his oversize chair. He assured the Dreschers that he expected Mark Winger's six years of undeserved freedom to end soon.

The following morning, Detective Jim Graham drove to Pleasant Plains at 7 a.m. and parked at his vantage point, half a mile from Mark Winger's home. He waited. Winger should be going to work within the hour. The detective peered at the house through his binoculars, a little more intently than usual.

"I didn't want him to get away or flee to Mexico— or go postal," he said.

Right on time, at ten minutes before eight, Mark Winger backed his Ranger out of his driveway. Unlike before, however, Winger did not zoom past the detective's car. This time, to Graham's surprise, Winger pulled up behind him and waited, his engine running.

Graham raised his newspaper but it was futile. He had been spotted. On this of all days!

"He was pissed that someone was watching his house," Graham said.

The detective had no choice. He pulled onto the road and drove towards Springfield. Winger did likewise, staying on the detective's tail.

"I'm being followed by Mark Winger!" Graham muttered to himself.

It was total role reversal. Winger followed the detective all the way to the police station, pulling beside him at the entry gate. Both men rolled down their windows. It was their first face-to-face meeting.

"I don't appreciate you watching my house," Winger shouted. "You're going to scare my family."

Graham started to apologize but Winger cut him off.

"Do you know who I am?" he asked.

"Yes, Mr. Winger, I know. I am Detective Jim Graham."

Winger told Graham to contact his attorney if he had anything further to say.

"Yes, Mr. Winger," Graham said, "I promise we won't sit on your house anymore."

Winger paused, waited a moment, then drove off triumphantly. Graham felt it was safe to make that promise on this particular day. By tomorrow there would likely be no reason to watch Winger's home. Graham drove to the courthouse. The grand jury was meeting at 9:00 and he was due to testify.

* * *

In Springfield, grand juries convene on the last Thursday of each month. Citizens called to duty serve four-month terms. The grand jurors who considered the Winger case, on August 23, 2001, were near the end of their term and well versed in the routine. Prosecutors presented evidence through a handful of witnesses, and if the jurors believed there was "probable cause" for charges, they issued an indictment.

Assistant State's Attorney Steve Weinhoeft presented two witnesses, Sergeant Doug Williamson and Detective Jim Graham. Williamson described the crime scene and how police at first believed Mark Winger's story. Later, he said, when the pieces did not fit together as neatly as they thought, the investigation was reopened.

A grand juror asked if Harrington's fingerprints were found on the hammer.

"I don't think the hammer was checked," Williamson answered.

"It wasn't checked?"

"Uh-uh."

"That seems kind of basic."

"Yes, it does." Williamson maintained his authoritative tone.

Most of Jim Graham's testimony focused on the forensics and Tom Bevel's analysis of the blood evidence. He also talked about Roger Harrington's note and Susan Collins's statement about overhearing Roger make an appointment. When Graham finished, Steve

Weinhoeft asked the grand jurors if they had any questions.

"I know that you were not the detective at the time," one of them said, "but with what now seems like over-whelming evidence, how did the city of Springfield screw up so badly?"

"That is a very good question," Graham said.

It was not unexpected, but he wished it hadn't been asked.

"I must admit, even though I wasn't the original officer, Mark Winger told a believable story. DeAnn Schultz had not come forward yet."

The explanation was good enough. Mark Winger was indicted and charged with double homicide.

Immediately after the indictment was issued, Williamson and Graham, armed with an arrest warrant, headed to the squat building in an industrial park that housed the Illinois Department of Nuclear Safety. Accompanied by three other vehicles, they pulled into the lot. They spotted Mark Winger standing outside by the front door.

"Winger made eye contact with us, his eyes got big, and he turned and ran," Williamson said later.

Winger disappeared into the building. Williamson and Graham ran from their cars and barged inside. There were two women seated behind a large reception desk, but Winger was nowhere to be seen. The detectives identified themselves and asked where Winger was, but the women were too stunned to answer.

"Where is Mark Winger?" Graham repeated loudly.

The echo of his voice died out and a whimper came from a room directly behind the desk.

"I'm in here."

The quivering voice unmistakenly belonged to Mark Winger. The detectives trained their guns on the closed door.

"Come out with your hands up!" Graham shouted.

The door opened and Winger stood there, dazed. Behind him, Graham could see a large chalkboard filled with incomprehensible equations.

"All that stuff on the board. Like Albert Einstein," Graham said.

This was the first time he had arrested a nuclear engineer. What a waste of brains, he thought. Why would someone so capable and well-off resort to such senseless violence?

Graham ordered Winger to the floor, but Winger stood frozen. Graham repeated the command as Williamson calmly inched toward the startled engineer. With that large frame closing in on him, Winger complied and dropped. Graham's heart raced as he grabbed his cuffs and ceremoniously secured Winger's hands behind his back. He read Winger his Miranda rights, then led him to the squad car. Winger was squeezed in the back between Williamson and Graham. Graham said they were there for Donnah.

Williamson glanced at the young detective, signaling they should not say anything for the rest of the ride. He understood Graham's excitement—no one had waited for this arrest longer than he had—but his experience cautioned him that they were a long way from conviction. In the six years since he responded to Mark Winger's 911 call, he learned to be patient and to stay in control. The police could not afford to make any more mistakes.

Correspondent Richard Schlesinger later asked Graham what he saw in Mark Winger's eyes. Graham said at first he saw a flash of fear, but that quickly changed.

"It was replaced with a very cocky smirk, a smirk that said to me, 'You'll never convict me. You'll never get me.'"

The detectives drove to the back of the jail, where television camera crews were waiting. They paraded Mark Winger around a little before taking him through a back door. Once inside, Winger was whisked to the basement, booked, and photographed.

"He was still smirking when the mug shot was taken," Graham said.

Doug Williamson let his old partner know that Mark Winger was in custody.

"You were kind of cheated out of the joy of arresting this guy," Schlesinger later told Cox. "What was it like for you to hear he was in jail?"

"It felt good. Because even though I wasn't there to close the case, it was me and Doug who did all the work to get it reopened."

"But here is a guy who you called a hero now in shackles. How did you feel about that?"

"It was a good feeling. My feeling stupid had been gone a long time. He didn't get away with his perfect murder. He caused a lot of people a lot of pain, and so did I by not doing my job. I promised that would never happen again. I felt worst for the Harringtons."

"Did part of you feel like 'I got the last laugh now'?"

"Oh, yes, but, being a religious man, I didn't gloat on that."

"Not even the tiniest bit?"

Cox grinned.

"Yes, I did. I'm not a perfect Christian. I enjoyed the fact that he was in jail."

Sara Jane and Ira were in the prosecutor's office when the indictment came in. In all the commotion, by the time they were taken to the basement, Mark and the posse surrounding him were already gone. The arraignment was postponed until the following Monday, and the Dreschers had too many other commitments to stay for the weekend.

"We didn't get an opportunity to see Mark in handcuffs," Ira wrote in his notes. "We'll see plenty of him at his trial, in about a year or so."

The Dreschers planned to be there every day.

Mark Winger was put in a cell in the Sangamon County jail. His bond was set at ten million dollars. Among other inmates, he stuck out like a sore thumb.

Now thirty-eight, the father of four had never been charged with any other crime. He had a lifetime of gainful employment and was earning $72,000 at the time of his arrest. Even in his orange prison garb, he looked nerdy. His receding hairline and large glasses added to the effect.

State's Attorney John Schmidt proudly announced that the arrest was the culmination of a long, arduous investigation. He deflected questions about the botched early investigation and stayed on message.

"I think we're quick to look for fault," Schmidt said. "But it is very important to look forward in this case."

No matter how reporters rephrased their questions, that was the answer they got. Ira was also getting the hang of handling the press.

"This news has devastated our family and we just hope that justice is served," he said. "I have no further comment."

That was perfect, Schmidt told him.

In the twenty months since the case against Mark Winger went public, neither he nor his wife, Jessica, knew exactly what evidence the state had against him. At first Mark was nervous, but as time passed, he grew increasingly convinced that he was off the hook. Jessica, however, spent every day looking over her shoulder, wondering if it was the day her husband would be taken away. The dreaded moment came on a hot summer day when, after a meal at McDonald's, Jessica took the children to the play area and let them burn off some energy. They were merrily running around when Mark's secretary called and said that the police had taken Mark away. Jessica, suddenly on her own, was beside herself. She would have to explain Mark's absence to the kids. Worse, she had to figure out a way to support them for goodness knew how long. She called her mother, who hit the road for Springfield within minutes.

That same day Jessica went to police headquarters. Detectives Williamson and Graham took her to a private room in the detective bureau. She asked what to expect.

The detectives bluntly told Jessica that the evidence against her husband was solid. She had a decision to make about her future. Only she knew how much she believed in her husband and how far she would go to stand by him. They suggested she may want to drain her joint bank accounts.

"She was overwhelmed and under a lot of stress," Williamson said, adding, "She did not defend him."

Instead, Jessica wondered out loud how, why, if there was such good evidence, the police had let so much time pass. Why was she left in the dark? She was now the mother of four young children.

Jessica had the unconditional support of her mother and brothers. The members of her church pitched in to help in any way they could. But at age twenty-seven Jessica was thrust into a situation that would test her in ways she could not yet imagine. She resolved to muster whatever strength it took to care for her brood.

Like Jessica, Jerry and Sallie Winger considered their child their first priority. They rallied support from anyone willing to give it, making sure that Mark had the best lawyer and whatever other resources he needed. But the ten-million-dollar bond was beyond their reach.

The Wingers wholeheartedly believed in Mark's innocence. Nothing in their lives had prepared them for this.

"Mark is incapable of having done the acts that prosecutor has said he has done," Jerry later told Richard Schlesinger. The source of Mark's problems was DeAnn Schultz.

"DeAnn Schultz had a real agenda. She was a woman scorned."

"She tried to break up Mark and Jessica," Sallie said.

The Wingers contended that DeAnn was jealous of Mark and Donnah and deluded herself into believing that she could take her best friend's place. When Mark rejected her, she became bitter. Her bitterness festered and resurfaced when she ran into Mark years later.

"You don't doubt that your son had an affair with DeAnn, do you?" Schlesinger asked the Wingers.

"Well, if you want to call it an affair, I think it was more like a dalliance," Jerry said.

"He called me that night when he ran into DeAnn," Sallie said. "He told me she wanted to resume the relationship, the relationship of which he wanted no part of. He was already married to Jessica. She said, 'I will make you pay.'"

"What do you think she meant by that?" Schlesinger asked.

"Exactly what happened."

"She came forward with insinuations of things that Mark had said about planning Donnah's death," Jerry said. "They were absolutely untrue."

The Wingers believed that Mark was a victim of a terrible coincidence of misfortunate encounters. Mark had his fling with DeAnn around the same time that Roger Harrington stalked and killed his wife. Years later, when DeAnn was unstable and bent on vengeance, she talked with a detective who had tried to make a case against Mark but was overruled by his superiors. This was the detective's chance to prove himself right.

The scenario was obvious to the Wingers, but they realized it would be an uphill battle to clear Mark's name. They were in it for the long run.

At his arraignment, Mark Winger pleaded not guilty. His attorney, Thomas Breen, requested that bond be reduced, as it was excessively high. Winger should be allowed to return to work and support his family.

"Mark Winger is a loving and caring father, a loving and caring husband, and an active member of his church and the community," Breen said.

Breen argued that Winger was not a flight risk.

"He went to work on a daily basis, knowing full

well there was some kind of cloud on the horizon," he said.

Breen said all Winger wanted now was to put the matter to rest. The truth would come out at trial. He killed Roger Harrington in self-defense.

"There is not a shred of credibility to the evidence the police have collected against him," Breen said. Tom Bevel's forensic report was not reliable.

John Schmidt countered that Winger was charged with two murders and had six years to plan his flight. The judge sided with the prosecutor, ruling that the ten-million-dollar bond was warranted. Winger would remain behind bars.

Roger Harrington's mother, Helen, who was watching from a back row in the courtroom, could not contain herself. She stood up and let out a yelp of approval. She was admonished by the judge and quietly sat back down.

Three days after that outburst, on the sixth anniversary of Roger's death, the Harringtons placed another memoriam in the newspaper. It read: "Although your death has interested many, it is your life we truly miss."

24

Countdown to Trial

No matter what people believed about Mark Winger, there was respect and sympathy for both of his wives. Donnah was an innocent victim, whoever killed her. Jessica was revered for her dedication to her children. But another woman who had known Winger intimately was reviled for her deeds. DeAnn Schultz was the target of public scorn as well as Winger's defense. She was also crucial to the state's case, so Jim Graham kept her at hand.

Their first meeting was over lunch at the Cracker Barrel. It was a shaky start.

"She was very nervous and so was I," Graham said.

DeAnn picked at her food, eating very little of it. Graham told her he would be her liaison with the police and they would keep talking as the case wended its way to trial. He sensed her tension. She was willing to play her role but had not realized how long the process would take.

There were many more meetings and many more

meals. Graham did his best to befriend DeAnn, but it was not easy. When Graham probed for more information, she was guarded and slow to answer questions. When she spoke, her eyes shifted constantly. It was clearly painful for her to conjure memories of her friendship with Donnah.

"Did you think that was guilt?" Richard Schlesinger asked Graham.

"Absolutely. That's exactly what it appeared to be."

Asked what she had to feel guilty about, Graham himself became guarded.

"How much did she know about the plan?" Schlesinger asked.

"I really don't know for sure," Graham said. "The things she said she knew were more than enough for any person to have incredible anxiety over feeling responsible, or partly responsible, for what happened."

Graham believed that Mark Winger used DeAnn, and she was vulnerable enough to believe the bill of goods he was selling. She truly thought they would get married and be together forever. He saw her as a convenient aide to help carry out his plans.

Whatever DeAnn's understanding of Mark's intentions were, Graham believed, in the end, she subjected herself to a life sentence of guilt. As he got to know her, he grew to respect her. It was gutsy to come forward and expose herself to everyone, including her own family, Graham thought. She also took a personal risk. Mark Winger was free long after she first spoke out, and if he had killed two people, he may not have hesitated to kill a third. In all their meetings, DeAnn never recanted a word of what she said.

"We did establish a friendship, so to speak," Graham said. "I liked her in a weird way. She had real remorse."

Police and prosecutors knew that DeAnn came with baggage. She had a history of psychiatric treatment. She took a long time to come forward. No one knew if she withheld information to protect herself. Winger's defense team was going to have a field day with her.

"In this line of work, you don't get the witness you want," Graham said. "You get the hand that's dealt to you."

DeAnn felt more comfortable with Graham than she did with Doug Williamson or any other of the cops. She showed up when he requested it and listened to what he had to say. But there was always a little bit of tension.

DeAnn Schultz understandably wanted nothing to do with the media. The *48 Hours* team was, of course, eager to talk with her. At first, she refused to answer our calls. But, with time, she relented and gave us background information over the telephone.

She seemed fragile and deeply troubled. She insisted she was neither a hero nor a victim; she was just someone who made some extremely bad choices. DeAnn knew people would judge her and there was nothing she could do about it. She did want to speculate about the crime. She said she feared sensationalizing a story in which there were real victims. But she realized that she was part of the story whether she spoke with us or not.

Shortly before we aired our program, DeAnn agreed to sit for an interview with Richard Schlesinger. Schlesinger puts almost everyone at ease and gets more out of an interview than just about anyone else in the business. The conversation with DeAnn, however, got off to an unusually rocky start.

We rented a hotel suite in downtown Springfield. DeAnn showed up on time but was visibly uncomfortable from the moment she sat down. She fidgeted under the bright lights and gripped the arms of the chair so tightly that her knuckles turned white. When Richard asked his first question, she held him in a steady, disapproving stare. Her voice was barely audible. Her words were fragmented, hardly the soul-searching we hoped for. A few questions later she stopped the cameras, upset about a question she did not comprehend. She appeared to be close to walking away.

We assured her that she could ask to have any question clarified and say as much or as little as she wanted to say. She was the only person who knew what she had gone through. She was the only one who could tell her part of the story. She sipped some water, closed her eyes, and took a deep breath. She agreed to try again. This time DeAnn pulled herself together. She answered each question in a deliberate manner, taking whatever time she needed to think it through.

DeAnn described Donnah as "very friendly . . . exuberant and full of life."

"I wish that she would have lived and I would have died. I would have traded places," she said.

"Why did you feel like that?"

"I still feel that today," DeAnn said, correcting Schlesinger's use of the past tense. "Because she did not deserve to die. She shouldn't have died. I didn't have a lot to offer other people. She had a lot to offer."

The morning after Donnah was killed, DeAnn said, she and Mark were together at the Datz home. He told her not to tell the police anything about their affair. As it turned out, DeAnn said, the police didn't ask pointed or probing questions anyway. They all but told her that they believed what Mark said.

"I was relieved, because it wasn't my job to decide whether or not he did it," she said.

"Did you believe it when the police said he wasn't involved?"

"Yes. At the time. I . . . believed it. I didn't believe that I could care about someone—love someone—who would be able to do anything like that. So, yes, I very much just went with what the police said. And I just let it go at that."

DeAnn said she had good reason to keep her secret. She did not want to hurt her family. No one knew about her affair with Mark Winger. But that also meant she had no one to confide to. As years went by, DeAnn said, her secret was killing her—literally.

"It became more difficult. I became very ill. I was hospitalized. I started drinking. I tried to overdose. I wanted to die," she said in a hushed voice, locking eyes with Richard.

DeAnn said she was surprised how quickly Mark cut ties with everyone from his previous life.

"He seemed to move on very quickly," she said.

She stated flat out that she had no idea whether or not Mark had been involved in the murder. All she knew was that she had information about him that no one else did and that was an "enormous burden."

"I knew that his marriage wasn't as good and wonderful as it seemed to be," she said. "In the back of my mind I kept hoping that someone would come and ask me so I wouldn't have to make the decision myself. It would be easier if someone just asked me."

"What did you want them to ask you?"

"Anything so that I could tell my story."

"What was it that was eating at you?"

"The questions. Not knowing."

DeAnn said the floodgates burst open when she saw Mark in 1998.

"I had been very sick that year. I still hadn't told anyone. And I saw him and just decided I had some questions. And that I deserved a few answers, I suppose."

When she spoke with Mark, he did not seem like the man she had known.

"He mentioned Jesus Christ as his savior. It would take something very drastic for the person that I knew to switch from his heritage and Judaism to Christianity." He told her that "Jesus Christ forgives all sin."

When Mark tried to persuade DeAnn to keep their secret, it backfired. She found the courage to come forward.

"I knew the police thought that he didn't do it, but maybe if they knew a little—just a little bit that I knew—there could be an investigation."

DeAnn said she was not proud of decisions she had made long ago, but she felt she was finally on the road to recovery.

"In your own soul, how do you feel now compared to the way you felt in those years?" Schlesinger asked her.

"I feel free. I didn't realize how powerful secrets can be," DeAnn said, letting out a long sigh.

DeAnn delivered on her promise to us. She sounded sincere. But there was no way to know if she had told us the whole truth. Maybe she still harbored secrets she kept to herself.

Shooting on location, the *48 Hours* team was getting a feel for Springfield. One time, when an outdoor shoot was called because of rain, we succumbed to the lure of Lincoln and took a tour of the house Abe lived in before leaving for Washington in 1861. We learned that Lincoln was the first president to sport a beard, that he milked his own cow, and that he and his wife apparently had a fondness for loud wallpaper with bold patterns.

One more detail: Lincoln stood six feet four inches—the exact height of Sergeant Doug Williamson.

Williamson and his protégé, Jim Graham, took us to the places more pertinent to our story. Williamson drove with us through the leafy subdivision where the Wingers lived. Graham showed us the silo he sat by while staking out his suspect. He drove us past the Illinois Department of Nuclear Safety, the site of Mark Winger's arrest.

Our most distant journey was to BART's home office in Cape Girardeau, Missouri. Owner Ray Duffey greeted us in the small wood-paneled waiting area. Duffey is not an excitable man but, years after the lawsuit against him was dropped, he was still visibly shaken by the experience.

"I feel a great sadness for both families," Duffey told Richard Schlesinger. "Roger's family lived so long with a black cloud over their heads."

Duffey suffered heart problems in 1997 that required bypass surgery. His wife attributed it to stress. His reputation had been badly damaged. He spent a lot of time assuring potential customers that his drivers were not crazy, but he still lost a lot of business. Duffey repeatedly made the point that his problems paled next to the victims' families, but the accusations still stung.

"We do, in fact, screen our employees. We just don't go out on the street and pick up the first guy that walks by and put him in a van. That was the way it was depicted."

After the interview, we retraced Donnah's ride home from Lambert Airport in St. Louis, one hundred monotonous miles on I-55. No wonder Roger Harrington engaged his passengers in conversation.

Producer Doug Longhini managed to wrangle an interview with the Harringtons in their home. We walked past three cats snoozing on the porch and knocked on the door. Someone peeked out from a living room window, behind a venetian blind that was crooked and bent from being moved too many times. We stood there for a few anxious minutes before Roger's sister, Barbara Howell, greeted us. She had become the family spokesperson.

Ralph Harrington sat alone in the living room on a worn upholstered chair. He wore a blue work shirt and breathed with the help of an oxygen tank. He smiled and nodded our way but seemed too sapped of energy to deal with us.

An eight-by-ten childhood photo of Roger, grinning, was displayed prominently next to a Bible on a small table near the front door. To the left was the kitchen, where Helen Harrington was hiding from us. She slipped out the back door, fed the cats, came back in, and let us know in no uncertain terms that she did not want to be on camera.

Richard Schlesinger sat down with Barbara at the kitchen table, which took up nearly the entire room. Barbara was TV-ready. Her makeup was expertly applied, her dark wavy hair fell to her shoulders, and she wore a neatly pressed black blouse tucked into her jeans. She made an impassioned plea for her brother and spoke about the frustration her family felt after his death.

"The police just brushed it off, like 'This is not important, we've got other things to do,'" she said.

Helen, tending to two large simmering pots on the stove, listened attentively.

"They treated us like dirt," she interjected.

Schlesinger was determined to get her on camera. After interviewing Barbara, he cornered Helen, backing her up against the refrigerator. Helen finally gave in but insisted they talk standing where they were, squeezed into a corner.

"Nobody would listen to us," she said. "So Ralph and I, when we got up in the morning, that was the first thing we'd speak about."

Her eyes reddened. She looked down at her weathered hands.

"Does it still hurt?" Schlesinger asked.

"Sure it hurts," she said. "We lost a twenty-seven-year-old son and no one would give us a reason."

In time, the family sat together at the table, showing us photos of Roger. Most were in outdoor settings.

"He's around fifteen there—it was a family camping trip," Barbara said, pointing to a picture her father held.

Ralph shook his head, his disbelief still raw.

"Really looks like a killer, don't he?" he said.

State's Attorney John Schmidt would not let us interview any prosecutor unless we spoke with the three who handled the case at the same time. The men sat side by side on a table in a courtroom. Schmidt did most of the talking, mincing no words about Mark Winger.

"He's a cold, calculating individual," Schmidt said. "He is also very intelligent."

Schmidt was familiar with and articulate about the people and the evidence. He would not budge on his refusal to publicly acknowledge past mistakes.

"I mean no disrespect," Schlesinger said, "but don't you want to know why the police didn't look at those Polaroids in 1995?"

"They took a second look. That's what police agencies are supposed to do."

"In reality, they didn't take a second look, they took a first look, because they didn't look in 1995—"

"They took, in my mind, a second look."

Schmidt clasped his hands around his knees, his bitten nails in plain sight.

Charlie Cox was more candid. By the time *48 Hours* spoke with him, he had retired from the Springfield PD and was the captain of police in a nearby rural community. Speaking softly in his simply furnished den, he readily admitted that his errors had hindered the investigation big-time.

"Were you embarrassed?" Schlesinger asked.

"Oh, yes," Cox said. "Very much so."

Cox was comfortable in his own skin and enjoyed the repartee with Schlesinger. But he never lost sight of the serious consequences of what he had done.

"I put a family through hell because of not doing the job as well as I could have," he said, referring to the Harringtons.

Cox's error made the case more difficult to prosecute. That made the story more interesting for us to report, but, from the former detective's perspective, it meant that Mark Winger might get off completely. It was a heavy burden to bear.

Word was that Mark Winger was not adapting well to jail life. He felt no need to adapt because he did not plan to be incarcerated very long. He was confident he would prevail in court. The legal pundits gave him good odds, noting that long delays tended to favor the defense.

"People's memories fade. The evidence is harder to find," one explained. He conceded that there was less public sympathy for Mark Winger than there was earlier, when he was hailed as a hero. He had lived under a cloud of suspicion for years.

Winger's attorney, Thomas Breen, fought to get two key pieces of evidence thrown out before trial. One was Winger's statement to the police, which was taken without reading him his Miranda rights. The state argued that Winger was treated as a witness that day, not a suspect. The judge agreed: his statement was fair game.

Breen also contended that DeAnn Schultz was incompetent to testify at trial, given her history of extensive psychiatric treatments. DeAnn suffered from chronic major depression, among other conditions. She had been treated with numerous prescription drugs, including Prozac, Zoloft, and Xanax. She overdosed three times in attempts to commit suicide. She underwent nineteen electroconvulsive therapy sessions.

The judge ruled that it was up to the jury to determine her credibility. She could testify.

Breen launched his own investigation. It included paying a visit to Donnah and Mark's old friends, Rabbi Mike Datz and his wife, Jo. Jo later wrote Ira Drescher an e-mail, telling him what happened.

"Thursday evening whilst busy baking cookies with the boys, the doorbell rings," Jo wrote.

Taken by surprise, Jo and Mike chatted with Breen and his investigator. They said they believed Mark was guilty but did not know very much about the evidence.

Jo did not sleep well that night, afraid that she may inadvertently have said something that hurt the state's case. The following morning she sought out prosecutor Steve Weinhoeft. It turned out he was in court, at a status hearing for the Winger case. Jo slipped quietly into a back bench to watch the brief procedure.

Jessica was there in the front row, staring straight

ahead. Jo tried but failed to catch her eye. She was not sure if Jessica purposely avoided her but would understand it, as they were now in enemy camps.

A short time later Mark was led into the room, wearing a gray jail uniform. His hands were cuffed behind him.

"He strode across the room with a huge smile on his face to Jessica, looking calm and confident," Jo wrote in her e-mail. "It was just awful."

Jo could not fight the mental image of this man violently beating her beloved friend. It gave her the chills. She herself had socialized with him frequently. Being in the same room with him unnerved her.

"I can see Mark if I'm prepared," she wrote in her e-mail. "But it caught me off guard, completely."

To Jo's relief, Steve Weinhoeft assured her that nothing she said to Mark's attorney would jeopardize their case. There were no secrets. By law, the state was required to hand over everything it had to the defense.

In another e-mail to Ira and Sara Jane, Jo asked about Donnah's dog, Stonewall. How come she did not bring him inside if she was afraid of someone harassing her? Where was Stonewall that day, anyway?

"NO ONE RECALLS ANYTHING ABOUT THE DOG THE DAY OF THE CRIME!" Ira wrote in his own notes. "If Stonewall was there, the police surely would have run into him either in the backyard or in the garage. You can't miss a 175 lb. mastiff!"

The detectives believed that Mark probably put

the dog in a kennel, in anticipation of carrying out his wicked plan. Unfortunately, it was too late to confirm that. Stonewall died a few years after the homicides and the veterinarian destroyed his records. His whereabouts on August 29, 1995, would remain a mystery.

Mark Winger's trial date was set for May 20, 2002. Knowing it would be stressful, Sara Jane and Ira Drescher took a breather, booking themselves on a cruise of the Panama Canal. They came home, re-packed, and set off for Springfield by car.

"You'll think I'm crazy for what I'm about to say," Ira said as they drove on the interstate. "I really think Mark is guilty. I saw the pictures. But I am kind of wishing for some kind of evidence that will exonerate him."

Sara Jane looked out the window, staring at the sunlight flashing between the trees. Ira had expressed exactly what she was thinking. She wanted the case to take one more dramatic twist.

"We were hoping that there would be some way that Mark could prove to us that he did not do this," she later told Richard Schlesinger. "That he would come out with a version of the story and it would say to us, 'Thank goodness, he didn't do this.'"

"Why were you so eager for him to prove that he didn't do it?" Schlesinger asked.

"Because we loved him. Because he was part of our family. Because Donnah loved him. Because they appeared to have such an incredibly wonderful marriage. Because in the eight years that we knew him, we never saw anything that would ever lead us to suspect that he could do such a horrendous thing."

She fantasized about the relief she would feel knowing that, in Donnah's last moments of consciousness, her husband came to rescue.

25

Presumed Innocent

In the days before the trial, Sara Jane Drescher steadied herself by writing her notes.

"I think I am numb right now," she wrote. "It is the calm before the storm. I vacillate from calmness to a stomach that does not stop churning."

She dreaded the thought of seeing Mark Winger in court.

"I think of the passing days and I shiver," she wrote. "One day closer to Monday. One day closer to a beginning that might not have an end."

She pulled herself together by focusing on Donnah's two sisters. She wanted to make things as easy as possible for them. On the night before the trial, she went with them to the Datz home for dinner. Ira, giving them time alone, took a long walk downtown.

It was a pleasant spring evening, but the streets were virtually empty. As well kept as downtown Springfield was, most people found it more convenient to go to the restaurants and multiplexes that popped up over the years in strip malls outside town. Ira meandered up one deserted street and down the next, listening to his footsteps—and his thoughts.

Steve Weinhoeft had warned him to expect surprises at trial and that a few memorable exchanges with witnesses could make or break a case. John Schmidt told him there would be highs and lows and it would sometimes seem that the prosecutors got their law degrees at Kmart. That did nothing to ease Ira's nerves. He feared that Mark would get off on some legal technicality. What would that do to Sara Jane?

Ira walked past the stately old capitol and through the landscaped park behind it. He wandered to the courthouse and then to the jail. He stopped and stared at the razor wire above him. Mark was somewhere inside that building.

The door to the police station was open. Ira walked into the vestibule. He kept to himself, aimlessly reading notices on bulletin boards. An officer came out from behind a glass enclosure and asked if he needed help. Ira told him why he was in town, that his wife was Donnah Winger's mother, and before he could say much more, his eyes welled with tears. He had finally reached his limit. So much for his macho pride.

The officer listened and consoled him. A half hour later Ira walked back to his hotel feeling back in control. He was grateful for the officer's time and kind words. He was good to go for trial.

"Ira has been wonderful," Sara Jane wrote in her

notes. "He is so wrapped up in this case. He is trying so hard to help the prosecution and the police. He told me that I have to expect good days and bad. There will be days when I feel as though we have lost the case. I can't give up."

Sara Jane was as ready as she was going to be. But she could not sleep. She was on the witness list and she worried how she would come across.

She got up and went into the other room to read but she could not stop thinking about the trial and the role she would play in it. Her body shook when she thought about identifying Donnah's picture in front of all those people. Then she thought about all the other witnesses.

"I pictured dots," she wrote, "lots and lots of dots and a Seurat painting came to mind. I was one of the dots in a painting. One meaningless dot. But put that dot in with millions of others and it makes a whole. I am part of the whole."

On Monday morning, May 20, Sara Jane and Ira walked the few short blocks to the courthouse. It was a characterless modern building, unlike the historic sites nearby. The wood-paneled courtroom had no distinguishing architectural features, but its acoustics were better than in older courtrooms, which made it easier to understand what witnesses were saying. Friends and family of everyone who felt the impact of the crime seated themselves in two rows of plain wooden benches.

Mark Winger's parents and brother took the front

row on the right side, behind the defense table. Jessica was there, too, dressed in a suit, with her long hair pulled neatly into a ponytail. Her mother sat at her side, and her brothers took the bench behind him. Members of her church filled in the other seats.

Ira, Sara Jane, and Donnah's other relatives sat in the front row on the other side, behind the prosecutors' table. There would be a few awkward encounters with the Wingers in the restroom area, but the two families—once so close—kept their distance. Mike and Jo Datz sat with the Dreschers, along with other friends. The Datzes promised to be there for every minute of the trial—and they kept their word.

"I couldn't possibly be anywhere else," Jo said.

The Harringtons sat behind the Dreschers and exchanged brief, polite greetings with them. It was the first time the families met. By then the state considered them all relatives of victims, but the Harringtons still felt like second-class citizens.

"Everything was Donnah, Donnah, Donnah," Helen said later.

Her son did not have the same public sympathy, she felt. But she knew he was on trial as much as Mark Winger was. This was his chance to be exonerated.

Mark Winger, flanked by his attorneys, wore a pressed dress shirt, with the top button opened. Now thirty-nine years old, he looked more like a member of the legal team than a defendant. Ira gazed at the back of his head until Mark turned around and returned an icy stare. Mark's arms were muscular, Ira noticed. He must be working out. But he was also getting jowly and a little thick around the middle. Donnah would remain forever young but Mark was aging.

Court came to order promptly at nine o'clock. State's Attorney John Schmidt began opening arguments by repeating the story Mark Winger told the police.

"Everything the defendant told the police is a lie," Schmidt told the jurors.

Winger lied, Schmidt said, when he maintained that he did not know who the man in his house was. Winger knew exactly who he was, because he had invited him there earlier that day. The man was Roger Harrington, and Winger lured him to the house so he could pin Donnah's murder on him.

Schmidt told the jurors they would hear from Mark's secret lover. She would testify that Winger told her his life would be easier if Donnah just died. He talked about how that might happen. Most telling, he told her that he "had to get that van driver into his house."

Schmidt's opening argument was strong, but so was defense attorney Thomas Breen's. Breen promised to discredit Winger's secret lover and show her to be a scorned, bitter woman. The entire case hinged on her, Breen said, and her false claims that Mark made incriminating comments. Before she came forward, the case was closed.

Breen said that the evidence would show that

Roger Harrington had a history of violence and mental health problems. He and only he committed murder that day. Mark Winger took his life in self-defense.

"I don't care if Mark Winger shot Harrington twenty times," Breen said. It was justified.

Breen told jurors that Mark Winger relived August 29, 1995, over and over "in his mind and his heart."

Breen then played the tape of Winger's call to 911 in its entirety. The audio was tinny and muffled at times, but Winger's anguished cries came through loud and clear.

"My wife is dying! . . . Oh, God, oh, God, help me!"

As the tape played, Winger lowered his head and seemed to sob. Breen clicked the cassette player off, and the sound slowly decayed until the courtroom was eerily silent.

"That was the state of Mark Winger on August twenty-ninth," Breen said. "That is the reality of it."

"It sure sounded realistic and genuine to me," Ira wrote in his notes.

The jurors followed instructions and did not share their thoughts. But they were shaken.

"It was heart wrenching to see what happened to those people," one juror later told *48 Hours*.

"Mark Winger just didn't seem at all like a cold-blooded killer," another said.

They had no problem presuming Winger innocent, as the judge told them to do.

"You've got this man who now has four kids. And

his life is going just the way he wants. You don't want to pull the rug out from under him," a juror explained.

Roger Harrington was already dead. It would be a lot easier to keep things just as they were than it would be to send Winger to prison for life. If the prosecutors wanted a conviction, they had better come up with damn good evidence.

Judge Leo Zappa was a fair judge who maintained control of his courtroom. Witnesses and jurors showed up on time. Attorneys did what they needed to do, but kept their bickering to a minimum. Sidebars were infrequent and quickly resolved. After opening arguments, the prosecution called nine witnesses the first day.

BART owner Ray Duffey led the pack. He was well prepared.

Duffey testified that he asked Roger Harrington for permission to give Mark Winger his phone number because Winger insisted on talking to the driver directly.

"Roger seemed very anxious to talk to Mr. Winger," Duffey testified. "He wasn't angry."

Harrington's roommate, Susan Collins, took the stand next. She was living in Texas at the time but was arrested in Springfield that morning on a four-year-old warrant. The charges were minor—relating to a bad check—but the arrest guaranteed that Collins would stay put for a while. There was no need to worry: she was eager to testify. Skinny and worn, she stood tall, raised her right hand, and swore to tell the truth.

Collins repeated her story about how Roger told her he would not get any more work until he resolved the complaint. On the morning of August 29, Collins said, she took a call from a man who asked for Roger. While Roger was on the phone, she gave him a bank deposit slip and he wrote down the guy's name and address on the back. She heard Roger confirm the time, 4:30.

"I heard him say, 'I want to get that taken care of. I'll be there,'" she testified.

Duffey and Collins set up the prosecution's central theme: if there was a meeting, there was a murder.

"Everything goes back to the meeting," Doug Williamson told Richard Schlesinger. "If Winger would've told us there was a meeting and the guy went berserk, this case would probably still be closed. That's not what he said."

Prosecutor Steve Weinhoeft had a theory. He believed that Mark Winger originally did intend to say there was a meeting, and that it went terribly wrong. But when the 911 operator unexpectedly asked him who the man in his house was, he was caught off guard. He slipped up and said, "I don't know who he is!" From that moment on, he was stuck with it.

Attorney Breen attacked Susan Collins's credibility. She reluctantly admitted she had a cocaine problem but said that was after Harrington died and she since had treatment. She did not deny that she and Roger smoked marijuana frequently, sometimes twice a day. They may have even had some early in the morning on August 29, before Winger called, she conceded. She got flustered when Breen tried to pin her down on exactly what she heard and the exact order she heard it in. But she held firm that she heard Roger set up a meeting.

"It was clear she was lying," Winger later told Schlesinger. He felt certain that the jurors would not believe this woman who was a close friend of Roger Harrington.

Even if the jurors did believe Collins, her testimony was problematic. She had said virtually the same thing in 1995 and the authorities ruled that Winger acted in self-defense.

During testimony, Winger took notes on a legal pad and conferred with his attorneys. He was a cool customer, alert and attentive, relaxed and in control. He spoke frequently and amicably with the bailiff who was assigned to watch him. Once in a while he pivoted his chair and exchanged a few words with his family. He smiled at Jessica and she smiled back at him. He exuded confidence. It drove Jo Datz crazy.

"He was cocky," Jo said. "He stared us down. He looked at me with glaring disapproval."

Officer David Barringer took the stand and described the crime scene. More important, his three Polaroids were offered into evidence. Other cops and paramedics who subsequently testified said that the bodies lay as depicted in those photos. The prosecution used two posters to drive the point home: one showed the bodies as they were found, the other as the police believed they would have been if Harrington was kneeling over Donnah and shot from the hallway, as Winger maintained. In that poster, Harrington faced the opposite direction. The defense got the witnesses to concede that Winger was distraught, implying he might have been too confused to remember the events exactly as they happened.

The first responders testified that they found Donnah lying facedown in a pool of blood. Sara Jane wondered why Mark would leave her that way if he had cradled her as he said he had. Her hope that the evidence would exonerate Mark was fading.

Several witnesses, including Amy Jaffe, testified about what Winger told them after the fact. They each told a different version of the story. A colleague who drove back from Tennessee with Mark said that, during their drive, Mark told her about Donnah's encounter with the shuttle van driver. Out of nowhere, the witness testified, Mark posed a morbid question.

"He asked me what I thought would happen if Donnah died."

Assuming he was worried about his child, she told him she did not think Ruby would be taken from him. She said that Donnah should let the dog inside, but Mark said Stonewall had a drooling problem and he did not want Donnah to have to clean up after him.

Winger's former neighbors also chipped away at his story. A man who lived across the street said he saw the car parked the wrong way in front of Winger's house at 3:50 p.m. It was significant, because Winger did not call for help until 4:30.

"What was going on in there between 3:50 and 4:30?" Steve Weinhoeft asked later.

Laurelee Smith, the next door neighbor, testified about hearing the single gunshot. That meant the two shots were not fired in succession, as Winger claimed. Smith's testimony was supported by the 911 tape, Weinhoeft told *48 Hours*.

"When the operator asked Winger if the man was still there, he answered, 'Yes, he's laying there on the floor with a bullet in his head.' Note, that's *a* bullet, a single bullet. Not two bullets. He fired that second shot after he hung up."

Under cross-examination, Laurelee Smith said that she spoke to Detective Jim Graham six years after the incident. The implication was that it was too long ago for her to remember the incident clearly. Once again, the jurors were reminded how much time had passed before Winger was considered a suspect.

Anyone observing Sara Jane in the courtroom saw an attractive, dignified woman. She did not hide her pain, but she did not call attention to herself. The first day went better than she thought it would.

"I saw the Wingers and I was okay. I saw Jessica and I was okay," she wrote in her notes that evening.

"I saw Mark and I was okay. I AM A SURVIVOR AND THEY WILL NOT DESTROY ME."

The following morning, Sara Jane was the first witness up. She walked to the stand with confidence. The gold silhouette of a female face—the pendant that had angered Mark when he saw it in the restaurant—hung from a chain on her neck.

"Donnah was sweet, kind, and beautiful," she testified.

Sara Jane told the jurors that the last time she saw her daughter was when she bid her good-bye at the airport in Florida.

When Schmidt finished his questions, Sara Jane prepared to step down. To her surprise, defense attorney Thomas Breen took the opportunity to cross-examine her. He asked about Donnah's marriage. Sara Jane said it seemed perfect.

Schmidt took the podium again and asked Sara Jane if she still saw her granddaughter. A tear fell down her cheek.

"No," she said softly. "Mark won't let me."

Helen and Ralph Harrington took the stand next. Helen testified that the last time she spoke with her son was the night before he was killed. Ralph told jurors that Roger was right-handed and wore his watch and ring on his right hand. The police took those items at the hospital, Ralph said, and returned them three weeks later. He put them in a box and did not touch them again until he gave them to Detective Jim Graham in 2001.

The prosecutors were planting a seed. Later a lab technician would say that, even under the microscope, there was no blood found on Roger Harrington's watch and ring. That made it unlikely that the right-handed driver had bludgeoned Donnah. It was a salient point but not the only one made by the Harringtons. As the Dreschers recognized all too well, Ralph and Helen bore the pain of parents who had lost a child.

At times the trail devolved into arcane disputes about gory evidence. Images from the crime scene were projected and scrutinized.

"Oftentimes, especially when they were showing slides, I would put my head down because I didn't want to see," Sara Jane told Richard Schlesinger.

"I would tell her when to look and when not to look," Ira said.

Nevertheless, Sara Jane heard the testimony about Donnah's injuries.

"I feel such pain!!" she wrote. "Knives stabbing into my heart. Although everyone has assured me Donnah never felt anything, I can't accept that. Whether she felt physical pain or emotional pain of walking in and seeing that Mark had killed Harrington, I don't know. She did feel pain and so do I."

Sara Jane shuddered when the hammer was introduced into evidence. There was no escaping the awful tool. It came up again and again. The jurors were shown the pictures of Mark's hands that were taken before he was allowed to wash up. They were bloody, but the slot between his thumb and index finger seemed clean.

"That's from gripping the hammer," Doug Williamson told *48 Hours*.

Ira Drescher's expansive notes reflected the nitty gritty battle being waged in court. He wrote furiously as each witness testified, adding commentary as he saw fit.

"Ira's personality is such that he wanted to be able to do something to exert some control over the process," prosecutor Weinhoeft said later. "He analyzed the case as a sports commentator would break down a big game."

"I guess it's a catharsis. It relaxed me," Ira said later. "It was a learning process too."

Sara Jane's notes were personal and impressionistic. They were heartbreaking.

"Emotions run from numbness to the beating of my heart so loud that I feel everyone will notice," she wrote.

She recounted the thoughts she had when the attorneys projected photographs of the Winger kitchen for the jurors to see. There was a picture of Sara Jane's now deceased mother near Donnah's handwritten note on the refrigerator. Sara Jane had thought of her as Donnah's guardian angel and, in that photo, she looked the part. Donnah must have enjoyed seeing her smiling face. Then, for a moment, Sara Jane's thoughts turned dark.

"I think to myself, why didn't she protect Donnah on the twenty-ninth?" she wrote. "I get angry . . . Mom, you let her down . . . you let me down!! But she smiles back at me and, as all mothers do, says that she understands why I am so angry, and no matter what, she loves me."

The more testimony Sara Jane heard, the more she believed Mark was the killer.

"As much as my heart would want him not to be guilty, my head was saying, 'Hey, you know, he is. He really is,'" she said.

By the end of the week, Sara Jane was dispirited.

"Today was not a very good day in court," she wrote, fearing the prosecutors were not making their case. She could imagine that Mark would walk away free.

Detectives Charlie Cox and Doug Williamson had testified. They wore suits and ties and sounded authoritative. But both men spent a lot of time explaining mistakes.

Cox testified about interviewing Mark Winger and how distraught he had seemed. He watched Winger drop to his knees when he was told Donnah was dead. Cox told the jurors that he recognized Roger Harrington as someone he had had a run-in with before. That clouded his judgment, he said, and it should not have.

During cross-examination, the hammer came out again. Breen waved it at Cox, asking if the detective had bothered to find out exactly what type of matter was on it.

"Hair? Tissue?"

Sara Jane cringed.

"It made me so sick it turned my stomach," she wrote later. "It was my child on that hammer. It was my skin, my blood."

Cox admitted he did not give the hammer to a lab. He also acknowledged that the medical examiner said that Donnah's wounds fit Winger's story. Cox explained that the medical examiner took what the detectives had told him into consideration when he made that judgment. They reinforced each other's beliefs. But, Cox said, the medical examiner also said there could be other explanations for the wounds.

"None of that is in your report, is it?" Breen asked.

No, Cox said, it was not.

Doug Williamson testified about the chaotic crime scene, the interview with Winger, Winger's request for a Diet Coke that sent him to the refrigerator, and the way that Winger put the drink down without taking a sip.

"I believe Mark was getting me to find Donnah's note that was hanging on the refrigerator," he later told Schlesinger. "It had not been located at that point."

Williamson told the jurors about the note he saw in Roger Harrington's car: the note that had Winger's name, address, and "4:30" written on it. Williamson also talked about interviewing Winger at Rabbi Datz's home and then going back to the house to fish Harrington's mug and cigarettes from the bag at the curb. He was suspicious and asked for permission to subpoena phone records, but his request was denied.

"I was told the case was closed and that there would be no further action by our agency," he testified.

Subpoenas were eventually issued in 1999 and the phone records revealed lengthy calls between Winger's motel room and DeAnn Schultz's home.

Sara Jane thought that Williamson did a good job on direct examination. But then he was cross-examined by Breen.

Breen picked apart everything that was said on the stand, comparing and contrasting the details to the police reports. In his report, Doug Williamson said that when Mark was being questioned, he asked for "something to drink." On the stand, Williamson said Mark asked for a Diet Coke. It was a minor point, Sara Jane thought, but she was concerned. The more Breen belabored all those little inconsistencies, the more likely he would successfully erode Williamson's credibility.

On the stand Williamson held his ground. Mark Winger asked for a Diet Coke, he said.

The more important issue was why Williamson's more seasoned colleagues considered the case solved.

"Trained professionals saw the same scene that we saw and they closed the case the next day," one juror later told Richard Schlesinger.

Sara Jane had another sleepless night. She turned to her notes. "How am I going to get through the next week?" She wrote. "Don't ask."

Donnah had been a popular woman in Springfield and her many friends and colleagues made sure that her mother and stepfather were kept occupied during the weekend. There were dinners and cookouts. Everyone shared their memories.

"Donnah gave the best hugs," one friend said.

Sara Jane agreed. There were lots of hugs during Donnah's last visit. It comforted her to know that her daughter was loved and appreciated.

That night Donnah was in Sara Jane's dreams: Donnah was more radiant and beautiful than ever. She wore bright red lipstick—a shade she never wore in life. Sara Jane could not remember what they were doing; she only saw that image of her daughter and that red, red lipstick.

"I have not seen her in my dreams in a long time," she wrote. "I think I touched her. I want to touch her!'

Court resumed on Monday and Sara Jane was once again face-to-face with Mark Winger.

"He was sitting there with a stupid grin on his face," she wrote later.

She prayed, not for a guilty verdict, but for the jury to be wise and just.

26

The Other Woman

The witness most people were anxious to hear was DeAnn Schultz. She came to court in a conservative dark blue suit with her shoulder-length hair neatly trimmed. But everyone knew this was the woman who had fooled around with her best friend's husband. DeAnn took a deep breath and prepared to tell her sordid tale.

"She looks well but seems very nervous," Ira noted.

DeAnn was granted immunity, so she did not have to fear incriminating herself. But she probably sensed the disdain so many people had for her. At best, she was a traitorous friend.

"It takes a special kind of bitch to do that," someone close to the case said.

Observers in the courtroom wondered if DeAnn was complicit.

"Do you believe she's culpable?" Richard Schlesinger later asked Doug Williamson.

"I don't know," he answered, shaking his head. "I don't know."

"What's your hunch?"

"My hunch is that she's more involved than she's telling us."

Ira strongly believed that DeAnn had played a role in the crime. But he realized that she was crucial to the state's case, so he purposefully caught her eye, smiled, and winked. DeAnn was grateful for any sign of support—especially from Donnah's family. Although she would never face charges of having any part in the murders, the trial was an ordeal for her.

Prosecutor Steve Weinhoeft questioned DeAnn and established that she was married to John Schultz for fourteen years, until they divorced in 2001. She worked in surgery before becoming a psychiatric nurse. Her first liaison with Mark Winger was in July 1995.

DeAnn bowed her head through much of her testimony. Winger looked straight at her. He took notes and kept his cool, betraying little emotion.

DeAnn told jurors that Mark made unsettling comments about wanting Donnah dead.

"I said I didn't want to hear anything more about anybody dying. I told him that I would cease to be a vital person if I thought that anyone was hurt," she said.

"Who talks like that?" Steve Weinhoeft later asked *48 Hours*. "Who says 'I would cease to be a vital person'? But those were the exact words she used when she first told us about it."

Weinhoeft believed that her consistent use of the awkward phrase made her more believable. In court, he asked DeAnn to describe the arrangements she and Mark had when they got together in town.

"Where would you normally meet?"

"In the parking lot of Jungle of Fun."

The locals knew Jungle of Fun to be a children's play area. DeAnn's face reddened and every muscle in her body tensed. Some spectators snickered.

DeAnn testified that Donnah called her on August 24, 1995, and told her about the strange conversation with the shuttle van driver. DeAnn stayed with Donnah that night and, while there, answered a telephone call from a man who asked for Mr. or Mrs. Winger. DeAnn said she offered to take a message, but the man said he would call back.

The next day, DeAnn said, Mark told her he had to get the driver into the house. When they spoke again, on the morning of August 29, he asked her if she would love him "no matter what."

After Donnah was killed, DeAnn said, she went to the Datz home to help take care of the baby. She slept on the couch and was wakened by Mark early in the morning. He seemed less concerned about Donnah's sudden death than the investigation into it.

"He said that it was going to be very high profile, that it was best for me to stay as far away from the police as possible. He wanted me not to say anything about us having an affair, that that would look bad."

"Did he ever make mention of any police detectives?"

"He mentioned that he thought that Detective Cox believed him."

The affair continued, DeAnn said, and they exchanged the symbolic rings. Then Mark abruptly broke things off in March 1996, when he returned from Africa. After that, her mental health deteriorated.

"It just spiraled down—I wanted to die. I didn't—I felt so bad, I did not have anyone to talk to. I pretty much figured that everyone would be better off without me," she said in a barely audible voice.

On January 18, 1998, DeAnn said, she "took a bottle of pills." She made three other suicide attempts that year. Then she had the chance encounter with Mark at the hospital and found the resolve to confront her demons.

"DeAnn, why did you try to kill yourself four times in 1998?" Weinhoeft asked.

"Because I couldn't keep those . . . there were too many comments and too many things that didn't make sense to me and I couldn't . . . I didn't . . . I didn't know what to do with the information. I was afraid to tell anybody and I was afraid not to. That's why I tried to kill myself."

"DeAnn surely could have stopped this all from happening, but she was dreaming of her new life with Mark," Ira Drescher noted. "And this eventually ate her up!"

"She came across as credible and sincere, despite being a flawed person," Weinhoeft said.

During cross-examination, defense attorney Thomas Breen went on the attack. He asked DeAnn why, if she felt that her best friend was in danger, did she keep it to herself? Why did she say nothing about her suspicions until more than three years after Donnah was murdered?

"I just could not believe that Mark would kill Donnah," DeAnn said.

Breen made the point that DeAnn painted Roger Harrington as a menacing character when she spoke to Mark while he was in Tennessee.

"Do you remember telling Mark on the phone that you thought this guy sounded like a schizophrenic?" Breen asked her.

"Something to that effect."

"You told Donnah that this driver needs help, didn't you?"

"It sounded that way, yes."

Breen also quizzed DeAnn about the phone call she took.

"I believe you described the voice on the telephone as monotone and suspicious, correct?"

"I believe I described it as slow and halting."

"That frightened Donnah a little bit more, didn't it?"

"It seemed to cause . . . yeah, give her reason for a little bit more concern."

DeAnn said it was Mark's idea to have her call the police and have them put a watch on the house.

"Do you remember telling the police that Donnah was a very trusting person and she fears the man will take advantage of the fact that he knows where she lives?"

"Yes."

The prosecutors did not object to this line of questioning. It implied that DeAnn had had a hand in the crime by making Roger Harrington seem more dangerous than he was. But that implicated Mark Winger as the mastermind.

Breen aggressively questioned DeAnn about her mental health history, going over all of her medications, all of her treatments, all of her doctors, and all of her diagnoses. DeAnn's discomfort made Jo Datz wince. She had no love for DeAnn, but she was embarrassed for Donnah's friend. Breen's strategy might backfire, she thought.

"My guess is that some of the jurors may have had problems at some point in their lives too," Jo said.

Whether or not Breen successfully undermined DeAnn's credibility with the jurors, he had one last point to make. DeAnn never claimed that Mark confessed to her. On the stand, she admitted she still didn't know if he was guilty.

"I've never concluded that," she said.

27

State of Mind

The witness after DeAnn Schultz was Dr. John Lauer, a psychiatrist who had treated her for her migraines, depression, and suicidal thoughts. Lauer said that DeAnn told him her secret in September 1998, about a month before her chance encounter with Mark Winger. He encouraged her to come forward with her information every time he saw her.

"I told her she wasn't going to get better unless she talked to her husband or the police about this," Lauer testified.

That November, after DeAnn made her fourth suicide attempt, Lauer visited her in the hospital.

"We had a very pointed discussion about her coming forth," he testified.

Another psychiatrist who reviewed Roger Harrington's case files also took the stand. He said that Harrington suffered from a personality disorder and chronic marijuana abuse, but the medical records did not indicate that he was dangerous. Harrington was eccentric, he said, but "Dahm" and his other fantasies were just a way to get attention.

Mark Winger's state of mind, in his own words, was entered into the court record through testimony he gave earlier. An assistant district attorney read aloud the deposition that Winger gave in his by then dropped civil suit against BART. Winger described what he felt when he came upstairs and ran to his bedroom.

"I heard sounds from the other room, I just had this sick feeling, you know, just nothing was normal. So I ran over to my nightstand and grabbed my weapon and went running down the hallway and saw the driver—actually, I didn't even know who he was at that point . . ."

The jurors also heard the answers Winger gave when BART's attorney, John Nolan, quizzed him about his interactions with Roger Harrington:

"Do you remember telling Mr. Duffey that you wanted to speak with Harrington?"

"No. What I remember is that Mr. Duffey said that the driver was willing to talk with me and release his number to me, that I said I'd like to do that."

"Why did you call him?"

"To just tell him that if he's the person that has been calling my house, to please stop, and that my wife is not his friend, nor does anyone in my family want to be his friend, just, you know, leave us alone."

"At any time did you tell Roger Harrington that

you wanted to meet with him personally to discuss the situation?"

"Never."

"Are you aware of a note that was found in Roger Harrington's car that had your address and a phone number on it?"

"Yes, I am aware."

Winger later told *48 Hours* he had no explanation for that note. He shrugged it off.

"Roger Harrington was crazy. I don't know why he wrote what he wrote on that note. I don't know why he went ballistic on my wife."

Expert witnesses play a unique role in trials in that they are allowed to offer their opinions while testifying. Other witnesses are restricted to describing what they saw or heard. Experts use their proficiency in a field of knowledge to help jurors understand and interpret evidence.

In the Winger case, there was a lot riding on the blood spatter testimony, which took days. It was the most challenging part of the trial to comprehend. Forensic scientist Tom Bevel's report—issued in 1999 as part of the civil case—seemed definitive: the blood spatter evidence contradicted Winger's account of the events. But, as predicted, the defense found another expert, Terry Laber, to dispute that. Bevel and Laber took turns explaining their complex theories to bleary-eyed jurors, who struggled to make sense of it all. Neither expert could talk about the significance of the body positions, as Illinois does not allow opinion based on "crime scene reconstruction." They were restricted to scientific analysis, which made their testimony even more difficult to understand.

Like Bevel, Terry Laber had solid credentials and was respected internationally. Like Bevel, his services did not come cheap, but he was Winger's best shot at making his case. Laber scrutinized Bevel's report, ordered some additional testing, and concluded that the physical evidence supported Winger's story after all.

Each expert used projected slides of the gory crime scene to illustrate his reasoning.

"The blood that is going up the wall, the further up you go the more elongated or elliptical it becomes," Bevel said, circling a laser pointer on particular spots of blood. "The blood is pointing in the direction of travel."

Bevel contended that the stains were consistent with blood being cast off from a hammer being swung in a north-south direction. Laber disagreed.

"My opinion is consistent that the assailant was swinging the weapon in an east-west direction," he testified.

The jurors' eyes glazed over as they grappled with the logic behind experts' arguments. The battle over the bloody clothing seemed, at first, easier to grasp. The issue was simple: whose blood was on whose clothing and how did it get there? Donnah's blood would have spattered the clothing of whichever man beat her. Laber said her blood was on Winger's shirt, but there was nothing sinister about it.

"What I found was contact transfer basically from one surface to another," he said. That could have happened when Winger cradled Donnah after the attack.

Bevel pointed out the two suspicious bloodstains on Winger's shirt he had noted in his report. He believed that they indicated that Donnah's blood had been cast off the hammer and flung there. Laber said there were innocent explanations for those spots too.

"I don't see any evidence of a cast-off pattern," he testified, saying that the same type of elongated drop "could come off a finger, a towel, or could be dripped there. If blood were falling straight, it would be perpendicular here, but"—he swiveled to face the jurors and demonstrated—"if I simply turn my arm, it is now at an angle, it is going to be elongated."

Laber also challenged Bevel's observation that none of Donnah's blood was found on Roger Harrington. He referred to last-minute DNA tests that were conducted in the early days of the trial at the defense's request.

"It turned out that the results were more favorable to the defendant," Steve Weinhoeft conceded. It was one of those surprises that he had warned the Dreschers to expect.

Donnah's DNA was, in fact, found on Roger Harrington's shirt. That, said the defense team, was an indication that Harrington had beaten her. The prosecutors suggested other explanations. Maybe Donnah's DNA got on Harrington when Mark Winger hit the driver with the hammer, which already had Donnah's blood and tissue on it. Maybe the paramedics contaminated the scene when they moved back and forth between victims.

Laber said one spot on Harrington's left sleeve was particularly incriminating.

"The DNA matched Donnah Winger and Roger Harrington, so it was a mixture of those two," he said.

Laber said that it was likely a contact stain and he thought it matched a similar stain on Donnah's shorts. That meant the two victims probably came into physical contact, which supported Winger's statement that Harrington was kneeling over Donnah when he was first shot, then rolled away.

In an interview with Richard Schlesinger, Bevel suggested another explanation for that spot. Bevel believed that before Winger shot Harrington the second time, he rolled the wounded man over. Winger might have transported some of Donnah's DNA to Harrington when he grabbed him to turn him.

When the experts were grilled under cross-examination, both admitted that blood spatter analysis was subjective. Both agreed that a complex, messy crime scene like this one made interpretation more difficult. But the prosecutors worried that the jurors would focus on one questionable bloodstain and lose sight of the bigger picture.

48 Hours producer Doug Longhini, who sat through the trial, thought the concern was legitimate. The jurors were given an overwhelming amount of information and pushed to their limit. They would have to choose which expert sounded most credible. The advantage, Longhini thought, went to the defense.

"Laber, at a minimum, raised doubt about the blood evidence," he told his colleagues. "His testimony did not prove that Roger Harrington killed Donnah Winger or that Mark Winger wasn't the real murderer. But the burden of proof, of course, is on the prosecution."

The defense called few witnesses. Dr. James Cavanaugh, a forensic psychiatrist who reviewed Roger Harrington's records, disputed the findings of the psychiatrist who testified earlier for the state. Dr. Cavanaugh said that Harrington had serious substance abuse issues and was delusional. He believed that Harrington had "an explosive personality" and was potentially dangerous.

Roger Harrington's ex-wife, Tari, testified about her brief marriage. She recalled three run-ins with Roger. Once, she said, he pointed a shotgun at her and told her to say good-bye. Another time he hit her in the chest: that was the fight that Charlie Cox broke up. The third incident was when Roger tried unsuccessfully to handcuff her.

"I wouldn't let that happen," she said defiantly.

Under cross-examination, Tari said Roger could also be pleasant. She never saw him show a bad attitude to or be violent with a stranger.

"You described him as a wimp, didn't you?" prosecutor John Belz asked.

"Yes," she replied.

Defense attorney Breen objected to the leading question, and the judge sustained the objection, but it was too late. A few jurors chuckled.

Mark Winger's brother, Greg, and mother, Sallie, testified briefly but neither were with Mark on the day of the crime. There was speculation that Mark himself would take the stand—he wore a tie on the last day of testimony—but he exercised his right to remain silent.

"THEY'D BE CRAZY TO PUT HIM ON THE STAND!!!" Ira wrote in his notes. "The State would eat him up!!"

In all, fifty-one witnesses testified over ten days. Before closing arguments got under way, Ira gave the prosecutors a list of the points he felt they should make. Assistant State's Attorney John Belz began, as virtually every prosecutor does in virtually every case, by imploring the jurors to use their common sense.

If Mark Winger had been so worried about someone stalking Donnah, Belz asked, why did he stay an extra night in Chattanooga? Harrington's car was seen at 3:50 p.m.: what was going on inside the house for the forty minutes before Winger called for help?

When Mark came upstairs, why didn't he turn the other way and follow the noise he had heard?

Belz also defended DeAnn Schultz.

"She didn't come forward for revenge," he said. "She came forward from guilt."

Belz did not want to take any chance that the significance of the body positions would elude the jurors.

"I felt like I had to lay down on the floor to demonstrate," he said. "So I did."

The jurors craned their necks to watch the prosecutor squiggle around the floor.

"There is absolutely no way it could happen the way the defendant said it did," he said, rising to his feet. "It's not only inconsistent with his statement, it's impossible."

Defense Attorney Thomas Breen took the podium and declared that the state had failed miserably to prove its case at all, let alone beyond reasonable doubt. Breen made repeated references to the blood spatter and to Roger Harrington's mental state.

"For what reason on earth would Mark Winger kill this beautiful woman?" Breen asked, holding up a picture of Donnah and panning it slowly so that each juror could get a good look.

The same investigators who testified at trial, he said, were there in 1995. They saw the crime scene. They saw Roger Harrington's note.

"They reported up and down that Mark Winger's version of events was perfectly consistent with the crime scene," he said. Nothing changed until DeAnn Schultz came forward.

Breen said DeAnn's mental problems made her unreliable. He came down hard on her, reminding jurors about her many medications, but he did not spare his client, either. Facing Mark Winger, Breen slowly raised his hand, pointed, and bellowed that Winger was "a pig."

"It was an act of lust, not passion," Breen said, lowering his arm and his voice. "He was ashamed, he is ashamed, and he has tried to make amends."

Breen suggested that Roger Harrington may have wandered into the house thinking he had an appointment.

"He calls out," Breen said. "Donnah runs out of the bedroom to see who it is, and there's a confrontation. Whatever was said, it was enough for Roger Harrington to grab a weapon."

Breen assured the jurors they would be proud of a not-guilty verdict.

The prosecution got the last word. State's Attorney John Schmidt delivered the rebuttal arguments.

Schmidt acknowledged that the blood spatter experts disagreed, which was why common sense was so crucial. He reached into a large brown paper bag and pulled out a pair of new-looking white sneakers with black laces and a pair of blue-striped sports socks. Bright red evidence tags hung from each item.

Schmidt put the footwear on the railing in front of

the jury. This is what Roger Harrington wore that day, he said. They were absolutely clean of blood.

"These are not the shoes and socks of a killer," Schmidt said.

It was a powerful moment of courtroom drama.

"This is where Schmidt shone," Ira Drescher wrote.

Mark Winger was unimpressed. When the jury left to deliberate, he felt more confident than ever. The police had changed their story. The state's star witness had mental health issues. His blood spatter expert had done a terrific job.

"What were you thinking?" Richard Schlesinger asked.

"'I'll be home for dinner tonight,'" Winger said.

"I remember seeing him sitting there, and thinking, 'Man, you are arrogant,'" Roger Harrington's sister, Barbara Howell, said. "'You are really arrogant.'"

She worried that her parents would be burned again.

"I kept praying. I kept going, 'Rog, if you're up there, you hear me—bring us good news. Bring us something good. You know, so Mom and Dad can sleep tonight.'"

Ira Drescher was pleased that the prosecutors had hit most of his points. But he and Sara Jane knew there was no way to predict a jury's verdict.

"I have tried to program myself and say that no matter what I will go back to Florida and resume my life," Sara Jane wrote in her notes. "Will I be able to do that?"

* * *

The jurors took a methodical approach.

"First, we cleared away the debris," one later told *48 Hours.*

By that, she meant that they discarded all the expert testimony because the experts canceled each other out.

"That went for the psychiatrists as well," another juror added.

Sifting through the other evidence was heart wrenching. The police work was an embarrassment to Springfield, they agreed, except for Officer Barringer and his Polaroids. Like the *48 Hours* team, the jurors tried to reenact the scene to understand why the bodies had ended up as they had.

"I kept waiting for the defense to give us an explanation," one said. "It never came."

As damning as the photos were, a few holdout jurors wanted more. The stakes were too high. Late in the evening, they asked to hear the 911 tape again. As the jurors shuffled into the courtroom, Ira Drescher eyed them nervously.

"That damn tape was very realistic to me and I felt the jury could be swayed by it," he wrote.

Mark lowered his head as his frantic words echoed in the room again. Deliberation resumed and the jurors were sent home at 10 p.m.

Shortly after assembling the following morning, the jury announced it had reached a verdict. Everyone crowded into the courtroom. The Dreschers and Harringtons felt their hearts race; their stomachs were tied in knots. The Wingers imagined hugging their son and taking him home.

Mark Winger was escorted to his seat by several burly deputies. Other guards stood by the door. For the first time, Jo Datz thought, Mark seemed ill at ease. Jo sensed that something had happened between him and Jessica during the course of trial. There was tension between them. Jessica sat with her mother and brothers and stared straight ahead. She was not smiling as she had been when the trial began.

The detectives stood nervously in the back of the courtroom.

Judge Zappa took the written verdict from the bailiff and studied it before reading it out loud.

"As to the charge of murder in the first degree against Donnah Winger. The jury finds Mark Alan Winger—guilty."

One of Donnah's sisters let out a wail. The judge read the rest of the verdict. Every count was the same: guilty.

Winger's parents sobbed.

Mark slowly turned to Jessica and mouthed, "I love you." Jessica closed her eyes and thought about her children. She was numb.

The Dreschers gasped and held each other, as did the Harringtons. They were hugged by relatives and friends. Jo Datz squeezed Sara Jane tightly, feeling both relief and horror.

"Oh, my God, he really did it," Jo said to herself.

Her husband, Rabbi Mike Datz, tried to make sense of it. If a single person could do so much harm, he thought, then one person could also do a great deal of good: a person like Donnah.

Ira turned to the rear of the courtroom and gestured his thanks to Doug Williamson and Jim Graham. Both detectives had tears in their eyes. Graham's eyes moistened again when Richard Schlesinger asked him about that moment.

"I still get emotional 'cause I can still hear 'guilty.' When you put several years into something, and it all leads up to that one second . . . It could have gone either way."

"Did you have a sense that you righted a wrong?"

"Absolutely, I felt I was part of that," Graham said. "I thought of the incredible pain the Harringtons went through burying their son as a murderer when it wasn't the case."

Doug Williamson tried ~~to~~ not to betray his emotions.

"It's sad for the families of both sides," Williamson said later. "You don't want to be too jubilant in there because it would be rude, it's not the right thing to do."

As Mark Winger was led from the courtroom, Ira could not control himself. He stood and stuck his fist out with a big thumbs-up. The bailiff scolded him and ordered him to sit. Before anyone got up, the Wingers were taken to a rear exit.

"I felt sorry for them," Sara Jane said. "They were wonderful people, wonderful to Donnah. I loved them for loving her."

Prosecutor Weinhoeft felt badly for them too. He kept a respectful distance throughout the trial, knowing they had their own grief. It was unfair, he thought, because they had done nothing wrong. They seemed like good people.

"I believe in all my heart that Mark will be vindicated," Mark's brother, Greg, told *48 Hours* later. "Unfortunately, his life is ruined without just cause."

The spectators filed out into the hallway, where reporters were waiting. Ira praised the detectives and that state's attorneys.

"My family will never forget their dedication to this cause," he said. "But this is no victory, as we still mourn the loss of our beautiful Donnah."

"The part of our heart that was ripped out on August 29, 1995, will never heal, and that's the way it is," Sara Jane said. She clutched the pendant that hung on her necklace. "Donnah loved everyone and was loved by everyone."

She reminded the reporters that there was more than one victim.

"I felt so much compassion for the Harringtons. They are wonderful people with so much pain."

A reporter caught Barbara Howell as she walked out the courthouse door.

"Today, justice has been served finally," Barbara

said. "My parents are doing wonderful. It was the greatest news they could have gotten."

"This should have been done seven years ago," said her father, Ralph.

Jessica Winger and her family slipped past the media throng and walked into the bright sunshine. Her mother reached for her hand, letting her daughter know she was not alone.

"Four families were in that courtroom," Karen said. "Three of them lost a loved one: Donnah's, Roger Harrington's, and Mark's. Our family is intact."

Jessica scowled. It was not what she wanted to hear at that moment.

"I was premature in saying that to her," Karen said. "But it was true. We had each other."

Karen's words would resonate with Jessica in the future.

The jurors who spoke with *48 Hours* said there were several deciding factors in their verdict. They believed that there had been an appointment and that Winger lied about it. DeAnn was credible. And Barringer's pictures were critical.

"The placement of the bodies: they couldn't be where they were if what Mark Winger said was true," one juror explained.

One of the holdouts later told Ira Drescher that he made up his mind after the 911 call was replayed during deliberation. Mark told the operator he had to hang up because his baby was crying, but when they listened to the tape, they did not hear any crying. The other jurors agreed.

"None of us heard the baby cry," one said. "But we did hear Roger Harrington moan."

28

Speaking Out

Charlie Cox was not in court the day the verdict was delivered. He was relieved to hear the news. Mark Winger almost got away with it, he thought. He might have, if Barringer had not taken his pictures, if DeAnn had kept her secret, if Winger had not sued BART, or even if he had simply chosen to move away from Springfield after the crime. His mistake was thinking that he could continue to fool everyone, including the lead detective.

"Admitting I was wrong was the hardest thing I ever did," Cox said. "It was also the most rewarding."

The sentencing hearing, two months after the verdict, was more or less a formality. Illinois law mandates life without parole for double first-degree murder. Nevertheless, the procedure lasted nearly two hours. The judge was given victims' impact statements from Donnah's and Roger's relatives. Defense attorney Breen filed letters from Winger's parents and members of his church. They begged for mercy, saying Winger was an exemplary family man committed to his faith. Many said they believed he was truly innocent.

Winger was led into the courtroom in leg shackles. They clanged as he walked to his seat.

"It was overwhelming to see Mark in prison clothes," Sara Jane Drescher said.

State's Attorney John Schmidt called Sara Jane to the stand and asked her how the crime had affected her family. Sara Jane had carefully thought about how to put her loss into words. She spoke from the heart, praising her daughter.

"She loved people and in return was loved by all who knew her."

Sara Jane talked about how well respected Donnah was at her job. Then she addressed her own grief. She told the court she had nightmares reliving the night when she heard the unbearable news that her daughter had been murdered. She spoke about her ongoing struggle to get through each day.

"I hear beautiful music and cry because I know she will never hear it again. I see a sunrise and I yearn for her so. A million times a day her face, her voice, comes into my mind. It has been seven years and I have learned how to go on, but there is a pain that will never go away." Sara Jane paused and dabbed at her tears.

"Do you know what I miss most? I miss touching her face and feeling the softness of her skin. I miss picking up a phone—"

She was about to tell the court about her Sunday-morning ritual with Donnah, but she could not go on. Crying, she left the stand.

"We both felt cheated," Ira said later.

Sara Jane might have said less than she had planned, but she came through loud and clear. Barbara Howell, Roger Harrington's sister, spoke next. She talked about the good times she had had with her brother and the bond they had shared. She cried when she spoke about the unwarranted shame her family had endured.

Before being handed his sentence, Mark Winger took the opportunity to address the court. He stood, faced the judge, and read from a nineteen-page handwritten statement. His hands shook and his voice cracked repeatedly.

"Roger Harrington killed my wife," he said. "I was there, and he did it. I don't personally need to be convinced by any evidence."

The Harringtons bristled. They could not understand why Winger was allowed to speak at all. Winger launched into an indulgent autobiography, rambling on about the way he first charmed Donnah and their perfect marriage. Then, he said, DeAnn "literally threw herself" at him and he was too weak to resist.

Contrary to DeAnn's testimony, Winger insisted he never loved her or told her he did. He praised Jessica for rescuing him from despair. But he came down hard on Donnah's family, especially Sara Jane. He blamed her for their estrangement and said that the Dreschers "threw my little family into the lion's den." He said that Donnah "must be turning over in her grave seeing what her family has done to me."

The Dreschers fumed. Winger continued. He blasted Mike and Jo Datz. "Here were former friends who claim to know God, but by their actions they deny Him."

Jo Datz looked at Mark's hands and felt a chill. These were the hands that had murdered her friend.

"As I stand here, I can only imagine that my wife Jessica is seeing me in much the same light as I saw Donnah seven years ago: helpless and paralyzed with panic," Winger said. "The desperation in my voice is much like Donnah's panting breaths as I desperately gasp for one more precious moment with my family."

The analogy was sickening to everyone who knew Donnah.

Winger twice mentioned his four children by name, once at the end of his speech, along with their ages, when he invoked them as a reason why the judge should find the "courage and wisdom" to "boldly set aside these verdicts."

Jessica cringed when she heard her children's names and ages being read in open court. She realized that Mark had always seen them as extensions of himself—"my children"—just as she was always "my wife." He was thinking of himself; this was not in their best interest.

Winger finally finished and sat down. As expected, Judge Zappa sentenced him to life without parole.

* * *

Winger had more to say. He agreed to talk with *48 Hours'* Richard Schlesinger. The prison rules were strict: one hour only, with Winger sitting behind Plexiglas and Schlesinger in a small booth facing him. The crew set up a monitor in the hall so that the producers could watch the interview as it happened.

Interviews with prisoners are standard *48 Hours* fare. The most brutal killers manage to be on their best behavior for the brief time the cameras roll. Guilty or not, inmates use the precious time to plead their cases. Not Mark Winger: he preferred to show off his male prowess, apparently unable to censor himself. It began when Schlesinger asked what had first attracted him to Donnah and he said, "Her body." It got out of hand when DeAnn came up. Smirking, Winger embarked on a raunchy play-by-play of just what DeAnn did to arouse him in the motel room.

"As I was standing up, my pants looked like a pup tent," he chuckled several minutes later.

He lamented that Donnah put him up to helping DeAnn with her marital problems, but assured us that he did not blame his wife for the fact that DeAnn came on to him. That was strictly DeAnn's fault, according to Mark Winger.

Schlesinger tried to redirect the discussion—we had a lot to get through and little time—but Winger would have none of that. His saga continued, in explicit language, making sure we did not miss his point that DeAnn was the aggressor. It was an obvious attempt to get back at her any way he could from behind prison bars. None of it was anything that we could—or would—ever use in our broadcast.

A growing crowd of prison guards gathered around our makeshift screening area. Winger was asked why the affair continued after Donnah died.

"What better way to get closer to my wife than through DeAnn?" he said. "I wanted physical contact with my wife. And I guess I thought maybe I could get that vicariously through DeAnn."

It is not easy to shock prison guards but Winger was succeeding. When he was asked what he went through the day of the crime, he switched from X-rated sex to X-rated violence, describing the victims' wounds in graphic detail.

He said that when he shot Harrington, the driver was rolling away, as he had told the police, but "he was also ducking like someone about to get bitch slapped. When I required my target he was no longer there, but he was . . . moving to my right." (So much for remorse for taking a life.) When he tended to Donnah, Winger said, he put a towel to her head. Sobbing and sniffing, Winger gave a vivid description of the human tissue that stuck to the towel.

"I was so angry that I got up and stood over Harrington and said, 'You motherfucker,' and shot him in the head," Winger said.

Schlesinger, suitably revolted, was determined to get material suitable for network television. He asked

Winger if he knew that Donnah was dying at that point.

"I knew she was in dire straits when I saw the inside of her head," Winger answered, sniffling. He looked up and added, "I just told the world something I never told anybody."

"What was that?"

"What happened between shot one and shot two."

It was a belated attempt to explain the time lag between gunshots, which Winger by then knew was strong evidence against him. He went on to talk about the "fountain of blood" that came from Harrington and then casually dropped the idea that he saw the paramedics move the victims. That was an attempt to explain away Barringer's photos. It contradicted the testimony of every paramedic who had testified at trial. It also meant that his forensic expert, Terry Laber, was working with an erroneous narrative when he analyzed the crime scene and matched it to Winger's story.

Producer Doug Longhini pointed out that Winger's latest claims rendered meaningless that critical contact stain that Laber found on Donnah's shorts.

"That stain could not have happened by contact under Mark's new version of his story," he said.

Laber theorized that the stain got there when Harrington knelt by Donnah and rolled away from her after he was shot. Now Winger said Harrington was ducking and moving away to his right. Perhaps he was trying to explain the distance between the victims he now knew could be seen in the photographs.

Longhini noted that, according to Mark Winger, DeAnn Schultz had lied at his trial. So had Charlie Cox, Doug Williamson, the other detectives, Susan Collins, Ray Duffey, Tom Bevel, and the paramedics. Just about everyone but Mark.

The time spent with Winger eliminated any lingering doubt the *48 Hours* team had about his guilt. Sara Jane had him pegged.

"He's a monster," she said. "He's a chameleon who portrays himself on the outside as one thing and really is something very different."

He was the nice Jewish boy who wooed Donnah. He was the dutiful, church-attending father who won over Jessica. Now, as a convicted murderer, he was part of the prison culture. It suited him well.

At the sentencing hearing, Jessica's brother George approached Sara Jane and told her she could see Ruby when she wanted to. Crying, Sara Jane thanked him. Ruby was seven years old. She was doing well, George said, and had not yet been told about her past. Jessica shielded her children from the notoriety of the case as much as she could.

"We made one huge mistake," Jessica's mother, Karen, said later. "Before the trial, we told the kids their father was coming home."

The younger children were too little to understand, but the older girls expected Mark to return. They sensed the turmoil. Jessica's family showered them with love and attention. George and Albert had tried to voice their suspicions about Mark Winger long before, but neither Karen nor Jessica wanted to hear it. Now, having sat through the trial, Karen was confused.

"The head believes before the heart," she said. "The pieces were not fitting."

Jessica's resolve was also beginning to crack. Mark had told her that everything in the case against him hinged on DeAnn's lies. But neither Mark nor she knew about other evidence—like Barringer's pictures—until the trial.

Jessica had been angry with the police for a long time. Now she wanted information from them. She called Williamson and Cox.

Cox remembered that Jessica cried a lot when she called. She told him she had issues with the trial that she needed to clarify. Cox sensed she was grasping at straws, trying to hold on to anything that would allow her continue to believe in Mark's innocence.

"She wanted to be consoled and reassured," Cox said.

Instead he told her that the evidence was overwhelming.

"I told her she was very lucky he was in jail."

Cox said he guaranteed that when things got rough for Winger again, Jessica would be his third victim. He had had no problem killing twice before. Jessica protested, reminding Cox that he once believed Mark. She asked the detective what had changed his mind to make him so adamant now. Cox restated his reasons and said that Winger was a master of deceit.

"I told her that he sold me, an experienced professional. She was in love with the guy. If he got to me, she certainly shouldn't feel guilty that she was taken by him."

The trial erased any doubt that Sara Jane had about Mark's innocence, but it also took its toll.

"My downtimes are spent reliving the trial and the things that I found out that I never wanted to know. I hope in time those thoughts will fade and I can only remember that Mark is in prison for the rest of his life and that we were a small part in putting him there," she wrote in her notes.

Sara Jane and Ira expanded their charitable efforts in Donnah's name. They raised more money for the clubhouse at the Joe DiMaggio Children's Hospital. The Dreschers also established Donnah's Fund for the organization Women in Distress.

"Unbeknownst to us, Donnah was a fatal victim of spousal abuse," they wrote in a letter announcing the fund. "We feel confident that Donnah would be proud to have a fund in her name so women who have been separated from their abusers could have the opportunity to make a new start in their lives."

Richard Schlesinger asked the Dreschers what they believed had motivated Mark Winger. Ira responded immediately, listing a litany of reasons he had mulled over for years: Donnah's inability to conceive; Mark's fear that she would take Ruby to Florida if they divorced; DeAnn; control. He elaborated on each.

"Mark liked to control everything. If he would have had to get a divorce, he wouldn't have control. He would have child support and everything else."

Schlesinger turned to Sara Jane.

"Do you have a sense of why he did it?"

"No. Absolutely not. I have no idea why he did it. I think it's a question that will never be answered in my mind."

Whatever Mark's motive was, Ira Drescher was determined to make his ex-son-in-law's life as miserable as possible. Ira sent him dozens of taunting "Dear Markie" letters (Markie was Donnah's affectionate name for Mark) on birthdays ("You look great in your latest ID picture. Isolation agrees with you!"), special dates ("I want to wish you well on celebrating your fourth anniversary of BEING ARRESTED AND LOSING YOUR FREEDOM FOR THE REST OF YOUR LIFE!"), and holidays ("Yesterday was Thanksgiving and we had fifteen over and Mom really did a great job with the turkey and all the fixins!!" "I was wondering how you are going to celebrate the New Year? Is Bubba going to stop by or are you going to his place?"). He sent picture postcards ("Here in Italy, I'm thinking of you and wondering if you've tried to commit suicide yet. The beach and the sun are terrific here"). Mostly, Ira wrote when he felt like it, which was often: "You are a powerless sucker . . . Your life is OVER!!" He signed them "Pop-I."

Ira tracked every legal move Mark made in long-shot attempts to overturn his conviction. Ira also kept in touch with prosecutor Weinhoeft, Detectives Williamson and Graham, and Rabbi Mike and Jo Datz. He debriefed the jurors. He spoke with the Harringtons every so often. And he made friends with a few prison administrators so that he could keep tabs on everything Mark did. Nothing would escape Ira.

Mark Winger never answered any of Ira's acerbic missives, but he wrote hundreds—maybe thousands—of letters to his wife. He wrote about himself and told her his thoughts. Sometimes he contradicted himself. He drew lots of pictures.

"Some were disgusting," Jessica's mother, Karen, said.

Jessica, concerned about her children, filed for divorce. Mark fought her tooth and nail, arguing his case in court via telephone. Jessica persisted and prevailed. She then moved to change her children's last name and was told she needed to go to a different court. She showed up armed with a magazine article about Mark Winger. The judge quickly approved Jessica's request.

Throughout it all, Ira kept lines of communication open with Jessica. Ira expressed concern for her predicament but said she would have to understand that he was certain that Mark was guilty. He told her why. He encouraged her to break away from him. Eventually, Jessica did.

"As time progressed, the pictures disappeared,"

Karen said. The children went on with their lives. Mark Winger faded away.

"Mark fooled us all," Jessica said. "I am sorry I did that to my family."

Karen's thoughts were more sobering. If the police did not reopen the case, she said, "my daughter would not be alive."

Jessica was increasingly appreciative of her family's support and patience. It took her years to fully absorb the evidence she had not been privy to until the trial. It took time for the shock to wear off.

"When you are emotionally involved, it is very difficult to see things clearly."

During the trial, her friends repeatedly told Jessica that they admired her strength. Looking back, she said, it was easier to believe in her husband than it was to face the truth. Breaking away was the hard part. That took more guts.

Her mother, Karen, agreed. She had watched Jessica blossom into a woman wise beyond her years. Karen admired the stamina and strength her daughter exhibited when she embraced the responsibilities of a single parent. Jessica had been dealt a rotten hand but remained positive. She got a job and put every penny earned toward her children. Thanks to her maternal devotion, Karen's grandchildren were happy, energetic, and kind.

"As always, my concern is for my kiddos," Jessica e-mailed this author when she was contacted about this book.

Jessica was upset because the publicity surrounding Mark Winger's case never seemed to die down. She had worked hard to reestablish her children's lives and their privacy. But Mark was not making things easy. Another case was brewing. He was about to be taken to court again to face new charges.

29

An Intricate Plot

In spring 2005, a convicted murderer doing time at the state prison in Pontiac, Illinois, sent a typed letter to a private investigator. Terry Hubbell claimed that a fellow inmate was looking to hire someone to kidnap one of the witnesses from his trial. That witness would be forced to tape a confession, then killed, with the death made to look like a drug overdose. Hubbell said that in his fourteen years of incarceration, he had met a lot of men with "crazy ass ideas." Most were "just blowing smoke." This one seemed real.

"He will find some one with the connection to do what it is that he is after," Hubbell wrote.

Hubbell said the inmate had worked out a complicated scenario. The money needed to pay the hit man would be obtained through a second kidnapping and a ransom extracted from "a friend who was loaded."

"This guy has no money left as his family spent it all on his trial," Hubbell wrote.

Hubbell said he was "willing to help stop this," but only for a price. Among other demands, he wanted

322 • Invitation to a Murder

his freedom, a home, two trucks, four Harleys, credit cards, and—he inked in as an afterthought—a job. His letter eventually led to a state police investigation. Hubbell cooperated, apparently settling for a transfer out of Pontiac.

The inmate with the elaborate plan was Mark Winger. His intended victim was DeAnn Schultz. The other target was someone Winger knew growing up who had ended up striking it rich. Winger was miffed at the man for refusing to post bond when he was arrested. Winger's idea was to kidnap the man's wife and children, collect a large ransom, then have the entire family killed. If there was money left over after paying off the hit on DeAnn, Winger wanted Ira Drescher killed too.

Before being killed, DeAnn would be forced to write letters and make an audio recording professing Mark's innocence and saying that she had lied. She would then be made to write a note to her current husband, making it appear that she had left her house on her own. Then she was to be taken away and dispatched.

Hubbell gave investigators a written statement in June 2005.

"I have known Mark Winger for approx 1½ years and he has worked his way around to asking me if I knew any gang members that maybe could have someone offed and from then on he kept after me and started to discuss it more and in detail . . ."

Hubbell answered written questions:

"Why does Winger want DeAnn Schultz killed?"

"So that once she has made the tapes and letters she would no longer be able to change her story."

"Why does Winger want [his childhood friend] and family killed?"

"Once he had any money that he could get out of him, he wanted them gone (dead) so that it could not be tied back to him."

"Why does Winger want Ira Drescher killed?"

"Because of the letters and postcards that he keeps sending him."

Hubbell also handed over nineteen pages of hand-written pages Mark had given him to type out. They included the letters that DeAnn would be forced to address to attoney Tom Breen, Mark's parents, his brother, his ex-boss, and Mark himself. The letter to Breen would be accompanied by a tape that DeAnn would be forced to record, a five-page statement that Mark wrote out.

DeAnn's coerced recording would offer a new explanation for what she had said at the trial. She would say that she loved Mark and felt betrayed when he dumped her for Jessica. She was distraught when she ran into him years later and confided her affair to her psychiatrist. She told her doctor some of her fantasies and he threatened to stop treating her unless she came forward. She would express her feelings this way:

"I guess I felt redeemed to hear an outsider blame Mark for my pain . . . I expected that going to the police would result in Mark losing his lawsuit, but I didn't know it would go into a murder investigation. I didn't imagine that I'd be dragged into it. But the police kept pressuring me to give more details. Eventually [Detective Jim] Graham laid out a scenario of what he believed happened and spelled out what he wanted me to say."

DeAnn would say she had no choice but to play along or else "Jim said that I could go to jail along with Mark."

DeAnn would say she fabricated everything she said to the police and at trial. "The truth is that Mark isn't responsible for killing Donnah . . . The truth is that Mark never made threats about Donnah dying."

The last paragraph of DeAnn's coerced statement expressed her relief to "finally get this off my chest."

DeAnn's letter to Mark would say, "I just wanted you to know that I have purged my conscience and confessed my sins."

Mark Winger's extensive written instructions showed his desire to micromanage the operation. There were phone calls to be made to set the scene for DeAnn's disappearance ("Have a *girl* call my mom and dad . . . ask for my brother's address . . ."). There was a list of items to "take from the target's home" to make it appear that DeAnn had left voluntarily, such as her purse, makeup bag, car keys, cell phone, and medication ("Check above kitchen cabinets, bathroom, nightstand"). There was a reminder to wear gloves while driving DeAnn's car but not to wipe her fingerprints from the steering wheel ("It will appear to be staged"). There was a warning, "DO NOT LEAVE BEHIND ANY OF THE PREPARATION MATERIALS (this is a show stopper)," and a note spelling out the last words DeAnn would hear before being killed. "You once told Mark that 'you don't fuck Bubba for no one.' Well, Mark wants you to know that he *is* Bubba, you stupid bitch."

Winger also suggested an "alternate ending (if possible)" in which Jim Graham would be framed for DeAnn's murder. "We would need to find a way to get DeAnn to lure Graham to some out of town place, like a bar. Then, plant some very incriminating evidence in his car (hair, blood)."

Prison inmate Terry Hubbell agreed to wear a wire and secretly record a conversation with Winger in the prison yard. This yielded more details on Winger's elaborate murder plot as well as insight into his mind. Winger, optimistic about overturning his conviction, told Hubbell that he would like to work for the "hit men" when he was released from prison. He said that when he first got out of college, he wanted to be a CIA hit man—not because he was into the law but because "I wanted to do some cold-hearted fuckin' shit, know I can pull a trigger."

The former state Department of Nuclear Safety engineer was charged with two counts of solicitation for murder. That news generated some topical "Dear Markie" letters from Ira, who expressed disappointment at being so low on Winger's hit list.

"I have to tell you how pissed I am with you as

you consider me to be in THIRD PLACE! Damn!! . . . I thought you rated me higher than that!!"

"I think this 6 years of your prison time has really WARPED YOUR BRAIN . . . BUT WHAT THE HECK . . . THAT'S WHY YOU ARE THERE!!! . . . YOU AREN'T TOO SMART TO BEGIN WITH!!"

Mark Winger was transferred to Tamms, a super-max facility that, according to the state prison website, "has been designated to house the department's most disruptive, violent and problematic inmates." Inmates placed there have "demonstrated an inability or un-willingness to conform to the requirements of a general population prison."

Winger was out of money. He was assigned a public defender.

30

Insurance

In May 2007, one month before Mark Winger's second trial, this author met Doug Williamson and Steve Weinhoeft at a popular downtown Springfield restaurant. Winger's case was one of the biggest they had ever handled and they were still familiar with every facet of it. Williamson, by then a lieutenant and soon to be deputy chief, was happy that he had never relented but sobered by the thought that Winger almost got away.

"Most murders involve drugs or alcohol in some way," Williamson said.

"Or they happen on the spur of the moment," Weinhoeft interjected.

Williamson nodded, then leaned forward to emphasize his point.

"This guy *planned* to beat his wife to death with a hammer. And he did it. I've never been around that before."

The case was not quite closed for Weinhoeft. He was helping the state's appellate attorneys prepare responses to Winger's requests for appeals. He was also called to testify at the new trial.

Williamson and Weinhoeft praised Ira Drescher for his tireless efforts. They had never dealt with anyone quite like him. They expressed ongoing sympathy for everyone in Donnah's life as well as those who loved Roger Harrington.

Helen and Ralph Harrington, married forty-four years, welcomed me to their home. Their wrongful-death suit was never revived, so they never collected any money. Helen worked part-time caring for the elderly in their homes. Her curly gray hair was thinning but she stood erect. She was a sturdy survivor. Ralph was ailing, his words hard to understand at times. He shook his head and repeated what he said when we first met.

"It made no sense. Roger was always fun-loving, laughing."

Roger's sister, Barbara, said her family forgave the cops but still could not understand how the case got so messed up.

"It had to be Mark Winger; there was no one else it could have been," she said. "You read about these things. It's always the husband."

Helen invited me to take a walk with her. I welcomed the opportunity to stretch my legs and feel the warm spring air. We walked past the now-quiet state fairgrounds, then turned onto nostalgic Old Route 66. Helen told me some history of the area, but mostly we talked about her current hardship and the heartache she still endured. This tough-as-nails woman seemed weary and vulnerable. She feared that Mark Winger would pull some legal maneuver to get out of prison. I told her that was unlikely, especially in light of the new charges against him. I promised to keep her up-to-date on the trial. Walking back, she said she was still bothered by the way her son had been portrayed in the media. She slipped me notes she wrote in longhand script on three letter-size pages.

"This is the Roger I knew," she said.

In part, those notes read:

"Corrective shoes, braces on his teeth . . ." "Wrote to President Reagan once and got a response . . ." "Roger came to my work. The girls were very impressed with him . . ."

"He had his job, his sunning in the park across from the airport, his paycheck. That was the Roger I knew."

Ira Drescher could not resist traveling to Pontiac, Illinois, in early June to attend Mark Winger's new trial. It was held in a nineteenth-century neoclassic-style courthouse with a beautiful clock tower. In the park behind it was an imposing life-size bronze statue of a young Abe Lincoln leaning against a split-rail fence. Lincoln had argued a few cases in another courthouse that stood on the site until it burned down.

Mark Winger's trial began on June 11. According to the charges against him, he was in the process of meticulously plotting the murders of five people:

DeAnn, his childhood friend, and the man's wife and two children. Counting Ira Drescher (funds allowing), there would have been six victims.

This time Ira had no problem envisioning Mark committing the crime. The plan was chillingly familiar: an elaborately scripted scenario designed to deceive, kill, and take down bystanders along the way. Mark devised DeAnn's coerced statement just as he likely dictated to Donnah the words she wrote in her complaint about Roger Harrington.

Mark's hands were shackled to a chain around his waist; his ankle chains were fastened to a hook in the floor. He wore a black sport jacket, white shirt, and large gold-rimmed glasses.

"He looked gaunt and pale and balder and grayer," Ira said. "He was surprised to see me."

Winger was probably even more surprised to see that Ira was sitting next to Jessica's mother, Karen, and brother Albert. Ira had always been fond of Jessica, and over the past few years they had developed a respectful relationship. Jessica had reached out to him and, on the anniversary of Donnah's death, told Ira that she was thinking of and praying for his family. She celebrated Donnah's life, she said, and the life she had given her.

"When all is said and done, Ruby was Jessica's salvation," Karen said.

Jessica had set out to help save Ruby when she first accepted the job as Mark Winger's nanny, and in the end that's what she did. Ruby was an integral part of a loving family.

Mark's murder-for-hire trial was the first occasion that Ira had to meet Jessica's mother and brother in person. He liked them too. Someday, he thought, he and Sara Jane might even get a call from Ruby.

It was a strange turn of events. When Donnah was killed, the Dreschers disdained the Harringtons as parents of a crazed killer. Then, during Mark's first trial, they came to know the Harringtons as the good people they were. At that time Jessica and her family were in the enemy camp. Now, five years later, they were friends. They had a lot in common: all were deceived and betrayed by Mark Winger.

"We commiserated about our thoughts and opinions and perceptions, which happen to be similar," Ira said.

Karen said that she had grown to appreciate Ira. She was grateful to him for his guidance. She understood why he sent those letters to Mark, even if she would never do anything like that herself.

Ira learned that Jessica's brothers never believed Mark and they had secretly hoped for a guilty verdict in 2002. In 2007 they all hoped for it.

The state's first witness, Steve Weinhoeft, testified that DeAnn Schultz was "an extremely important witness" in Winger's double-murder trial. Terry Hubbell, the convicted murderer, took the stand and talked about Winger's alleged intricate plan. The jurors were shown the nineteen handwritten pages Winger had given him to type. They listened to the hour-long conversation Hubbell had secretly recorded in the prison yard.

"I'd like to cut her fuckin' tongue out, put it in a jar," Winger was heard to say, referring to DeAnn. He didn't care where she was buried, he said, "as long as it's fuckin' thirty feet."

Under cross-examination, Hubbell said that his reward for coming forward was a transfer to another prison. His mother got $3,250 in exchange for his wearing the recording device.

During a break, Mark was led out of the courtroom. Ira described the moment in an e-mail. "I looked him straight in the eyes and told him, 'Mark, have a good life . . . but let's face it: YOURS IS OVER!!' Boy, did that make me feel good!!"

The following day Winger took the stand in his own defense. His attorney asked him about the vulgar language he had been heard using. He turned to the jurors and apologized.

"I am very ashamed of that. It's not the way I was before I came to prison. I was very nice and charitable and kind."

Winger did not deny writing the detailed scenario but said he had been duped by Terry Hubbell, who egged him on.

"I never had any intention for it to be carried out," he said. "It was an interactive process of Terry and I. Just talking BS. You know, and fantasizing."

Winger said Hubbell gave him information to put in as part of the fantasy.

"I sit in my cell twenty-three hours a day. It is cathartic. I write things. I just fantasize. I got a lot of anger and bitterness. I should not be in prison. Should never have been convicted."

It took five months to write the nineteen pages, Winger said, and as time passed, Hubbell showed increased interest. Winger said he feared Hubbell and worried that the inmate would find a way to harm his children. So, Winger said, he kept the fantasy going. There was no option.

"You have to be tough. You can die in prison. All the nightmares you have heard about it are true."

He insisted the plan was pure fantasy and that he "never thought for a minute that any of that was going to occur."

The cross-examination was simple and to the point.

"What was your degree in college?"

"Physics."

"That is not an easy course of study, is it?"

"No, sir."

"And Terry Hubbell outsmarted you?"

"He did in a way. I mean, he scammed me."

Karen understood Mark Winger as she never had before.

"It's ego, ego, ego," she said. "His ego is his enemy."

Mark was convinced he was smarter than everyone

else. He could make people believe him. She once did. Hearing him now, he was extremely transparent. She hoped the jurors would see through him too.

In closing arguments the prosecutor argued that only Winger stood to gain from the plot. The defense attorney did not have much to work with.

"Is it a plot?" he asked. "I think not. It's just craziness. He has nothing else to do, and he thought he was allowed to fantasize."

The jury wasted little time, taking only three hours (including lunch) to reach its verdict: guilty. At sentencing, Winger proclaimed his innocence: the detectives had lied in his first case and the detectives were lying in this case too. He said that "educated men get fooled every day." He was sorry he had shared his fantasies with Hubbell, who duped him for his own purposes.

"This case was too important to lose for some very powerful people, especially down in Springfield," Winger said, painting himself as a victim. "To satisfy their lust for pain, they have stowed me away."

He complained about prison conditions. He said he expected his unjust conviction to be overturned. The judge admonished him.

"Your life shows, at least since 1995, that you live in your own world and try to make your own rules."

The judge sentenced Winger to thirty-five years on each count, saying he was a "very dangerous individual and threat to the public." The sentence was to be served concurrently with Winger's natural life sentence for the double murder. Even if he was some-how granted a new trial for murdering Donnah and Roger Harrington, he would remain incarcerated.

Karen said the conviction was an "insurance pack-age" for her family. She at last felt that everyone was safe. It was highly unlikely that Winger would ever walk free. He would have to face the consequences of his actions. The new conviction also wiped away whatever shred of doubt that any of them had about Mark's guilt. Even after paying such a heavy price for his crime, he concocted another nefarious plan.

"Mark made costly choices when he had everything: a loving wife, a great job, a beautiful baby, and won-derful in-laws—things everybody dreams of," Karen said. "And when he lost everything, when he had nothing, he still made bad choices."

There was talk that Winger had turned back to Ju-daism. Whatever his beliefs were, he would have a lot of time to reflect. Publicly, he continued to deny doing anything wrong and insisted he was framed. Only he knew what he really thought. Only he knew what was in his mind and in his heart when he lay alone at night in his cell.

The murder-for-hire scheme was foiled. Mark Winger would be limited to two victims, both with families devoted to keeping their memories alive. Roger was loved and his family now rightfully had the sympathy of the community. Donnah was remembered by the many people whose lives she had touched. A new generation of her family was told about her remarkable life.

In 1995, Mark Winger chose the inscription for Donnah's grave. When he was exposed as her killer, Sara Jane had the inscription changed. The new one was a quotation written by Maya Angelou:

Nothing Can Dim the Light That Shines From Within.

AUTHOR'S NOTE

The following names are pseudonyms: Ruby, Jessica Walters, Karen Walters, George Walters, and Albert Walters.